THE RESILIENT ENTREPRENEUR

From Crisis to Enlightenment

Rachel Doern

First published in Great Britain in 2025 by

Bristol University Press
University of Bristol
1–9 Old Park Hill
Bristol
BS2 8BB
UK
t: +44 (0)117 374 6645
e: bup-info@bristol.ac.uk

Details of international sales and distribution partners are available at
bristoluniversitypress.co.uk

© Bristol University Press 2025

British Library Cataloguing in Publication Data
A catalogue record for this book is available from the British Library

ISBN 978-1-5292-0117-8 hardcover
ISBN 978-1-5292-0120-8 paperback
ISBN 978-1-5292-0119-2 ePub
ISBN 978-1-5292-0118-5 ePdf

The right of Rachel Doern to be identified as author of this work has been asserted by her in accordance with the Copyright, Designs and Patents Act 1988.

All rights reserved: no part of this publication may be reproduced, stored in a retrieval system, or transmitted in any form or by any means, electronic, mechanical, photocopying, recording, or otherwise without the prior permission of Bristol University Press.

Every reasonable effort has been made to obtain permission to reproduce copyrighted material. If, however, anyone knows of an oversight, please contact the publisher.

The statements and opinions contained within this publication are solely those of the author and not of the University of Bristol or Bristol University Press. The University of Bristol and Bristol University Press disclaim responsibility for any injury to persons or property resulting from any material published in this publication.

Bristol University Press works to counter discrimination on grounds of gender, race, disability, age and sexuality.

Cover design: Designed by Ben Read, rendered by Nicky Borowiec
Front cover image: Shutterstock/aarrows

Contents

List of Figures, Tables and Boxes		v
About the Author		vii
Acknowledgements		viii
An Introduction to Entrepreneurs in Crisis		1
1	Understanding Resilience	12
PART I	**Strategies Entrepreneurs Use That Strengthen Resilience**	
2	Distraction	29
3	Expectation Management	45
4	Positive Self-talk	64
5	Positive Reappraisal	79
6	Situation Selection and Modification	99
7	Offsetting Resource Losses	115
8	Leaning Into Social Support	135
PART II	**Strategies That Can Compromise Resilience and How to Manage Them**	
9	Denial	153
10	Rumination	166
11	Behavioural Disengagement	176
PART III	**Conclusions**	
12	The Resilience Work We Can All Do	189

Appendix A: Additional Commentary on the Implications of the Research	203
Appendix B: Additional Commentary for Studying Entrepreneurs in Crisis and Resilience	208
Notes	213
Index	239

List of Figures, Tables and Boxes

Figures

4.1	Shifting negative self-talk towards positive self-talk	76
10.1	Shifting from vague concerns to more specific concerns	174
12.1	Resilience work	190

Tables

2.1	The focus, form and implications of distraction strategies	41
2.2	Guiding questions for an acceptance-based distraction strategy with a lowercase 'd'	42
2.3	A distraction log	43
3.1	Broad categories of news entrepreneurs in crisis have a tendency to wait for and their expectations	51
3.2	Guiding questions for a more deliberate expectation management strategy	60
3.3	How emotions and behaviours link to examples of crisis-related news	61
3.4	Managing expectations log	61
4.1	Guiding questions for a more positive and constructive self-talk strategy	75
4.2	A self-talk log	75
5.1	The focus and significance of positive reappraisal strategies	95
5.2	Guiding questions for positive reappraisal strategies	96
5.3	Positive reappraisal prompts	96
6.1	Guiding questions to help us adjust our situation	110
6.2	Using situation selection and modification to diminish crisis-related stress at work	111

6.3	A situation monitoring log	112
7.1	Guiding questions for developing strategies to offset resource losses	131
7.2	The focus of and barriers to strategies for offsetting resource losses	132
7.3	An offsetting resource losses log	132
8.1	Guiding questions for creating a more deliberate strategy for leaning into social support	148
8.2	Leaning into social support log	149
9.1	Guiding questions to protect yourself from denial	162
9.2	The 4 Cs of denial busting	162
10.1	Guiding questions to protect yourself from rumination	173
10.2	A rumination log	174
11.1	Guiding questions to protect yourself from prolonged behavioural disengagement	183
11.2	A reengagement log	184
12.1	Resilience work checklist	198
12.2	Resilience work strategy overview and application	199

Boxes

2.1	Actionable takeaways for distraction	43
3.1	Actionable takeaways for expectation management	63
4.1	Actionable takeaways for positive self-talk	77
5.1	Actionable takeaways for positive reappraisal	98
6.1	Actionable takeaways for situation selection and modification	113
7.1	Actionable takeaways for offsetting resource losses	133
8.1	Actionable takeaways for leaning into social support	150
9.1	Actionable takeaways for protecting yourself against denial	164
10.1	Actionable takeaways for protecting yourself against rumination	175
11.1	Actionable takeaways for protecting yourself against behavioural disengagement	185

About the Author

Rachel Doern is Reader/Associate Professor of Entrepreneurship at Goldsmiths, University of London. She researches crisis management and resilience in an entrepreneurial context. Her work has been published in academic journals and has appeared in the popular press, including the BBC and *Los Angeles Times*. She grew up in Canada but eventually swapped the snow for the rain, moving to the United Kingdom where she received her MSc from the University of Strathclyde and her PhD from the University of St Andrews. She lives in London.

Acknowledgements

There are so many people I'd like to thank, and I know what follows will only scratch the surface.

I'd like to express my deepest thanks to all the entrepreneurs I've had the privilege of engaging with, who have shared their personal and compelling stories with me. I've learned so much from you.

A special thanks to those friends who read through the book and commented on its contents and design, who also happen to be entrepreneurs. Thanks for your generosity, for sharing your time and valuable opinions with me, especially Ben Lucas (who read the book more than once), Mona Hayat, Catherine Riney, Ben Gillam and Fahim Pour. A shout out to the talented Ben Read, my graphic designer friend, for your hands-on support with formatting the book and with the cover of the book. I am very grateful to all of you. You have made the writing process a more enjoyable one.

Thanks to Monica Chakraverty and Paul Roberts for your enthusiastic and astute editorial guidance on aspects of the book's structure. Also, and especially, for serving as a valuable sounding board.

Thanks to the team at Bristol University Press, particularly Isobel Green, Ellen Pearce, Paul Stevens and Amber Lanfranchi, for your continuing support, kindness and flexibility throughout. For this I'm greatly appreciative. And thanks to the reviewers for your helpful comments.

Thanks to my students for listening to me go on about resilience over the years and for engaging in activities that sometimes touched upon different aspects of resilience, as featured in the book. Thanks also to my wonderful colleagues at Goldsmiths University of London, including the brilliant members of the research and knowledge exchange team who have supported me and have promoted my interests in entrepreneurs and resilience, like Anthony Crowther.

ACKNOWLEDGEMENTS

A heartfelt thanks to Rob and Hazel for your patience and encouragement over the years. Thank you not only for giving me the time and space to work on the book, but for giving me a reason not to. Hazel, you are a lovely human being and my inspiration. I'm so proud of you.

And thanks to my parents, extended family and close friends for instilling in me the confidence to write the book in the first place. Your companionship has been so meaningful and motivating to me.

An Introduction to Entrepreneurs in Crisis

On a warm summer night in August 2011, Sofia, a veteran London bar owner, peered out of the front door of her small business and gazed in horror at what she saw.

> The high street was like a warzone. Everything was burning. Every single shop was smashed.

Rioting, prompted by the fatal shooting by police of a 29-year-old black man, Mark Duggan, had resulted in chaotic scenes across London. A woman jumping from a burning building and a neighbouring family business in flames would become vivid and enduring images in the media.

Most business owners had been prevented from re-entering their premises by police cordons. However, like some others, Sofia was inside her business at the time. Behind her was her teenage son and some friends. She quickly pushed the door closed and locked it.

Soon after, she heard noises on the street. The rioters were making petrol bombs. They set fire to three cars just outside Sofia's front door. A sense of dread swept over her and she switched off the lights.

> We were standing there in the corridor thinking, 'What are we going to do now? We are trapped! We can't go anywhere.'

Now, there were 300 people outside. And only moments later the door of the bar was smashed open and the angry rioters poured in.

> I was thinking, 'Where can we escape? If we go upstairs, we are trapped!' I could see they were setting things on fire. I shouted to my son, 'Let's go to the kitchen!' We locked ourselves in the kitchen and went right to the back where there was a metal shutter where deliveries would be made. But there was no space for the five of us on this corner. The rioters were right behind the shutter, burning the bins. And then they jumped on the flat kitchen roof. That's when I heard them shout, 'Burn it! Burn it!'

Somehow, Sofia, her son and their friends managed to flee that night without harm. Her beloved neighbourhood bar – her decades old business – was looted and badly vandalized but escaped being burned down. Some other businesses were less fortunate. Sofia was comforted by the support she and her husband, Jim, had received from the community.

Sofia's story, and many others like it, can teach us about the fortitude of everyday entrepreneurs. Their stories also broaden our understanding of resilience in important ways.

Intuitively, we all have an understanding about resilience. We sense it's a good thing. We see it as something we want and, perhaps, more importantly, as something we need.

This book addresses fundamental questions about the resilience of the individual, focusing on an entrepreneurial context and discussing what we can learn from entrepreneurs. How can entrepreneurs become mentally, emotionally and practically better prepared for the crises they will inevitably face? What strategies might help when times are tough, or to endure and surface from crises? What strategies can compromise resilience and what can we do about them?

People have often tried to understand entrepreneurs and what these individuals have in common. And while entrepreneurs can differ enormously, what clearly unites them is their tendency to encounter a lot of challenges and their need and desire to adjust so that they can keep going.

I've been studying entrepreneurs for more than 20 years. In that time, many entrepreneurs have shared their rich and compelling journeys with me. Like Sofia, many have grown and developed during the most difficult periods in their personal and professional lives. And understanding just how they have adjusted can help to guide others in pursuit of resilience. Drawing on their experiences I show that resilience can be developed, like a muscle or a capability. Like them, we can all make adjustments that influence how we think, feel and act. I refer to this as 'resilience work'.

Throughout the book I discuss research, examples and strategies relating to resilience work, posing questions and devising exercises for the reader. I draw attention to those strategies entrepreneurs take that can strengthen resilience, such as distraction, leaning into social support, positive self-talk and reappraisal, and those that can compromise resilience, including denial and rumination. I also point out the sometimes subtle, distinctions between what can help and hinder.

What *is* an entrepreneur?

Perhaps, like me, you're fascinated by entrepreneurs. Who are they? What do they do – and why? During the last 20 years, I have observed how the term 'entrepreneur' can provoke extreme reactions. It's a word some of us proudly embrace, while others shy away from. It's a word the media commonly associate with risk-takers, visionaries and heroes. But it's also one we sometimes connect with tech geniuses in hoodies and sneakers, or even villains, greedy figures in shiny suits who are interested in turning a profit at any or all costs, perhaps set on world domination.

Some entrepreneurs themselves take issue with the word. One of the interviewees for this book made a point of distancing herself from the term. 'I'm not Elon Musk!' she said, worried that the label could be misleading. 'It sounds like you have to make so much money.'

As a consequence of this, we've created other labels to distinguish among the different kinds of entrepreneurs, like social entrepreneurs, 'ecopreneurs' and craft entrepreneurs. So, the meaning of the word depends partly on who you ask. Steve Jobs, the co-creator of Apple, is often referred to as an entrepreneur. But Anthony and Tom, the co-owners of 'Good as Gold', a small specialty coffee shop in London, are entrepreneurs too.

Commonly, an entrepreneur is understood to be a business creator or owner. An entrepreneur is someone who identifies, examines, and exploits a business opportunity.[1] Entrepreneurs include the self-employed. They have the agency, authority, and responsibility to make business decisions. They develop strategies in response to challenges.

Entrepreneurs *in crisis* are those individuals who create, own or manage businesses affected by a crisis or those who may be impacted by a crisis not directly related to the business, but which might have implications for the business. For example, consider the entrepreneur who has a health crisis or who has experienced a personal loss but must continue to direct and manage their business.

Why resilience matters and inspiration for the book

This book emphasizes how entrepreneurs can adjust to a crisis and be more resilient. A crisis can be professional or personal in nature, broad in scope or small in scale, internal or external to an organization, and major or minor in terms of impact. Like the riots described earlier, a crisis can arrive suddenly, generating uncertainty, ambiguity and time pressures for those affected.[2] A crisis is any adverse event that has the potential to create significant stress for the individual,[3] overwhelm their ability to cope,[4] and disrupt their wellbeing.[5] Stress often manifests as a kind of 'physiological and/or psychological arousal' that occurs when we perceive a threat to something we value and 'that threat taxes or exhausts the resources' we have available to confront it.[6] Resilience, in turn, is about our ability to recover swiftly from stress or to resist its negative effects altogether.

Resilience has been an enduring theme in my work with entrepreneurs. It's a topic that appears not only in my research, but also in my teaching, public speaking, mentoring, coaching and consulting. For the last couple of decades, I've been talking about the resilient entrepreneur to entrepreneurs and other business leaders, colleagues and friends, as well as to my students.

I first became interested in the study of entrepreneurs and resilience when I was undertaking research for my doctorate back in the noughties. I was looking at how entrepreneurs in transition market economies – particularly small business owners – respond to certain barriers to business growth, among them the repeated attacks on their businesses by opportunistic parties, including state officials. For example, I learned that Russian entrepreneurs could face more than 30 inspections a year from different agencies, few of which were planned or represented official business.[7] My discussions with entrepreneurs uncovered that these interactions often created much distress and negative emotions in entrepreneurs. Such interactions dampened their motivations to grow for fear of attracting unwanted attention. At the same time, and despite the difficulties, those I spoke to had managed to carry on, finding ways of navigating the business environment.

Then, in the summer of 2011 while living in North London, I witnessed first-hand the devastation inflicted on local businesses like Sofia's during the London riots. The riots began on 6 August, spreading quickly from Tottenham, a North London borough, to 22 of the 32 boroughs across the city over several days, and beyond London to several English cities. The rioting lead to fatalities, injuries, and the loss of homes and businesses.[8][9] A few thousand businesses, mostly small, independent shops and some chain stores and franchises, were severely vandalized, looted, and, in some cases, burned down, deeply impacting the business owners and the staff who ran them and the local communities they served. The process of business recovery for many riot victims took several months or years.

The morning after her business was ravaged, Marie, the 40-something-year-old owner of a children's clothing shop, spoke to me about seeing the damages for the first time:

> You know just before a storm is about to happen the birds go quiet? It was really quiet and I guess it was so early in the morning, but there were quite a few people around because people were curious. The fire brigade was there. Lots of police. There was a distinct burning smell, a smouldering smell, and a burnt-out car. It just looked like a film set. And lots of people. It was just disorder and chaos and just weird. A really weird and surreal morning. And, you know, lots of people gathered on the green and then I started to see my things just strewn all over the green. A little hat or coat hanger. One of the firemen started to help me pick some stuff up. And I saw somebody that I knew and he was crying, so I started crying. And then the fire brigade let me go underneath the cordon to see the shop ... The windows

were smashed but they were not shattered. The glass was still there. And the doors weren't even that damaged, it didn't look like … So, anybody looking at that would just think, 'Oh it's just got a smashed window'. And then, as I opened the doors, we did have blinds that pulled down and they were, they, I don't know what happened to those. They weren't there. And I just opened the doors and was met with this scene of total carnage really.

In contrast to my earlier research, the riots represented a one-off attack on businesses with long-lasting consequences. I started to explore studies on crisis management and resilience more deeply, noting the advances, gaps and limitations within these research streams. Then, two or three months after the riots, and again two years later in 2013, I interviewed entrepreneurs like Sofia and Marie, who were directly impacted. I began to understand just how significant a crisis could be to these individuals personally and learned more about the implications for their wellbeing, something that had not been sufficiently documented. I further uncovered that the ways in which they managed their distress and negative emotions allowed them to continue or, in some cases, thrive.

Later, in the spring of 2020, like many others, I became interested in how the ever-evolving coronavirus pandemic was impacting entrepreneurs. Many of them, like me, had to find a new way of operating while juggling the pressures of life and family. For the vast majority who were forced to significantly alter their operations or close for a time, it became a long waiting game.

In addition to the social and economic components of the London riots, the COVID-19 pandemic included a spiralling health crisis. This presented some similar and some different challenges. In the spring of 2020, COVID-19 was declared a global pandemic by the World Health Organization. With some exceptions, lockdowns were imposed by governments around the world, enforcing strict social distancing rules and forcing the closure of non-essential businesses.

In England there were three official lockdowns between March 2020 and the spring of 2021.[10] I interviewed entrepreneurs affected by the pandemic, and some more than once. I also conducted a weekly diary study to capture the experiences of a group of entrepreneurs, which began just prior to the first lockdown and continued over the next 15 months. These investigations enabled me to examine the thoughts, feelings and behaviours of entrepreneurs in crisis over time. The pandemic and its associated lockdowns demonstrated to me the twists and turns a crisis could take, and the corresponding highs and lows, which often stretched entrepreneurs to their limit.

On the cusp of the first lockdown, brought into force on 23 March 2020, Robert, the 30-something-year-old owner of a successful café, made three diary entries which together highlight his growing uncertainty, distress and discomfort around keeping the business open:

> Up until March 20th: Feeling very up and down. Waiting every day for the 5pm press briefing. It's very stressful as nobody knows what's going on. Staff are desperately trying to ask questions for answers that I don't know. But trade remains quite steady.
>
> March 20th–22nd: Feels like we're in limbo. Positive news regarding employees being paid 80% [of their salaries in accordance with the furlough scheme initiated by the government], but trade still consistent. More pressure from the public to close despite the shop still feeling busy, albeit with restrictions in place. We worked at [name of market] which was unbelievably busy and didn't feel right. It didn't feel safe putting myself in front of hundreds of people while the shop was quieter. Feel very guilty making employees work, even though they all agreed to.
>
> March 23rd onwards: Unbearably stressful, probably one of the worst weekends I can remember. Constantly torn between needing to keep my business going but then feeling like I should shut for the public good, even though the big supermarkets can stay open? Eventually decided to close on 23rd ... We agreed collectively it didn't feel right to open.

With little warning given of when lockdowns would come into effect or how long they would remain, combined with the need for last-minute changes, many entrepreneurs like Robert experienced feelings of anger, frustration and anxiety. This was especially true for those running customer-facing businesses. How these entrepreneurs personally dealt with the crisis is deserving of attention.

How is being an entrepreneur *different*?

This book is a culmination of those investigations with entrepreneurs and, importantly, findings from previous studies on crises and resilience from different parts of the world. In the former case, I draw insights from a pool of more than 100 interviews and 200 weekly diaries I conducted with entrepreneurs in crisis.

Most of these entrepreneurs were running small to medium-sized enterprises (SMEs) with fewer than 250 employees. In the UK, of the 5.5 million registered private sector businesses, more than 99% are classified as SMEs; 1.4 million of which have employees and a whopping 4.1 million are managed and operated by a single individual.[11] A similar distribution is common across the world.

These businesses operate with greater resource constraints than large businesses. Even so, the individuals responsible for them tend to be resourceful. For example, during the pandemic many of the restaurant owners I spoke to had created shops inside their businesses, weekend super clubs or flourishing e-commerce platforms to sell ingredients. But what really makes all these entrepreneurs special is that their identities are often entwined with their businesses, creating additional pressures on them, and making threats to the viability of their businesses all the more personal and impactful. Anne and Jacob, both affected by the London riots, are cases in point.

Anne's bespoke handmade clothing shop had just reopened when we met. It had been boarded up for months for repairs. When their stock was destroyed, Anne and her mother and business partner Chloe took on the enormous task of re-making all of the formal wear themselves. Anne explained to me why she and Chloe were motivated to keep going:

> On the face of it, it's property. It's things, but, it's our livelihood and it depends on what kind of value you place on it. I mean everybody does something. This is what we do.

Jacob, the 50-something serial entrepreneur and owner of a high-end branded clothing store ransacked by rioters, had similar views:

Owning your own business, I couldn't put it into any sentence. To me, it's as important as the blood that flows through my veins. This business is everything I'm about. Everything that's in here has come at a cost and I'm passionate about what we do.

Many entrepreneurs like Anne and Jacob regard their businesses to be a key part of who they are. They see their businesses as their babies, or as their home away from home. For them, finding a way to continue during a crisis, or in its aftermath, is a priority.

Why is this book important?

Entrepreneurs like Sofia, Marie, Robert, Anne, Chloe and Jacob are people who don't often spend time in the spotlight. Most popular business books about entrepreneurs or business leaders focus on the ascent of those who are already well-known or celebrated. This book is concerned instead with the vulnerability and resilience of the people who make up the overwhelming population of entrepreneurs: the *everyday entrepreneurs*. Their stories of resilience are relatable, and their strategies can inspire us to think more about what we are all capable of.

This book brings to light what entrepreneurs in crisis *do* to diminish their distress, to maintain healthy functioning and to be more resilient, so that they might carry on. Previous research has concentrated on the actions entrepreneurs or business leaders have taken to mitigate the negative effects of a crisis to businesses,[12] or on the capabilities and resources that are required for businesses in crisis to adjust.[13] The emphasis, it seems, has been on what matters to resilience at the organizational level,[14] something I've found in earlier studies on both risk management and continuity management.[15] With the exception of studies that focus on the personality traits entrepreneurs possess that might make them more or less resilient – such as self-efficacy,[16] perseverance, and optimism[17] – less is known about the resilience of entrepreneurs in crisis at the individual level. Until now, little has been understood about what entrepreneurs 'do' to develop their resilience and to adjust personally to a crisis. Highlighting the kind of 'resilience work' entrepreneurs undertake is crucial, not only because their business is important to them and their families, but also to their many stakeholders, especially their team and their community.

In their many forms, individually and collectively, crises have the potential to create significant distress. They can directly affect households. They can disrupt the flow of goods and services on which many depend, not least of which the entrepreneurs who operate them. This book draws together previous research on individual resilience from different crises – human-induced crises like riots and terrorist attacks, health crises grand in scale or closer to home, natural disasters such as flooding and fires, economic crises, environmental and organizational crises. In many cases, states, governmental and humanitarian organizations, insurers, the community and the like must intervene to support entrepreneurs and their businesses through a crisis. I provide examples throughout the book of the important role these institutions play in recovery, often alongside the actions of entrepreneurs.

Crises, it seems, have been a fairly consistent feature of the civic and commercial landscape and people have adapted, drawing on certain strategies, intentionally or otherwise. To shed some light on how entrepreneurs adjust to crisis, I draw from different fields of research, predominantly psychology. Not only can prior learning from psychology and other areas help explain just how entrepreneurs in crisis adjust, but it is the case that stories of entrepreneurs in crisis can more broadly demonstrate, and even extend, concepts and strategies relating to resilience.

And, of course, it has become increasingly evident that crises are not going away. This should serve to warn and reassure us at the same time. At this very moment, millions of people are dealing with some sort of crisis and its companion, uncertainty. You may be managing a crisis at home or at work, a local tragedy that has struck your community or a national emergency. The World Economic Forum[18] cites natural disasters and extreme weather events, warfare, economic downturns, a failure to adapt to climate change, dwindling natural resources, and cybercrime as posing significant threats to our way of life. Further, it suggests that we are on the brink of a 'polycrisis', when the collective impact of disparate crises combine to exceed the sum of each part with devastating consequences. The next crisis, it seems, is brewing. It may be small and personal in scale. It could be larger than we could imagine. Developing a readiness to respond to crisis is becoming a necessity in our hyper-connected world. And the research and practical exercises featured within the book may be a resource for all those preparing for a crisis, or those who may be at the beginning, middle or end of a crisis.

★★★

Resilience, therefore, is an important and timeless topic, one that everyone can practice and benefit from. This book will provide you with some of the insights and tools to start.

The structure of the book

Chapter 1 lays the groundwork. It provides an overview of different concepts and research streams relating to resilience. It is intended to help us better understand resilience and, critically, to recognize resilience when we see it. Thereafter, the book is structured in such a way as to allow you to dip in and out as I describe the strategies commonly adopted by entrepreneurs in crisis. In Chapters 2–8, I discuss those strategies that minimize distress and strengthen resilience. In Chapters 9–11, I consider those strategies that can potentially compromise resilience, depending on how they're employed or for how long. Throughout, I reveal what we can learn in each case.

Chapters 2–11 each define the featured strategy, describe the form the strategy takes and discuss when it's effective (or problematic), drawing from theory, prior research and different examples. Importantly, each chapter includes powerful stories of entrepreneurs in crisis who utilized the strategy, the role it played and its implications. Each chapter also highlights, through reflections, guidance, exercises and actionable takeaways, what entrepreneurs can do to engage with the strategies (or to protect themselves from their negative implications).

In the concluding chapter, Chapter 12, I summarize what I mean by 'resilience work', discussing some of the key lessons and how you can start to implement them. I provide some Additional Commentaries at the end of the book for practitioners as well as academics, advisors and policy makers working with this topic, stakeholders and the family and friends of those affected by crisis.

1

Understanding Resilience

We've all used the word 'resilient' at one time or another to refer to family members, friends, colleagues, acquaintances or public figures who have experienced their share of life's hard knocks. This might include those who have had very difficult upbringings. Those who may be battling with personal illness. Those who have lost loved ones. Been laid off. Struggled career-wise or financially. Endured a series of bad relationships or unfortunate, even catastrophic, events.

Think of the following comment made by a work colleague in casual conversation over lunch: 'My friend Amelia is so resilient. Despite being made redundant more than once and experiencing other personal setbacks, she's managed to run a business and raise three great kids all on her own.' But what does it really mean to warrant this label, to be resilient like Amelia, or like Sofia, Marie, Robert, Anne, Chloe and Jacob, whose stories I captured in part at the start?

What is resilience?

George Bonanno, a leading psychologist on the topic of resilience, defines resilience as our ability as individuals, when we are experiencing a highly disruptive event, 'to maintain relatively stable, healthy levels of psychological and physical functioning' across time, despite transient perturbations (or in simpler terms, the occasional uneasiness), and our 'capacity for generative experiences and positive emotions'.[1] Resilience, therefore, is about recovering quickly and easily from stress. Hence, its popular association with the notion of 'bouncing back' or even 'bouncing forward'.

Resilience can also involve resisting the ill effects of stress from adversity altogether.

Resilience is often associated with a range of concepts which provide us with a deeper understanding of its meaning, such as healthy functioning, protective factors and positive or flexible adaptation. Each helps us think about resilience and how we can work towards it.

Healthy functioning

From a mental health perspective, resilience has been described as maintaining healthy functioning across time, both through adversity and in the long term.[2] This feature of resilience makes it somewhat unlike recovery, where, following adversity, 'normal [psychological or physical] functioning temporarily gives way to threshold or subthreshold psychopathology (for example, symptoms of depression or posttraumatic stress disorder), usually for a period of at least several months, and then gradually returns to pre-event levels'.[3] This means that whereas an individual in recovery may experience depression and an inability to function for a period of time, before eventually returning to a position of homeostasis (a balanced state), the resilient individual experiences very little disruption by comparison[4] and maintains more consistent levels of healthy functioning.[5] Resilient individuals might experience some symptoms of posttraumatic stress, including negative emotions, but the duration of that stress is limited.[6] Negative emotions, in this case, tend not to affect them significantly.[7]

Resilience as healthy functioning tends to incorporate concepts such as psychological and physical wellbeing, positive emotions and posttraumatic growth. We can also learn more about healthy functioning by thinking about what constitutes unhealthy functioning.

Healthy functioning is often concerned with maintaining our psychological and physical wellbeing,[8] both of which are important to resilience. Research suggests that when we are psychologically healthy, we tend to be satisfied with our lives and to feel a sense of purpose. We're able to actively solve problems, experience mastery, higher levels of positive affect and lower levels of negative affect;[9] 'affect' being an umbrella term capturing both moods and emotions but one that I often use in the book interchangeably with the term emotions. When we are physically healthy, we make healthy choices.

Staying physically active, eating well and ensuring we get enough rest, are all examples.

As noted, healthy functioning is partly about our ability to experience positive emotions.[10] Positive emotions have a particularly important role to play in resilience[11] because they can help to quiet or undo some of the negative emotions we might experience during or following an adverse event.[12] Expressing gratitude, joy or love for others and being able to laugh or see the humour in a difficult situation can help us diminish painful feelings of grief, anger, frustration or fear. At the same time, negative emotions have value and should not be dismissed. They signal to us that something is wrong and deserving of our attention.[13] Nevertheless, negative emotions, if prolonged, can direct our attention to the emotions themselves, obstructing our thinking in the process, and potentially narrowing our range of responses. Certain positive emotions, alternatively, can serve to build more resources, social or otherwise, and generate creativity by expanding the thoughts and actions that come to mind, as outlined in Barbara Fredrickson's broaden-and-build theory.[14] Frederickson suggests that joy, for instance, can expand our thought-action repertoires by creating a desire in us to play and push the boundaries, whereas pride broadens the urge to share our achievements with others or to seek out future achievements. For these reasons, strategies that diminish or manage negative emotions and enhance positive emotions in a crisis will be valuable to resilience.

A great illustration of this dynamic comes from the second instalment of the Pixar film *Inside Out*, a coming-of-age story about a girl and the different emotions in her head – including Joy, Anger, Fear, Sadness and Disgust – who help her navigate certain situations, including key life transitions. SPOILER ALERT for anyone who hasn't yet seen it. In the sequel, we are introduced to new characters, including Anxiety. Reilly, our 13-year-old protagonist, who is in the throes of puberty, learns while on her way to a hockey camp with her two best friends that they won't be attending the same high school as her in the autumn. Anxiety's influence over Reilly in this situation produces mixed results. On the one hand, Anxiety helps Reilly prepare for a critical hockey match designed to showcase her talent, not only potentially earning her a spot on her coveted team but providing her with a new group of friends who attend the same high school. On the other hand, Anxiety does so at the cost of Reilly's sleep and peace of mind as she vigorously competes with her two best friends in the process, forsaking them to impress her newer, older hockey friends. Importantly, at the film's climax, Anxiety, consumed with fears of Reilly failing to qualify for the team and navigating high school alone, spins out of control, becoming immobilized, unable to think or act. Luckily for Reilly, the character Joy intervenes, reminding her of all the special times she's shared with her old friends and just what they have meant to her. Joy takes Anxiety by the hand and out of her negative spiral, helping Reilly move towards a positive resolution during the final stages of the hockey game.

Healthy functioning is also about posttraumatic growth. It's here where the notion of bouncing forward comes into play. Posttraumatic growth captures the positive aspects of going through a crisis for the individual, personally/or and professionally. In a natural disaster, of which flooding and earthquakes are examples, posttraumatic growth can manifest as a feeling that we've made a positive contribution to the recovery effort by becoming more informed about crisis victims and survivors, or by gaining a better understanding what factors can help or hinder rescue operations.[15] It might entail improving our professional competence in some way, like becoming more skilled at managing business teams during an evolving crisis, such as the COVID-19 pandemic. Posttraumatic growth also might involve developing new possibilities, paths, behaviours and interests.[16] At the same time, resilient outcomes don't always provide the opportunity or need for posttraumatic growth, although they can be valuable and help us adapt to a crisis.[17]

In contrast to healthy functioning, unhealthy functioning in adversity can be explained by the presence of mental distress or mental illness. While acute stress is expected in crisis situations, unhealthy functioning may result when our stress is prolonged and our recovery is incomplete.[18] Broadly speaking, unhealthy functioning might involve posttraumatic stress symptomology (PTSS) which is associated with poor psychological and physical health. Poor psychological health can take the form of depression, anxiety, irritability, anger, constant worrying, poor memory and judgement, and focusing on the negative. Poor physical health can include difficulties eating and sleeping.

Posttraumatic stress disorder (PTSD), which depends on the experience of a traumatic event, is one of the most frequently studied post-crisis mental health conditions.[19] PTSD tends to involve repeatedly experiencing the trauma weeks, months, or even years later. More specifically, those individuals with PTSD tend to have negative thoughts and emotions and tend to avoid situations that may prompt them to recall the trauma, which some suggest might reinforce rather than assuage negative perceptions.[20] Research on disasters, a kind of crisis, suggests that a third of disaster victims may experience PTSD; for children, these rates may be even higher.[21]

After PTSD, depression is the second most frequently studied mental health condition following a disaster. Depression can have many symptoms, including feelings of sadness and a loss of pleasure in things once enjoyed. Situational depression tends to be more common after a crisis than clinical depression. Populations affected by disasters frequently report PTSD or depression, as well as other mental health conditions such as anxiety, panic disorders or substance use disorders (such as alcohol and drug use disorders), and physical symptoms such as headaches, fatigue and abdominal pain.[22]

Some research suggests that the absence of psychopathologies such as PTSD, depression and anxiety following a disaster or crisis more broadly, is an indicator of resilience.[23] However, this definition of resilience also has its limitations in that it doesn't capture the experience of individuals who don't exhibit psychopathology but who do have low level symptoms and impaired functioning at work, home and/or school, with some negative impact on their quality of life overall.[24]

Protective factors

The notion of protective factors is also important to our understanding of resilience. Work on resilience and protective factors can be traced back to groundbreaking studies on adults with schizophrenia and studies of children and adolescents with early experiences of trauma. In the latter case, critical research carried out by psychologists including Norman Garmezy,[25] Michael Rutter,[26] Emmy Werner and Ruth Smith[27] has investigated why within populations of young people those who have endured catastrophic life events, parental mental illness, violence, maltreatment and socio-economic advantages, different strategies might be adopted for dealing with such difficult situations, and such strategies may be either maladaptive or adaptive in nature. Psychologists have found that the presence or absence of protective factors have an important role to play.

Protective factors are regarded to be those characteristics or resources that promote positive adaptation in adversity and modify the risks associated with exposure to adversity.[28] Over time, psychologists have identified several 'protective factors' or attributes that we might possess at the individual level (such as self-esteem or a positive temperament), familial/group level (such as cohesive or responsive caregiving) and societal or community levels (such as peer networks or supportive communities). Together these protective factors can form a constellation of protective variables for individuals affected by adversity and make them more resilient in turn.[29]

It can be helpful to think about what your own protective factors might be and how have they have helped you. In my teaching I have, on occasion, asked my undergraduate and masters' students to reflect independently on what they believe to be their own protective factors. Common responses have included being optimistic or solution focused, and the critical role played by family. I reckon that my own protective factors would be much the same, along with key friendships.

Protective factors have been identified in studies on crises and crisis workers as those factors that mitigate the harmful effects of crisis events on these individuals. For instance, health care workers dealing with SARS (severe acute respiratory syndrome), which caused an epidemic in several countries between 2002 and 2004,[30] and police officers dealing with the 2004 Madrid bombings, which targeted commuter trains a few days before Spain's general elections, killing 193 people and injuring more than 2000,[31] have shown that lower levels of posttraumatic stress symptoms coincide with higher levels of crisis training in handling infectious disease outbreaks and training in managing terrorist attacks, respectively. Similarly, firefighters who provided assistance following Hurricane Katrina in 2005, which killed nearly 2000 people and displaced over a million more,[32] reported fewer depressive symptoms if they were living with their families at the time.[33] Federal employees with more confidantes reported fewer posttraumatic stress disorder (PTSD) symptoms following the 9/11 attacks in New York City.[34] These examples suggest pre-crisis training and social support are crucial protective factors that can make people more resilient in a crisis.

Positive adaptation and flexible adaptation

The concept of adaptation is frequently associated with resilience. Adaptation captures how individuals, organizations or communities respond to stressors and the decisions and actions they take to return to an equilibrium state following adversity. While some of us might be unscathed by an adverse event and not need to adapt, those directly affected typically engage in adaptation.

Resilience is often described as positive adaptation to adversity.[35] For the individual, positive adaptation can take the form of certain responses, cognitive, emotional and behavioural responses; and more often still, and as my own research suggests, a combination of all three. Positive adaptation is important in that it can translate into desirable outcomes following adversity, such as (a) maintaining healthy functioning, (b) engaging in a process of recovery and (c) achieving better-than-expected outcomes.[36] In the latter case, for example, it may be that after being made redundant, getting into a retraining programme leads to a more fulfilling and better paid position.

Protective factors have been linked to positive adaptation in times of adversity. A case in point is the Deepwater Horizon oil spill in 2010, the largest recorded marine oil drilling disaster in history. The spill was preceded by an explosion which sunk the rig and led to the deaths of 11 workers; 4 million barrels of oil flowed into the Gulf of Mexico over a period of 87 days before the leak was capped off. A study of the Deepwater Horizon oil spill found that for the Gulf Coast communities affected in Texas, Mississippi, Louisiana, Alabama and Florida, social networks served as a protective factor that promoted positive adaptation in most individuals.[37]

While positive adaptation is a necessary part of resilience, flexible adaptation may also have a valuable role to play.[38] Several scholars, including Cecilia Cheng[39] and George Bonanno,[40] have argued that successful coping in adversity is not so much about adopting specific coping strategies per se, but about our ability to flexibly adapt these strategies to the stressor at hand; strategies which might involve finding ways of expressing certain emotions or suppressing those emotions when needed, and doing so in healthy ways. For example, losing a loved one can be especially difficult. Flexible adaptation in this case might include carrying on with certain responsibilities or routines in the aftermath, such as going to work and focusing on the tasks at hand, or participating in certain social engagements or activities, but separate to this, also having the time and space to speak to friends or family about the loss, expressing and sharing one's grief. Therefore, being able to flexibly adapt is also important to resilience and should be considered alongside positive adaptation.

★★★

Resilience has also been conceived of as a personality trait, an outcome and a process. Each research stream tells us more about resilience and its form and function.

Resilience as a personality trait

As a personality trait, resilience is seen as something stable that we as human beings possess, like hardiness,[41] or having a predisposition towards positive emotions,[42] and a sense of humour.[43] We can think of hardy individuals as those who are able to see both the benefits and losses associated with a difficult situation and as being able to manage more effectively as a result.[44]

As a trait, resilience is often linked to certain characteristics like hardiness, but also to 'self-efficacy',[45] a belief that one is able to perform certain roles/tasks or achieve certain outcomes, 'self-esteem',[46] a confidence in/or opinion of ourselves, and a 'locus of control orientation', particularly a feeling of being in control of certain outcomes.[47] One study has shown that individuals with higher levels of self-efficacy tend to use more coping strategies than those with lower levels.[48]

Research on resilience as a trait has tended to investigate the personality characteristics possessed by individuals who are subjected to traumatic events, characteristics that mitigate the negative effects of such events and promote their adaptation.[49] Studies have looked at whether the presence of self-esteem can protect individuals who have experienced childhood maltreatment from depression.[50] Or if bereaved individuals who score high on trait resilience might experience grief symptoms such as cognitive intrusions and health deficits in more transient than enduring ways.[51]

Historically, a focus on personality traits has dominated resilience studies. Even to the detriment of acknowledging other important influences on our personal and professional lives, such as families, communities, organizations and the greater context.[52] An emphasis on personality traits implies that our capacity to navigate stressful events is either abundant or deficient[53] – that we have the capacity to cope, or we don't. For these reasons, while traits are important, I think it's unhelpful to look at traits alone. We should also consider resilience as an outcome and a process.

Resilience as an outcome

Defining resilience as an outcome tends to focus on the 'state of being resilient'.[54] This perspective of resilience has been captured, in part, by the resiliency model.[55] The resiliency model assumes that when certain systems are disrupted, different pathways might be taken as individuals engage in a process of reintegration or regulation, which can lead to different outcomes in turn.[56] We may experience resilience, for instance, when certain protective characteristics or resources are present such as self-esteem or peer support, and when we undertake coping strategies such as emotion regulation; all of which can serve as a buffer to limit the disruption or associated low levels of dysfunction.[57] Moreover, some of us might also go on to develop healthier coping mechanisms or even to grow following adversity, as suggested earlier by the notion of posttraumatic growth (PTG).

Two years after the London riots, Anne spoke to me about how, in addition to being a business owner, she was inspired by events to become a writer, focusing on 'socio-political issues':

> It was just a useful thing for me to do to just think about communities and community collusion. So, I thought well, that is a good way of channelling things, so it doesn't kind of fester into any kind of toxic energy. Because it was really easy to kind of talk about, well, this is urban decay, and this is what you expect: this is urban decay. But that's fine if you want to throw it out there but if you are ... still having a business, still having a presence in an area of urban decay it might, for me, I decided, it might be more constructive to think about inverting the narrative.

This may not be the case for everyone, however. Outcomes for some following a crisis event might be negative. That is, without enough characteristics or resources in place and healthy coping strategies, we may either improve, but over a long period of time, or adjust in an unhealthy or maladaptive fashion and be worse off than we were prior to the disruption.[58] Unhealthy or maladaptive coping mechanisms might include, but are not limited to: substance abuse, social withdrawal, and those generally focused on suppressing emotions.

Nevertheless, even within this outcome stream of resilience research, it has been argued that it can be unhelpful to think of individuals as either resilient or not. Rather, we should reflect more on the different possible trajectories, and what a good outcome following adversity might look like,[59] given the event in question and experiences of the individuals involved.

Resilience as a process

Alternatively, as a process, resilience takes on a more all-encompassing role. In this case, resilience is depicted not so much as something we do or don't possess, or do or don't achieve, but as a capability that we can develop over time by adjusting our thoughts, behaviours and emotions.[60]

Within this research stream, resilience is regarded as a way of thinking, a kind of mindset we can foster in ourselves to resolve problems, look for the opportunities, and accept making mistakes, failing or falling short; the type of mindset that encourages us to start over or try again.[61] As a case in point, Sofia, the bar owner I spoke to after the London riots, said to me: 'If it is some [kind of] crisis I just work harder and I don't think about that and then, finally, you resolve the problem.'

Resilience as a process is also a way of acting that enables us as individuals to utilize our own internal resources and external resources to adapt to adversity,[62] and to build up and maintain our resources before, during and after adversity.[63] This might include forging strong connections to members of the local community, which can serve as an important source of support for an individual and their business. Following the riots, Sofia felt supported by members of the public and her customers, the local council and the police. She explained to me that often people 'were coming in and asking' how she was, and that she 'received so many flowers and so many chocolates and so many cards'. The police were also helpful, she said, 'making sure that we feel safe'.

Resilience in this process view is further about learning how to regulate emotions in stressful situations in order to make decisions and take actions. Emotion regulation is about influencing the emotions we have and when we have them to shape the way we feel.[64] This might necessitate changing our thinking and behaviours as well. By reframing the riots, putting things in a positive light, Sofia was able to diminish her negative emotions somewhat and carry on. 'Well, I'm back', she said. 'They didn't really damage us completely and people were really supportive as well.' Other ways of regulating our emotions might include reflecting on what we've learned from a difficult situation, distracting ourselves which could take the form of watching a funny film or clip on YouTube or by seeking out certain people or events which make us feel positive or inspired.

A focus on the mechanisms that lead to resilient functioning[65] within this process stream of research has further led to the design of prevention and intervention strategies for promoting resilience.[66] Examples of these strategies are often found in studies of resilience in elite athletes. One such strategy is to encourage athletes to engage in de-catastrophizing upcoming events in an effort to increase their coping skills and to undertake more comprehensive planning.[67] This might involve leading the athlete through the process of identifying the worst-case scenario (such as a runner tripping or a cyclist crashing) and potential outcomes (such as injuring oneself, falling behind or losing the race), followed by the best-case scenario, the most-likely scenario, and a programme for managing oneself and the environment in relation to each situation.

Take another example, that of being at risk of redundancy. This might involve not only reflecting on the redundancy process and our rights, but contemplating the possibility of losing our job and not finding another job quickly or one that is desirable. Other possibilities might include not being made redundant or being made redundant but landing our dream job shortly thereafter. Speaking to people around us, exploring the alternatives, drawing on support and taking care of our mental and physical health are things we can begin to do to manage the effects, either way.

Research on resilience as a process also looks at certain mediating processes, such as how or in what ways people draw on protective factors, certain characteristics or resources (such as support from family/friends), to achieve better-than-expected outcomes.[68] In this case, if two individuals in the same company have been made redundant and one has a wider social network of personal and professional connections than the other, they might be able to bounce back more quickly.

Entrepreneurs and resilience

As I noted in my introduction, existing research on entrepreneurship in times of crisis is often concerned with organizational resilience, as opposed to individual resilience, even though entrepreneurs' resilience can impact firms' resilience.[69] Entrepreneurs and their personal experiences are rarely the focus. Nevertheless, interest is growing in entrepreneurs and resilience more broadly, beyond the context of a crisis. There is some research available on the topic which concentrates on the antecedents of entrepreneurial resilience (such as traits, experiences or contexts that may make resilience more likely) and on the outcomes of entrepreneurial resilience. However, few studies explore what entrepreneurs can do to be more individually resilient. And research on resilience as a process, it seems, is sparse. Next, I discuss two systematic reviews[a] on entrepreneurial resilience and what's been done to advance our understanding and the gaps.

The first systematic review of the literature on entrepreneurial resilience was conducted by Korber and McNaughton.[70] When it comes to the antecedents of resilience, they found that studies have focused on intrinsic factors related to entrepreneurs or their businesses. There are certain traits or qualities which entrepreneurs might possess, including optimism, perseverance, or emotional intelligence which is about understanding our own emotions and the emotions of others, what triggers them, and how we can regulate emotions or shift our behaviours, accordingly. It could be the case, for instance, that entrepreneurs with more emotional

---

[a] Examine research on a topic (collating studies according to certain criteria) to unpack the main themes.

intelligence can build stronger relationships with different groups of stakeholders (like family and friends, as well as staff, customers or community members), by empathizing more with their needs. And these relationships might prove to be critical to their resilience. However, Korber and McNaughton suggest that research has not explored how entrepreneurs might tap into these traits or qualities during periods of adversity to be more resilient. They further argue that while individual resilience has been theorized to play a role in organizational resilience, this assumption has not yet been tested.

A second systematic review of the literature on the resilience of entrepreneurs was carried out by Hartmann and colleagues[71] who found that certain personal and contextual factors help entrepreneurs cultivate psychological resilience. Personal factors include personality traits, once again, but also learning experiences, personal experiences, commitment, attitudes and behaviours. For example, my own studies[72] and those carried out by the likes of Simon Stephens and colleagues,[73] have uncovered that entrepreneurs' prior experiences of a crisis enabled them to be more resilient. I've spoken to many entrepreneurs over the years who, while dealing with a present crisis, reflected on how a professional or personal crisis in the past had prepared them more mentally, emotionally and practically for what was to come next. Like David, who dealt with a shop fire years before the London riots, or Anthony who had lived through his wife's cancer diagnosis. Other personal factors identified from previous studies as being important to resilience include emotional capabilities such as emotion regulation, cognitive capabilities such as creativity and behavioural capabilities which include the likes of seeking out social support.[74] Contextual factors linked to cultivating entrepreneurial resilience incorporate the external and internal business environment, resources, social networks, and support.[75] Yet, upon examining the research reviewed by Hartmann and colleagues, it seems that these studies have neither fully explored nor provided rich accounts of how entrepreneurs utilize personal and contextual factors to achieve resilience or what they can do.

Beyond the antecedents of resilience, Hartmann and her collaborators also examined different outcomes of resilience for entrepreneurs, specifically regarding the initiation of, engagement with and performance of entrepreneurial endeavours. For instance, resilience has been shown to have a positive influence on the intentions to start a business and is seen as something that can be nurtured by entrepreneurs.[76] Resilience has further been found to increase the agency of entrepreneurs in a crisis.[77] These studies suggest that by examining entrepreneurs in crisis, we can learn more about individual resilience. At the same time, to date, previous studies are unclear about how entrepreneurs can nurture resilience or how resilience can enable them to respond to a crisis.

★★★

My aim over the following chapters is to build on the idea of resilience as a process, shining a light on how entrepreneurs in crisis develop resilience, like a muscle or as a capability, what I refer to as 'resilience work'. I show how, through their examples, we too might build our resilience. I suggest that resilience work is comprised of adjustments that impact on our thoughts, feelings and behaviours. These adjustments can be made to where we hold our attention, to how we think of ourselves, others or events, to the situations we face and to our resources. Distraction, for one, is a valuable strategy that entrepreneurs use to shift their attention, as we will see in the next chapter.

PART I

Strategies Entrepreneurs Use That Strengthen Resilience

2

Distraction

Robert left university in his early 20s to pursue his passion for coffee. On 16 March 2020, a week before the first COVID-19 lockdown was imposed by the British government, the now 30-something-year-old owner of a popular café in Southeast London shared with me his growing concerns. 'We didn't build being shut for 2, 3, 4+ weeks into our plan for the year' or 'an overall slowing down of our regular customer base'. Robert felt his anxiety becoming more palpable by the day:

> Probably this weekend I started getting very concerned. My biggest concern is we don't have the capital to survive a long period of closure. I'm also worried about myself and everyone else that works for us, how they'll be paid.

Three days after the first lockdown announcement on 23 March 2020, he wrote in his diary that it had been 'unbelievably, unbearably stressful' for him, with 'people crying' and asking him 'constant questions about pay', which were difficult to answer. Robert was pensive, deliberating over whether to close the café temporarily or carry on, while adhering to social distancing requirements:

> Hospitality, in general, can be pretty stressful, or certainly, from my own personal perspective. I find certain instances stressful and hard to handle. What's been particularly hard about COVID-19 stuff is that you seem to have two polar groups. Those who think that you're absolute scum for being open, despite

> them not understanding the financial implications for us when we're shut. I found people via social media saying things like that we should shut upsetting. And I felt that they were coming from people whose entire financial dependence wasn't at stake. I'm not saying that they aren't potentially right but when there was, and essentially still is, nothing for businesses who have to close on the table – it's extremely hard to decide to call it quits and close the door. Then you have another group of people who don't seem bothered. They don't seem to respect why you've put certain measures in (why you won't accept keep cups for example) and in general, seemed quite sneery about the whole thing. Again, not respecting that we were putting those measures in place for both our safety and theirs. While they might be going out for a coffee and it might be the only personal contact they have with someone all week, we were seeing hundreds of people a day and our risk inside the shop was greater than theirs.

Ten days later, he shut his doors. Robert was feeling good about his decision:

> We were still trading and although sales were down by about 20%-ish, we could have continued with a bit of a plan and a few furloughs. We unanimously decided to close because it didn't feel right being open, most of us didn't feel comfortable exposing ourselves to many people each day, regardless of any changes to the serving structure.

While the café was closed, thoughts about staffing, payroll and general finances played on his mind:

> I'm mostly concerned for all the other employees who are now earning 80% of their salaries. At the moment, I'm cautious about saying 'oh we'll pay your other 20%' because we don't know how long this is going to go on for and what trading might look like on the other end.

At the same time, Robert was spending more time with his family and working around the house, which was pleasant. 'When I can discount the financial implications, it's actually really quite nice and relaxing being at home. I have never spent this much time at home. Ever.' He described some of the things he was up to that shifted his focus away from his financial worries: 'We've been doing lots of odd jobs around the house that we've talked about doing but never got round to. I've cooked with my son.'

Distraction can be an effective course of action as a short-term reprieve in a crisis. Several entrepreneurs in crisis shared with me how they used distraction to manage their negative feelings.

What is distraction?

Distraction is any task or stimulus that shifts our attention and, in so doing, interferes with the generation of negative emotions by taking our attention away from the 'emotionally salient aspects of an emotion-eliciting event'.[1] This might involve focusing attention on the non-emotion relevant aspects of the situation, like when you're nervous about speaking in front of an audience you take in the design of the room or what people are wearing; or when you shift your attention away from the immediate situation altogether,[2] such as checking your phone or your emails during the break. Distraction, therefore, is a form of emotion regulation that relies on directing our attention within a given situation in order to influence our emotions.[3] In some cases, the external environment cannot be altered. We still need to do the presentation, for example. It can't be avoided. Turning towards our internal state can be useful in these circumstances and help us manage stress.[4]

There are many kinds of possible distractions. Watching a funny film, spending time with friends, exercising, playing sports or a video game, baking, drawing and gardening can all serve as distractions. Yet, it seems that some forms of distraction are more effective than others. Research has shown that more cognitively demanding or absorbing tasks or stimuli are especially good distractions, better at regulating negative emotions.[5] Cognitively demanding or absorbing tasks might include learning a new skill, such as a new language or how to play an instrument. For me, learning to play the guitar, even for a mere 10–30 minutes in the evenings, is something I do that occupies my focus. Challenging games or problem-solving activities are other examples.

Even understanding humour can also be quite cognitively demanding as our attentional resources are required to 'get the joke'.[6] Take the example of one of my favourite kids' jokes, the one I'm not allowed to say in front of my daughter anymore. *Question: Why did the banana go to the doctor? Answer: Because it wasn't peeling well.* Getting the joke in this case requires you to think both about the features of a banana (that you tend to peel it before eating it), and why you might go to the doctor (because you're not feeling well). I've never thought about it before but maybe this is precisely why I liked watching amusing interview clips with performers, actors and comedians especially. Because it's not only entertaining, but it can be quite engrossing.

To test whether humour is indeed an effective distraction from negative emotions, Strick and colleagues[7] carried out an experiment with 90 university students which involved presenting these individuals with a series of either neutral or negative pictures followed by an unrelated humorous stimulus, or a positive but non-humorous stimulus, and asking them to report their feelings. Researchers found that, in the short term, the more that the humorous stimuli engaged attentional resources, the better they were at regulating the negative emotions that emerged in response to the negative pictures. For this reason, they suggested that exposure to humour can help individuals attenuate painful feelings in the moment, but not necessarily longer term. It might also be the case that humour elicits positive emotions which can help alleviate negative emotions.

During the pandemic I became more aware of the powerful effects of humour. I remember how, on one occasion, after having spent ages preparing dinner, my partner, somewhat deflated, described the resulting meal he had prepared as being little more than 'approachable'. I don't know why, but in a time of enforced social distancing, his choice of wording was a source of amusement for me, one I reflected on and took as an indication that we had been isolating for too long.

When is distraction most effective?

Distraction has been shown to be effective when the emotional intensity of a situation is high, as in the case of a crisis and following a loss; the loss of a loved one, income or home. Natural disasters like earthquakes can be especially difficult for those affected. They not only create measurable social impacts for residents but have enormous economic and environmental implications.

Japan, Indonesia, China, The Philippines, Turkey, Peru, the United States, Mexico, Italy, Haiti and Chile are some of the world's most earthquake-prone countries. Many of them sit on the 'ring of fire', a tectonic belt of volcanoes and earthquakes around the edges of the Pacific Ocean. On 27 February 2010, Chile experienced a massive earthquake measuring 8.8 on the Richter scale. The earthquake, which could be felt in countries as far away as Brazil and Argentina, created tremendous damage in its own right. It also triggered a massive tsunami and over a thousand landslides. Tsunami waves measuring 8–50 feet high completely devastated the Chilean town of Constitución.[8] Damage to infrastructure, businesses and homes was significant, with around 370,000 homes affected, more than 500 people were killed, and there were 56 disappearances.[9]

Wlodarczyk and collaborators[10] studied a group of volunteers who were directly affected by the chilling events instigated by the earthquake in Chile, over half of whom reported that personal or family property had been destroyed. The study revealed that for these individuals, distraction was a common strategy employed to manage their emotions, diminishing negative emotions and bringing about more positive emotions. This took the form of frequently engaging in pleasant communal activities such as preparing meals together, eating and drinking together, and going for walks. Researchers found that these activities boosted the wellbeing of volunteers and even led to posttraumatic growth, a feature of resilience as discussed in Chapter 1. Therefore, this study shows that distraction can be used as either an individual emotion regulation strategy or a communal one.

Distraction is more effective as a short-term strategy because it is not as costly to implement in the short term as other strategies such as reappraisal, which require more cognitive resources. In Robert's case, deciding to make a meal or playing with his child didn't necessitate a lot of thought whereas trying to reframe the pandemic and its impact on his business would have, much more so. Distraction may be less cost-effective to implement in the long term, however.[11] This means that the value brought about by a distraction, especially a one-off distraction, may decline over time.

Distraction is more effective if it takes place before we appraise a stressor and negative emotions begin to surface.[12] If I receive news from my boss or a work colleague that I might be made redundant while I'm travelling to a football game, the match might serve as an effective distraction from the negative thoughts and emotions that might otherwise emerge, at least for its duration.

Previous research suggests distraction may be more effective when we encounter an emotional stimulus only once (such as an unpleasant social interaction with a sales clerk), whereas reappraisal, a strategy which requires reframing – as discussed later – might be more effective when stimuli are encountered more frequently.[13] Applying this logic to entrepreneurs in crisis like Robert, in the first few weeks of the first lockdown, cooking and spending time with his family was an effective distraction which enabled him to shift his negative thoughts away from the pandemic. This strategy may have proven to be less effective as a long-term strategy, however, as the lockdown was extended or as the second and third lockdowns were introduced. But still helpful as a short-term fix.

Distraction may be a particularly effective emotion regulation strategy when we combine it with an attitude of acceptance,[14] as a temporary redirection rather than outright avoidance of a negative situation and its corresponding negative emotions. Distraction may be effective when we are willing to reconnect with the avoided emotion eventually,[15] rather than engaging in emotional suppression, which is a more maladaptive than adaptive strategy. Several studies on depression, including those by Morrow and Nolen-Hoeksema[16] and Park and colleagues,[17] have shown that distraction can help protect individuals against negative outcomes in the short term. However, because distraction doesn't change how we deal with situations in the future, it can be a harmful or ineffective strategy in the long term,[18] leading to negative health effects.[19] In the latter case, for example, Kross and Ayduk found that even a few days after distracting people with depression, the positive effects wore off.[20] For Robert, distraction offered a short respite from his financial worries, but it didn't resolve such problems and he still needed to address them.

Monitoring distraction

Following the insights I gained from entrepreneurs in crisis who employed distraction to adjust, listing and reflecting on my own distractions, what they are, why I use them and their consequences, has been a revealing exercise. Currently my go-to distractions include watching interview clips on YouTube, usually with the late-night talk show hosts, going for a walk or playing the guitar. During the pandemic I started walking every day as a way of dealing with the rising workload and not having much alone time. It's something I still do now that gives me a boost. I tend to watch YouTube on occasion, while I'm having lunch, when working at home or feeling tired. I find it enjoyable and a welcome break in short bursts, but if I do it for too long it drains my energy. Finally, playing the guitar is something I do in the evenings on occasion to be creative and end the day well. When I play, it evokes a lot of positive feelings and really transports me. These reflections reminded me of a friend who, when she was at risk for redundancy, started going to a hot yoga class a couple of times a week when her stress levels were sky-high. She told me the practice had been nothing short of 'transformative'. The distraction log and other tools at the end of the chapter can help you monitor your own distractions, their implications, when you might be using them and why.

The role of distraction

Entrepreneurs in crisis, like Robert the café owner, resort to distraction when negative emotions are especially high. This was often the case just after businesses were damaged during the riots or when new regulations were introduced during COVID-19. In such situations, distraction gives these entrepreneurs the space to do other things and to take a needed break by shifting their attention. Some forms of distraction can be more effective than others however, depending on whether the distraction is adaptive or maladaptive. When distraction is more adaptive than maladaptive, focused on accepting the difficult situation and negative emotions, rather than avoidance, it can make appraisals of the environment seem less threatening, at least in the short term.[21]

Next, I discuss a few examples of how entrepreneurs in crisis use distraction to minimize their distress and strengthen their resilience. I label these sub-strategies with a lowercase 'd' when distraction is employed in an adaptive fashion, as a strategy of acceptance, and with a capital 'D' when distraction is used in a more maladaptive manner, as a strategy of avoidance. Periodic distractions with a lowercase 'd' were found to be most helpful, creating short-term relief.

Acceptance-based distraction with a lowercase 'd'

Nearly a year into the pandemic in mid-February of 2021, Liam who was in his late 50s and the owner of a Central London consultancy specializing in research for public sector projects, wrote in his diary about how he was struggling with the third lockdown:

> For me personally, I think I have found it [this lockdown] harder for various reasons. It being the winter, dark and gloomy weather and the whole experience feeling like a very long, slow, and unpredictable process. Less scary than the first time round, but more tiring. Professionally it hasn't made much difference, other than that. The impacts on our staff, are the same as how I feel. And so, maintaining morale is a challenge for all of us.

Liam felt as though the crisis had 'taken the spark out' of him and his staff who had all started working at home after closing their offices in the first lockdown. 'In terms of demands on me as a manager, I think the first time round it was about creativity, flexibility and crisis management. This time it's about resilience, wellbeing and morale.' He felt he was able to keep going, by 'trying to think of new things' to keep staff connected and energised, but also by spending more time with his family and 'doing as much outside exercise as possible, mainly running, walking and cycling'.

Anthony dreamed of a career in medicine but after having a family he began working in the markets and holding down different jobs to make ends meet. After starting up several temporary shops across London, he was finally able to scrape together enough money to purchase the lease on a space in Southwest London which became a discount shop. He later turned it into a successful shop specializing in seasonal items and decorations for various occasions. Like Liam, Anthony was in his late 50s when we met for a coffee not far from where his business had once been. On the day after his business of 15 years was burned down during the London riots, Anthony, quickly shifted his attention toward the charity he had also started, which he was enormously passionate about:

> It wasn't the best night's sleep. I must admit. But I wasn't going to let … anything put me down … But then the

next morning the media circus started ... So within, you know, a few hours, I was in a TV studio ... from a TV studio to radio studio, to interviews with everyone. And right then I thought, 'Publicity. Hey, [name of charity]!' So that was it. My whole focus then was just to use the publicity to raise the awareness for charity. And that's what I did. 'Cause at that stage I had no idea what would happen. I knew I was insured, but, in my mind, it could be ages until I re-open again, so I've got to use the publicity for [name of charity], and I did.

While Anthony accepted the devastating blow to his business, he wasn't going to let it keep him down. He quickly shifted his focus toward something else that was especially important to him and gave him much joy – his charity. Interestingly, focusing on the charity seemed not entirely to be about diverting attention away from the emotionally salient aspects of the riots or focusing attention on the non-emotionally relevant aspects of the situation or even shifting attention away from the immediate situation, as previous research implies. Instead, it was also about using the negative situation and negative emotions generated and directing them toward something positive, which in turn enabled him to experience positive emotions. Anthony accepted the damages to his business and took advantage of opportunities to raise awareness for his charity.

Focusing on the charity was also an effective distraction for Anthony for several reasons. First, the strategy was implemented before he had made a full assessment of the damages to his business. Second, it created positive emotions – a sense of pride, joy, and passion – that balanced negative emotions. Third, it was absorbing and cognitively demanding, which increased the likelihood of the distraction successfully regulating negative emotions. Problem solving around how to continue supporting the charity financially now that its main source of income, the shop, was out of commission, was a positive source of distraction. Fourth, it was a useful short-term strategy in that Anthony was able to temporarily divert his attention away from his main business and return his attention to it when necessary. At the same time, as a short-term strategy it had positive implications for the charity and its continued viability, making him feel more positive in the longer term. Fifth and finally, by focusing on the charity Anthony was able to keep what had happened to his shop during the crisis in perspective. It enabled him to focus some of his energy on his bigger goals, which was to help people in need.

This example suggests that distraction does not automatically divert attention away from negative emotions or do so completely. It also shows that when distraction is rooted in acceptance and employed temporarily, it might have positive implications not only for the short term, but also for the longer term if the situation is positively reappraised. However, if Anthony was to continue employing distraction as a strategy in the longer term, focusing on the charity and the positive emotions it evoked instead of directing needed attention to the business and the damages incurred, the consequences for the business and the charity it supported could have been bleak.

Avoidance-based distraction with a capital 'D'

Like Anthony, Dylan's business had been burned down during the London riots. Dylan who was in his early 50s when we met and the co-owner of a longstanding furniture store in South London, spoke tearfully about watching the demolition of what remained of the business he had grown up in:

> To come back in the morning having seen it just a bit smoky and to go away have two hours sleep and come back the next day, when it was light, and see it, was horrible. Played in there as a kid, and my daughter had played there in the shop. It was terrible, terrible ... And then the bulldozers turn up to knock it all down. They knock it all down and it goes all quiet. They turn the diesel engines off and it just went still. Deathly quiet once they knocked it all flat. That was difficult.

In that moment, Dylan employed a seemingly subtle distraction to manage his emotions, filming the demolition on his phone. He explained, 'It was easier to do that then to look at it. Rather, looking through the iPhone, looking at it through that, you are dispassionate. Looking at it directly, and there's a whole wave of emotion. [He coughs and wipes the tears from his eyes.]' This strategy enabled

Dylan to suppress the negative emotions of anger and sadness associated with the business being torn down by focusing attention on the matter-of-fact side of the event, through the filter of his smartphone. This form of distraction did not help to elicit positive emotions. It did, however, require very few cognitive resources from Dylan, making it easy to implement on the day.

While distraction in Dylan's case helped him get through the immediate situation by enabling him to view the adverse event more objectively, when we spoke about the demolition of his business a couple of months later, the negative emotions remained and had yet to be processed. This is evident in the way Dylan described the demolition as 'horrible', 'terrible' and 'difficult' and was visibly upset in the retelling of the story. Avoiding his emotions in the short term offered Dylan a sense of momentary relief, but it was not necessarily an effective strategy longer term. Among other things, it did not elicit positive emotions, something Anthony's approach appeared to do.

Entrepreneurs like Joseph utilized distraction at different junctures of an evolving crisis. Joseph, who was 40-something when we met, started his first pub in Southeast London with an investment from his parents in the early 2000s. The pub was a success but after his rent doubled more than a decade in, he decided to sell it and to turn his attention to his second pub in Southwest London which he founded a few years before. During the pandemic, Joseph wrote in his diary almost seven months after the first lockdown about the 'no mixing' rule; a COVID-19 regulation which specified that groups of more than six people could not mix in public: 'The new no mixing rule is potentially disastrous. The government is not supporting us at all, it is only damaging. The opposition are not helping, nor is the Mayor.' He continued, 'The other people I know who own similar businesses are mainly communicating in swear words now.' He explained how he was managing the difficulties:

> I bought some grass for the first time in a few years! … It's come down to positivity and pot (pot luck!) but it's all I've got left at the moment – so I'm bloody going with it!!! The smoking takes the edge off just a bit right now, for the odd release – but I'm not thinking it will be a long-term thing.

Joseph was quick to state that his strategy for suppressing negative emotions was something he was doing in the short term only. A few months later in February 2021, the negative emotions persisted alongside the practical challenges. Joseph wrote that he had been feeling 'philosophical, with sporadic homicidal flashes' and suggested that he had turned to other forms of distraction, such as spending time with his family and watching certain TV shows for some immediate relief: 'What made things easier was *WandaVision* and *Marcella* – have kept me entertained.'

These examples show that, similar to what was observed in previous research, avoidance-based distraction does not appear to be as effective as acceptance-based distraction, in that it doesn't help entrepreneurs in crisis process negative emotions.

What can we do to engage in distraction more effectively in a crisis?

Often, we're told distractions are bad, that we should avoid or manage distractions. Countless books and blogs have been written to advise us about how we can stay focused and be more productive without succumbing to distraction. This might be through greater planning, meditation and/or sleep. But sometimes, and as the research on entrepreneurs in crisis presented here suggests, distraction can be useful, especially when it is adaptive, employed intentionally and for a limited time.

The following example illustrates these points nicely. While presenting at a conference for female entrepreneurs and intrapreneurs run jointly by Goldsmiths University of London and NatWest Bank, creatively named AdvanceHer, I asked audience members what forms of distraction they might use. One participant mentioned doing crossword puzzles. She said, 'because when you're starting your own business you can get overwhelmed on certain days that things aren't working out and you can get stressed'. She explained, 'So, I just take a 10-minute break. I bought a crossword puzzle book. I really focus and sort some puzzles through the books so I'm away from digital medium, TV, gadgets or any such things so I consciously sit down to solve that.' For her, doing crossword puzzles had rejuvenating effects.

To engage in distraction with a lowercase 'd' more effectively, we can firstly reflect on the forms of distraction available to us, and those we

Table 2.1: The focus, form and implications of distraction strategies

Distraction strategy	Focus	Examples of distraction	Implications
Distraction with a lowercase 'd': Acceptance-based distraction for entrepreneurs in crisis.	Accepting but temporarily interrupting negative emotions (willing to engage).	Connecting with others socially; doing exercise (walking, running, cycling, yoga or other activities); undertaking creative tasks (cooking, art, or other crafts); working on other professional initiatives; pursuing hobbies.	Broad perspective, incorporates the bigger picture; feeling refreshed; feeling better able to engage with whatever comes next; may lead to an improvement in wellbeing; may lead to posttraumatic growth.
Distraction with a capital 'D': Avoidance-based distraction for entrepreneurs in crisis.	Avoiding or suppressing negative emotions altogether (not willing to engage).	Excessively scrolling through social media; alcohol/drug use; engagement in any activity, including the ones in the previous row, that becomes compulsive and leads to a failure to work or to engage with work or other important responsibilities or aspects of one's life.	Narrow perspective, not focused on the bigger picture; feeling less able to engage with what comes next; may be linked to posttraumatic stress symptomology.

Table 2.2: Guiding questions for an acceptance-based distraction strategy with a lowercase 'd'

What is my attitude towards distraction?	• Do I accept that things are difficult now and that I don't know what exactly will happen next? • Is my attitude toward the crisis or aspects thereof one of acceptance or avoidance? • What is my rationale for using distraction? My plan?
What is my rationale for using distraction? My plan?	• Am I distracting myself in order to provide temporary relief? • Am I willing to do the work to engage with my negative situation and emotions, or am I trying to evade the situation and my negative emotions altogether?
What is the nature of the distraction – the activities or tasks I am engaging in?	• Are the activities/tasks I'm engaging in neutral and unrelated to the crisis? • Are the activities/tasks I'm engaging in related to the crisis in a positive way? • Are the activities/tasks I am engaging in absorbing or not? • How much time am I spending on these activities/tasks – a few minutes/hours, a day, a week?
What are the consequences of the distraction?	• Are the activities/tasks I am engaging in providing temporary relief? • Following the distraction do I feel more refreshed and better able to reengage with the crisis, or less able or unable to reengage with the crisis, indicating that I may need to rethink this strategy? • Is the distraction giving me space to grow as an entrepreneur, manager or individual generally? • Is the distraction facilitating my ability to work or to make work-related decisions, or is it interfering with my ability to work or to make work-related decisions? • Is distraction the best strategy I could be using at the moment?

Table 2.3: A distraction log

Distraction examples	The nature of the distraction	The rationale for using the distraction	Consequences of the distraction in the short term, in the long term

may have used in the past or are using more currently. We can consider the examples provided here and learn from them. As Table 2.1 suggests, we can think more about the two main types of distraction strategies – those rooted in acceptance and on processing negative emotions, and those focused on avoidance and on suppressing negative emotions – the focus of each, the forms they might take and their implications.

To use distraction more effectively we can also interrogate our attitudes towards the distraction and our rationale for employing it. Depending on our answers to these questions and our responses to Table 2.2, distraction may be regarded as helpful or hindering, as something to discontinue, employ in the short term or manage in short bursts longer term. Keeping a distraction log will help you examine which distraction strategies are most effective (Table 2.3). In Box 2.1 I've also included three actionable takeaways that you can perform on a more regular basis.

★★★

Distraction can be useful. While distraction is about adjusting attention in the moment to diminish stress, expectation management is focused on adjusting thoughts about the future, as we see next.

Box 2.1: Actionable takeaways for distraction

- Practice distraction with a lowercase 'd': When your negative emotions are heightened or your energy is flagging, shift your attention temporarily

to something different, something absorbing. This can help you reset and return to the issue at hand a little more refreshed.
- Plan for distraction: Throughout the day and week, schedule in regular breaks and activities. This not only creates a good balance, but solutions to problems can often be found by stepping back.
- Replace ineffective distractions: Look at the kinds of distractions you currently use. Replace distractions that drain your energy with those that give you energy. Replace distractions that serve to suppress negative emotions with those that acknowledge the need to process them.

Chapter summary

- Distraction is a form of emotion regulation that interferes with the generation of negative emotions by shifting attention away from the emotion-generating aspects of a situation, including a crisis.
- Distraction might be more effective in a crisis at particularly tense junctures and when it is more cognitively demanding and employed in the short term, so that negative emotions may be processed eventually and not suppressed, allowing us to adapt positively.
- Distraction is an effective short-term strategy for those entrepreneurs who employ it in an adaptive fashion (with a lowercase 'd'), to give them space to do other things. Even avoidance-related distraction (with a capital 'D') can be effective if applied knowingly in the short term and where space is created to process the negative emotions eventually.
- To engage in distraction more effectively, we can reflect on the kinds of distractions we have utilized in the past and to what effect, reflect on the focus and implications of acceptance- and avoidance-related distractions, and ask questions to identify our attitudes towards and rationale for the distraction and evaluate the implications of such for recovery.

3

Expectation Management

When Sam and I first met he was in his early 50s. Sam had moved to the UK a couple of decades prior, working in offices before starting his own businesses in the hospitality sector. He had built his North London pub from scratch a few years prior, something he was immensely proud of. On the first night of the London riots, he had heard earlier in the day from customers that 'there was some kind of protest taking place in front of the police station' and 'a police car burning there'. Sam closed the pub around 10 or 11 pm and went home. On returning to the pub a short while later he said:

> I found one of my main doors open, all my furniture burning on the road, and I came inside. It was completely dark inside. I saw a lady serving herself at the bar, so I tried to approach the lady, and I say, 'what are you doing here?!' All of the windows here, where we are, these on the front side were completely smashed up, there were no windows and some gangs, some people were coming in through the windows.

Sam then noticed something or someone that really startled him. 'Because it was dark and one of the guys was coming through this window, I think he has a weapon in his hand and I say, "now I have to go and hide myself"'. Sam ran up the stairs watching helplessly from above as people filed into his pub, ripping out his TV screens and smashing bottles. Looking for a quick exit, he climbed out of a window and made his way down the drainpipe to the neighbours.

When I visited Sam mid-afternoon a couple of months later, his pub was empty and in a state of repair, slowed down by a lack of funds. There were no customers and little to no furniture or stock. Sam scrolled through his phone, talking me through pictures of the pub he had opened only a few short years prior, filled with people, big screen TVs and shelves of alcohol. He flipped through images of the street the morning after the riots. 'You can even see how the street looks sad', he said, while the inside of the pub was like it had been 'hit by a bomb'. When speaking about the tables and chairs taken outside, 'broken and burned', he started to cry. Sam was 'waiting for the day to get everything back', waiting for financial compensation from the police fund, payable to those whose properties had been damaged, or goods destroyed or stolen under the Riot Damages Act of 1886:

> Sometimes it's not easy to talk about it, to be honest [his voice gets quiet]. Sometimes it's not easy because we are still … We are still in shock. Why? Because we didn't expect this to happen, and even by today's date … the government is saying that it is going to take a few weeks to help people. We are still waiting for the Riot Damages Act to compensate. I did apply to that fund and until now we are waiting. There isn't anything coming yet … So, every single shop here is still waiting for the Riot Damages Act from the police to come through.

As Sam's account suggests, waiting for news can be especially difficult. In circumstances such as these, expectation management was a common strategy employed by entrepreneurs in crisis, and it played a role in their resilience. While as human beings we all manage our expectations at one time or another, we might not fully appreciate why doing so is useful or its implications.

What is expectation management?

An expectation is a strong belief we possess that something will happen in the future. Like Sam, I might expect as a business owner to receive financial compensation from the state or insurers quickly following a crisis. In other situations, I might expect to get a promotion at work, or to win a race. Alternatively, I might expect to be overlooked for promotion or to come in last.

When future outcomes can't be determined because there are too many possibilities and we can't foresee what will happen, uncertainty results.[1] Expectation management is triggered in these conditions when uncertainty is high and perceived control is low, but some planning is still required.

Take flooding for instance. Something that afflicts many parts of the world. In September 2023, Storm Daniel tore through several countries including Greece, Turkey, Bulgaria and Libya. In Libya, one of the worst areas affected by flooding, more than 11,000 people were reported dead, over 10,000 unaccounted for and thousands displaced.[2] Flooding can create significant distress for flood victims, posing risks to physical health, including infections, respiratory diseases, and mental health. The negative effects on wellbeing from the loss of a home or business may persist for several months or years, especially for those who reside in areas prone to repeat flooding, such as the UK.

One particularly damaging flood took place in the winter of 2013, and over January and February of 2014 in Northern England. Severe storms and extensive rainfall destroyed infrastructure and around 7,800 homes and nearly 3,000 businesses, creating disruptions to critical services (400,000 properties were left without power) and causing the deaths of five people.[3] A study commissioned by the Federation of Small Businesses in 2014 found that small businesses in flood-hit areas collectively incurred damages totalling approximately £830 million. That same year, there were reports of homeowners and business owners waiting for water levels to recede, for their floors and walls to dry out and to be rewired, refitted and/or re-plastered, for government support and to return to 'normal'. The expectations of flood victims likely influenced their ability to cope.

Expectation management can serve to reduce the distress we experience in response to uncertainty.[4] Other ways of coping with uncertainty include distraction, as noted previously, reappraisal and support seeking, which I cover in later chapters. While expectation management is not widely discussed in the crisis management, entrepreneurship, or broader management literatures, it has received some attention in economics,[5] health studies[6] and psychology.

Most contemporary research on expectation management comes from studies about waiting for uncertain news, which is an anxiety-provoking time.[7] Research carried out by Kate Sweeny, a psychologist and key player in this area, shows that expectation management can help individuals cope with uncertainty which can be uncomfortable and interfere with certain tasks.[8] Together with her colleagues, Sweeny has studied a range of situations involving waiting for news, including law graduates waiting for their bar exam results,[9] undergraduates waiting for midterm exam results,[10] and adults trying to conceive[11] or waiting for diagnostic tests.[12]

To illustrate, Wilson, Rankin, Ludi, and Sweeny[13] studied patients waiting for life-altering medical results, specifically those relating to a breast biopsy. Researchers interviewed patients prior to their biopsies and had them complete daily surveys after undergoing the procedure. They asked patients to indicate the likelihood that their biopsy results would turn out fine to ascertain whether patients were preparing for the worst or hoping for the best. Researchers then measured distress by asking patients how happy, sad and anxious they had been that day, and whether or not they had any somatic symptoms such as an upset stomach or dizziness, or repetitive thoughts about breast cancer. Researchers found that more optimistic patient expectations negatively predicted distress, meaning that those with positive expectations were less likely to be distressed. Moreover, researchers also uncovered that distress appeared to follow a U-shaped pattern, with high levels of distress appearing at both the beginning and end of the waiting period.

Expectations, therefore, are important. Expectations have the power to guide our emotions and behaviours both during and after a stressful situation. Take another example, that of losing your job. If I expect that after losing my job finding another job will be easy and I might be able to access the support I need, I might feel more positive and less anxious about the transition. At the same time, I might not expend too much effort to find another job or only take small steps in this direction initially. However, if I expect that finding another job will be difficult and that I will have to navigate the process on my own without any support, I might feel more anxious about the transition. In this case, I might give up altogether or work to find ways to manage my negative emotions and create a plan of action. This illustration captures some of the key principles of expectation management.

As indicated in the study by Wilson and colleagues,[14] and the job loss example outlined, there appear to be two key strategies of expectation management. The first is about maintaining low expectations and bracing for the worst possible outcome. While this strategy can create more anxiety for us in the interim, it can also help us manage our reactions to bad news should it arrive, both minimizing disappointment and increasing the likelihood of positive reactions if the news is good.[15] While spending time with friends and their teenage children on holiday, one of which was nervously awaiting their exam results (GCSEs), I saw how this strategy played out before and after the big day. The second strategy, positive expectation management, is about embracing a sense of hope and optimism. This strategy helps us manage anxiety during the waiting period but potentially sets us up for a fall if we receive bad news, increasing our chances of feeling disappointed.[16]

Two years after the riots, when we met again, Sam was still carrying out repairs on his pub. Despite his hopes for a quick turnaround, it had taken more than a year to be compensated by the police fund and, in addition, he received a lot less than he had claimed for: 'I tried to make repairs, I did the most I could, and I was just waiting and I was expecting to, to, to get compensation early, but I was, I just keep repairing and building and you can see that until now I'm still building'. Deeply disappointed he said:

> I have to accept it to save my business. Otherwise, I was going to sink. It is exactly the same as if you leave somebody for two weeks without eating, and you come and say to the person, 'Listen, I've, I have cockroaches here for you to eat'. That person will eat cockroaches.

When is expectation management most effective?

As discussed, expectation management may be an effective strategy when uncertainty is high, and when we are waiting for important or difficult news and our perceived control is low. Expectation management is likely to be more effective when we apply it at the beginning or end of a waiting period, when distress is likely to be highest, as noted by Sweeny and her co-researchers.[17] There is often a downward shift in our expectations in these moments in order to protect ourselves.[18]

Positive expectation management might be more effective when optimism is tempered. That is, while optimism is generally believed to carry more risks than pessimism and some have argued it is an unwise as a strategy on its own,[19] my research suggests that cautious optimism rather than purely positive expectations might be a good way to go as it maintains some hope for the future but also encourages people to take action at the same time. Both strategies, managing low or positive expectations, might be useful in a crisis, but each comes with trade-offs.

Monitoring expectation management

Like entrepreneurs in crisis, we're all waiting for uncertain news at one point or another. It could be news about work, a relationship, our health, studies, home, finances or otherwise. When we put in an offer on a home several years ago, I was beyond excited. Everything was going well. All background checks had been completed and the contracts were in the hands of the lawyers. And then something unexpected happened. Because we had yet to sell our property, the homeowner started working with a second estate agent and, within a week, they had sold their property to someone else. I was gutted. I've learned from this example, and especially from the stories that follow, that our expectations and their implications are important. Later I include several prompts and activities you can use for unpacking and managing your own expectations.

The role of expectation management

Entrepreneurs in crisis like Sam possess a range of expectations regarding what will happen in the future. While a lot of the broader questions entrepreneurs might have around business recovery are likely to be similar, such as 'will things get back to normal?' or 'when will things get back to normal?', there are likely to be some variations between individuals depending on the kind of crisis they encounter. During the pandemic, for instance, entrepreneurs were waiting for information about changing or lifting restrictions, vaccines, COVID-19 rates and financial protection.

Based on my research with entrepreneurs in crisis, Table 3.1 highlights some broad categories of news entrepreneurs have a tendency to wait for and their expectation management strategies.

Table 3.1: Broad categories of news entrepreneurs in crisis have a tendency to wait for and their expectations

Waiting for news	Low expectations	Positive expectations
About whether or when the crisis event will end	The crisis will not end soon	The crisis will end soon
About whether or when the crisis event will reoccur	It is likely the crisis will reoccur	It is unlikely the crisis will reoccur
About whether or when we will get back on our feet operationally/financially	It is unlikely we will get back on our feet or do so anytime soon	We will get back on our feet and we will do so soon
About whether or when things will return to normal	It is unlikely things will return to normal or do so anytime soon	Things will return to normal and do so soon
About whether and when customers will return following a crisis event	Many customers will not return	Many customers will return
About whether or when we will receive support from stakeholders such as employees, insurers, the government, customers, community members	We are not counting on support at all or anytime soon	We are counting on support and believe it will come soon
About whether we will be able to take advantage of opportunities created by the crisis	We will not be able to take advantage of opportunities	We will be able to take advantage of opportunities

Entrepreneurs in crisis tend to rely on both low expectations and positive expectations. For the entrepreneurs in crisis I connected with, low expectations have served to manage uncertainty about when a crisis in question might end, when things might return to normal and whether the crisis will reoccur. As with prior research, these low expectations tend to be associated with negative emotions such as fear and anxiety in the interim. Some of the entrepreneurs I worked with managed the uncertainty surrounding the crisis with positive expectations, especially in relation to business recovery and future performance. In these cases, positive expectations tend to be associated with a sense of hope and a kind of cautious optimism, also in the interim.

Maintaining low expectations

William, the 50-something owner of a popular pub and live performance venue in South London, grew increasingly anxious about the possibility of an extended first lockdown during the COVID-19 pandemic and what it would mean for his well-established business. William was particularly concerned that continuing restrictions imposed by the government in response to the crisis would mean closing his business for good. A few weeks into the first lockdown he wrote in his diary:

> The longer the lockdown continues, the more we will need to look at liquidating the business. It will be a very sad day for all. The government has stated clearly that venues, pubs, clubs, theatres, restaurants, cinemas, gyms will be the last out of lockdown with social distancing restriction in place. The not knowing strategy is causing much of the hospitality industry distress.

In August 2020, a few months later, William made a point of noting how he was also waiting for news about when he could begin hosting live performances once again:

> We are still waiting and have no indication from the government about indoor live performances which are vital to this venue. There seems to be sense of urgency

> that the hospitality industry is on the verge of collapse ... I feel my responses and my temperament have changed over the last two reports [diary entries]. We tend to stay out of the political frame, but I am becoming increasingly frustrated how the government are dealing with this on a day-to-day and week-by-week basis.

For businesses like William's operating in the hospitality industry, there were many changes to restrictions and delays in announcing new restrictions. He clearly described how difficult it was to wait for such uncertain news, causing him and others much 'distress'. William's pessimism about the pandemic grew, especially as it related to social distancing restrictions and the absence of COVID-19 grants for small businesses with rateable values[a] over £51,000. This fuelled his own efforts to lobby for more local and national government support, and after a time, to carry out his own fundraising which was successful. Prior research suggests that managing expectations appropriately and taking pre-emptive actions in the event news is bad can minimize negative consequences.[20]

I found many examples of entrepreneurs relying on low expectations to manage the uncertainty of business recovery during the pandemic especially, and whether customers/sales would return to pre-crisis levels, thereby enabling businesses to get back to 'normal'.

Robert, the café owner whom I referred to earlier, was focused on reopening his business a few weeks into the first lockdown and concerned about what it would mean for him in terms of how he managed his business and his financial situation going forward:

> Probably finding myself a little more stressed as we start thinking about re-opening. The first few weeks were a bit of a holiday and now the real work is going to start again. Which is slightly daunting, knowing that the business we have built, the way we were used to operating is going to change – all more negatively. I will be working the same, but earning less money.

---

[a] Business rates are based on a property's rateable value, determined by how much it would cost to rent the property for a year.

Consistent with Sweeny's work, Robert's stress went up as his reopening date neared. Closer to the end of the waiting period, he had lowered his expectations to avoid disappointment. This is evident in the description of his state of mind prior. The diary excerpt that follows also shows that after the waiting period had ended and he had reopened the business, Robert experienced positive emotions. Yet, his negative feelings did not diminish entirely, a few months after the first lockdown:

> It's been good having money coming through the account again, it seems that at the moment we are trading pretty positively. There haven't been a lot of difficulties this week ... This current microcosm is great. We're working less, the work is less hard and stressful. We have less people, we eat together each day, the weather's nice and we are taking relatively good money. But I'm sort of waiting for it to all end. Once furlough ends and the government aid is used up and it starts raining again – it's going to be a very different picture.

Robert's low expectations had positive results. Following the reopening of the business, he reported feeling more positive and less negative, that things were going well, they were trading 'pretty positively' and the work was 'less hard and stressful'. However, rather than subsiding completely, his anxiety was redirected to other worries: waiting for the furlough scheme to end and for the good weather to change. Dealing with a number of uncertainties at the same time is not something prior research on waiting and expectation management tackles, which tends to focus instead on one key concern. Nonetheless, this is something that entrepreneurs in crisis tend to experience, which is reflected by the intricacies of running a business and the need for entrepreneurs to wear many hats.

Some entrepreneurs also employed low expectations to manage the uncertainty around whether or when the crisis might reoccur, a notion that created anxiety. A handful of those I spoke to who were affected by the London riots in 2011 expected more rioting in the future. Three months after the riots, I had the following exchange with Mark, the owner of an electronics shop in South London that had been operating for decades and was looted and vandalized by rioters:

> Every time I walk through the door I wonder if all the stock's going to be here. That's the way it is at the moment. I think it will happen again at some stage. Because we had, I don't know if you remember the Brixton riots, some years ago? So, it seems to spring up every so often. You'd think that the police would control it a bit better this time so it wouldn't get out of hand like it did. With so many people affected, it makes you wonder … The police response was, from my point of view, at the time, was non-existent. I sat in the café hanging on to, trying to phone up, you know the 101 line [police, non-emergencies]. They weren't answering that. I got so fed up with that. I did the 999 [emergencies] and they told me there were so many people affected by this they weren't even going to attend.

While the passage of time can help ease concerns of a crisis reoccurring, negative feelings can persist for some. Engaging in routine coping behaviours can help alleviate anxiety. For example, Anne, the 30-something year old co-owner of the bespoke clothing store in Southeast London cleared out during the riots, continued hiding stock at the end of every working day, even two years later.

Finally, consistent with prior research, I found that while low expectations can create anxiety in the interim, in some circumstances they created more enduring positive emotions longer term. For example, entrepreneurs in crisis with low expectations around financial compensation benefitted when the outcome was positive. This was the case for the father-daughter team, Nathan, in his late 50s, and Wendy, in her 30s, who owned a small shop specializing in electrical goods and appliances in East London. The business had started with Nathan's grandfather who did electrical work in people's homes in the evenings alongside his day job. Sometime before the First World War, he bought a small shop that sold bicycles and radios, adding electrical contracting work to its portfolio. Nathan's father concentrated on the retail side of the business and his uncle on the contracting side, which Nathan later disposed of after taking officially taking over. While Wendy and Nathan were feeling initially doubtful that they would be compensated fully by insurers after the riots, even two years on they spoke positively about the relief they felt when insurers came through in the end. Wendy said: 'We was thinking, "Oh God, what's our insurance gonna go up to?" But it didn't happen at all.'

Maintaining positive expectations: cautious optimism

Joseph, the London pub owner who had been running his business for over a decade, felt optimistic about the pandemic initially. A couple of weeks into the first lockdown he wrote:

> For now, it's a bit of a wait. I'm finding it hard to visualise how this unfolds, how things look starting up again and until I feel I can visualise it will be hard to put plans into action … I think I have some slightly nagging urges to diversify … I do feel rather positive despite the precarious climate as we head further into the unknown … but I tend to work off instinct more than anything.

Two months into the lockdown, Joseph was still feeling good:

> I have confidence that we will be okay in all this. I'm not panicking. I believe my venue is adaptable to social distancing and my business is strong enough to come back. I've always been a bit 'Little Red Hen'.

As this quote suggests, Joseph's positive expectations around recovery helped minimize his distress in the short and medium term. In his own words, he was 'not panicking' at the time. He saw his business as 'adaptable' and 'strong' enough to withstand changes brought about by the crisis. A few weeks later, Joseph reported that his positive feelings continued while he was adjusting to the new normal:

> It's become clearer all the time and I like it more and more – absolutely loving the challenge and not really scared it will go wrong. It's adaptable – has to be adaptable. More bookings, more apps, more table service.

Increasingly, Joseph felt he knew what to expect and what was coming next. And yet, as mentioned in the previous chapter, six months on, new regulations led to frustration and elevated his anxiety levels. In October 2020, he wrote in his diary, 'Having already lost the best part of our trading schedule … the new no mixing rule is potentially disastrous. The government is not supporting us at all, it is only damaging.' As he received more information about how the new regulations would affect his business, Joseph began to experience negative emotions, as he could not adjust as he had hoped. This was also the case for Daniel, who came to London from overseas more than a decade before the pandemic to study cooking. In his early 40s, the founder-chef of a restaurant spoke of how changing legislation and further lockdowns had eroded his optimism:

> The first lockdown I think we were all very apathetic, optimistic, we said, "oh it's just a virus it's going to pass, let's enjoy some time off, you know?" Everybody had that and we were talking about, we were obviously in lockdown, but we were, I was in touch with all my team, we were doing Zoom parties and quizzes and a really, really, different atmosphere, because the government tending to help. It was all very clear. But when things start to go wrong in the end of the first lockdown where they decided to ease the restrictions and you're allowed this, you're not allowed that, you're allowed this, you're not allowed that and we tried to do deliveries but we're not really a restaurant for deliveries, so that didn't work and then a fail after fail after fail. But towards the summer when Eat Out to Help Out[b] came, it was like a ray of light. Everything started to kick back off, amazingly. Optimism came back, so yeah, it was great.

---

[b] Eat Out to Help Out was a scheme initiated by the British Government over August 2020 whereby participating cafes, restaurants, hotels and other establishments selling food on-site for immediate consumption were provided with 50% off the cost of food and/or non-alcoholic drinks between Mondays and Wednesdays. Its purpose was to drive sales on more quiet days of the week to facilitate business recovery.

> Then November lockdown, boom, second time. This time with the looking onto Christmas, which is a biggest month of the year for us, but obviously very upsetting because November is a very busy month as well. But that was okay, they told us November just to save our Christmas trade. Then we opened a Christmas trade and 10 days, third lockdown, for five months [laughs]. The third lockdown was the toughest one because there was like, people lose optimism. People were very sarcastic, pessimistic about everything. I had a lot of mental health issues among my team, and myself, to deal with.

Most examples of positive expectation management from entrepreneurs in crisis were associated with hope and what I refer to as 'cautious optimism', which reflected an awareness of the challenges, rather than either a purer form of optimism or pessimism. A case in point, Brian, the owner of a design consultancy in Northeast London, was optimistic a few weeks into the COVID-19 crisis about his business's future and ability to recover, but was also careful to acknowledge what had to be done in order to keep the business afloat as the situation was still precarious:

> I do believe our performance will reach pre COVID-19 levels and we can exceed them. However, this will be because we are redefining our offerings and bringing new offerings to deal with the impact of COVID-19. The business has a runway into 2021, but if the economy takes a significant hit/lockdown was extended for another 6 months, it would be very challenging for the cash flow of the business. We would need a loan or investment to help.

Sweeny suggests that the two strategies, low and positive expectations, can co-exist.[21] In a more enduring crisis such as the pandemic, where a number of uncertainties compete for one's attention, it might be especially useful to utilize both strategies at the same time. For instance, Laura, a restaurant owner in West London who was in her late 40s, said that while she had low expectations about business profitability during the latter half of the pandemic, her expectations for the business overall were positive. She explained how she was tabling her concerns for the interim, directing her thoughts and energy towards the quality of the food and service over which she had some input:

> We would like to say, you know, it [the future] looks very bright and we're very optimistic about it, but like in any business, you're only as good as your last meal you serve ... Profitability is not our focus right now – we just want to break even and if there's a profit, great – until the tourists come back, the offices come back and there is some sort of normalcy, which we don't know what it is. Our focus is keeping the brand and keeping the levels – service levels that we have, the quality levels – that's our focus for the next 3 months and then we hope by winter, if things are normal and there's tourists back, offices back, then we can, you know, consider and look at the model and say, 'Okay, now we need to focus on making a profit', because at the end of the day, the business is not just to pay wages and bills. You know, we want to make a profit. We want to be profitable.

As Laura's quote illustrates, entrepreneurs in crisis can feel cautiously optimistic by holding both low expectations and positive expectations at the same time, and directing their efforts to areas where they might have the most control or where their actions might matter most. Earlier research on expectation management appears to focus less on the behavioural implications.

Similar to prior research, I found that positive expectations around a crisis gave entrepreneurs hope and a sense of relief. When their positive expectations were met with positive outcomes, there were no issues. However, when their positive expectations were met with negative outcomes – for example, when the crisis continued, support was not forthcoming, or they could not take advantage of opportunities provided by the crisis – these individuals became extremely discontent. Returning to an earlier point, the initial belief that their work and lives would return to normal quickly might be one reason why so many felt flat and fatigued the longer the COVID-19 crisis continued. Some entrepreneurs, however, anticipated a more drawn-out crisis or learned to expect such with time, adopting an approach that was more cautiously optimistic.

What can we do to manage expectations more effectively in a crisis?

We all hold expectations for the future. This is no big surprise. What's less obvious, however, is that the expectations we formulate and when, can have implications for how we feel and what we do, regardless of whether they are positive, low or somewhere in between.

To engage in expectation management more effectively, we can use the question prompts presented in Table 3.2 to reflect on the kinds of expectations we currently hold, the potential implications of these, and how we can go about creating a more deliberate expectation management strategy by asking certain questions. Table 3.3 shows how different expectations may be associated with certain feelings and actions. Documenting the uncertain news we're waiting for and examining our expectations can also help (Table 3.4), as can applying the actionable takeaways in Box 3.1 regularly to give us a feel for expectation management as a strategy for building resilience.

We can also seek to strike a balance between holding low expectations and positive expectations. Sweeny's body of research

Table 3.2: Guiding questions for a more deliberate expectation management strategy

Unpacking expectations	• What kinds of uncertain news am I waiting for? • Are my expectations about this uncertain news positive or low (bracing for the worst possible outcome)? • Are my expectations shaping the way I feel? • Do I feel positive and calm or negative and anxious? • Are my expectations affecting my behaviour for better or worse?
Creating a more deliberate expectation management strategy	• Can I adjust my expectations more broadly or at certain times? • Can I maintain a cautious optimism? • Can I do things while I'm waiting for uncertain news that might help me to prepare better for either a good or bad outcome?

Table 3.3: How emotions and behaviours link to examples of crisis-related news

Expectation	How might I feel?	What might I do?
If I believe the crisis will end soon (positive expectation) …	I may feel relieved in the interim, like I can stick it out.	I might hold on, take action in the short and/or medium term.
If I believe the crisis will go on (low expectation) …	I may feel angry, upset, or frustrated, like I want to give up or like I want to dig in.	I might give up, find ways to manage my negative emotions, and/or think about what I can do longer term.
If I believe I will be supported by stakeholders (positive expectation) …	I may feel grateful or relieved, like I can stick it out.	I might hold on and take action in the short and/or medium term to reach out.
If I believe I will not be supported by stakeholders (low expectation) …	I may feel angry, upset, or frustrated, like I want to give up or dig in even further.	I might give up, think about where else I might receive support, or think about what I can do on my own.

Table 3.4: Managing expectations log

What uncertain news am I waiting for?	What are my expectations?	How are my expectations making me feel?	What can I do/should I do in the interim?

suggests that this balance can be achieved by maintaining some degree of optimism in the initial waiting period and then moving more towards pessimism just prior to receiving the news, hoping for but not expecting a positive outcome. For entrepreneurs, this might mean remaining hopeful that government support will be forthcoming, but exploring other forms of funding in the interim should government support fail to manifest.

In speaking about expectation management with my entrepreneurship students and gauging what they would do while waiting for news about a hypothetical pitching for funding competition, one said, 'I think I'd feel sort of in between high and low expectations.' He explained that where the chances of success were lower because the competition was high, 'I would be confident' but 'I would not have my expectations so high it would stop me' from seeking out other opportunities so he would 'not over-commit to that one opportunity'. Another agreed that their expectations would vary according to the information available, like how many people applied.

Whether we pursue a strategy embracing positive expectations, low expectations or some combination of the two when awaiting crisis-related news, we should be aware of how we are framing the future, how this framing is making us feel and act, how intentional we wish to be in managing our expectations and trade-offs between the different strategies. So, for example, a few of my students have reported that they tend to maintain positive expectations about their grades and that this as a strategy makes them feel 'more relaxed' before their marks are disseminated.

While expectation management may not always be a conscious strategy, it can be. A handful of entrepreneurs I spoke with possessed an awareness that they were intentionally keeping their expectations low. Amir, the owner of a clothing store in North London affected by the London riots, wasn't sure his business would be viable in the long term following extensive damage to his premises. When we spoke a few months after the riots he was focused on taking one step at a time:

> You don't know what happens tomorrow. I believe [in the] day to day. Don't make plans for the future. I'm going to get disappointed. Life is short. Go for [the] day to day. I believe that.

★★★

The main takeaway from this chapter is that our thoughts about the future can impact on our feelings. Using this knowledge and acting accordingly can help diminish stress. Next, we turn to positive self-talk, another strategy entrepreneurs used to adjust their thoughts in a crisis.

> **Box 3.1: Actionable takeaways for expectation management**
>
> - Practice cautious optimism: When faced with uncertain news, think about maintaining a sense of hopefulness for the future while also creating a Plan B. This will help you manage any negative emotions you might experience in the lead up and give you options later.
> - Scrutinize your expectations: Frequently reflect on whether your expectations are serving you or if they require some adjusting. You may be more prone to adopting one strategy over the other (low expectations, positive expectations), but it might not be helpful in all cases.
> - Know when to manage your expectations: Manage your expectations at the beginning and end of a waiting period to deal with the uncertainty, directing your energy elsewhere while you wait.

Chapter summary

- An expectation is a strong belief that something will happen in the future.
- Entrepreneurs in crisis hold certain expectations about their recovery.
- Expectation management is one way in which individuals can manage uncertainty in a crisis and adapt, enhancing resilience to the potentially negative effects.
- There are two key strategies of expectation management – maintaining low or positive expectations – and each has implications for how we might feel and act in a crisis.
- Entrepreneurs in crisis tend to hold either low expectations or positive expectations that exhibit a 'cautious optimism' which, while hopeful, still reflect the challenges they face.
- To better adapt to a crisis, we can document the different pieces of information we are waiting for and whether our expectations are positive or negative, strike a balance between each and maintain an awareness for how expectations influence emotions and behaviours.

4

Positive Self-talk

In the spring of 2001, Brian, the 30-something-year-old owner of a design consultancy for commercial interiors in Northeast London, was forced to make redundancies. 'I was hopeful that we would be able to capture all the business that was delayed as a result of COVID-19. Now I realize that's impossible, and we just need to be the right size' to 'capture' what business we can 'for the next 18 months'. He added, 'A year is a long time in crisis. So, there is a level of acceptance about the situation.' This was not something Brian wanted or saw coming three days before the first lockdown came into effect, when he told me about his 'contingency planning'. 'There are so many moving parts around whether there is a lockdown or not, the financial assistance on offer from the state and the duration of any measures,' he said. 'We are a well-run business and so there has been no need of panic,' he added optimistically. But a few weeks into the lockdown, Brian was finding the situation quite 'challenging' personally, particularly 'the emotional aspect of dealing with people' due to concerns around health and financial security.

Taking a step back, Brian reflected in his diary on how he had been managing his team so far, despite the mounting financial and regulatory constraints: 'I've proved myself on being caring, putting people first and building a great culture. I passionately believe this is what a business should be.' Brian positively assessed his performance as CEO. He felt good about rising to the challenges of the pandemic and exhibiting qualities that he valued. Rather than position the crisis as a threat to the business, he ultimately saw it as a chance to build a great culture and, also, a new direction: 'This crisis will present numerous opportunities,' he said. 'My job is to make sure the business can take as many of them as possible.'

Despite the difficulties brought about by the pandemic for his business, close to a year after the initial lockdown, Brian reported, 'I still feel there are opportunities to innovate and create and change the market we operate in, so plenty of reasons to still be excited.'

How we frame events is important. While the stories we tell ourselves are unlikely to make everything better or bring an end to a crisis, they can shape our feelings and behaviours. In a similar vein, the self-talk of entrepreneurs in crisis is critical and can affect their plans for recovery. Think of the differences between the kinds of statements an entrepreneur might utter in a crisis, such as 'I can get through this and I have been through tough times before', 'I'm managing well under the circumstances' or 'I'm doing what I can', versus 'Everything is falling apart', 'I'm not capable of doing this on my own' or 'I can't find my way back from this'. These are all examples of self-talk. While self-talk has not been investigated in entrepreneurship research previously, several entrepreneurs in crisis whom I interviewed or collected diaries from utilized and benefitted from positive self-talk.

What is self-talk?

Self-talk is the conversation we have with ourselves. It's that small voice in our heads or what we say about ourselves out loud.[1] Self-talk is a reflexive activity focused on self-regulation.[2] This means that self-talk helps us interpret our feelings and manage our reactions, and is a way of giving ourselves instructions and encouragement.[3]

Self-talk has been explained partly by social cognitive theory,[4] which follows that those thoughts we formulate through our interactions with the world around us can shape our view of reality, encouraging us to behave in ways that align with our expectations. So, if, for example, we've observed that hard work eventually leads to a promotion and more pay, we might be inclined to work harder. If, on the other hand, we see that hard work doesn't bring such benefits, we might withdraw our efforts. Self-talk enables us to reflect on our experiences and develop self-efficacy – the belief that we can perform certain tasks, accomplish our desired goals and adapt our behaviour.

To date, the bulk of research on self-talk has been conducted on athletes. Think of the tennis player who says to themselves before a match, 'You're fierce. You're prepared. You've got this'. James Hardy has written extensively on the topic, creating a picture of self-talk in athletes,[5] critiquing research on the topic[6] and investigating negative self-talk in this population.[7] Hardy and others, like Van Raalte,[8] Hamilton[9] and their collaborators, have found athletes use self-talk to improve their performance and confidence, learn new skills, cope in difficult situations, regulate arousal levels and maintain or increase drive, and that positive self-talk enhances performance more so than negative self-talk. Beyond sports, self-talk has been linked to leader effectiveness,[10] academic performance[11] and professionals working in high-stress situations, such as surgeons[12] and firefighters.[13] Self-talk has been acknowledged but not researched extensively in crises.[14]

There are different dimensions of self-talk. As noted, self-talk can be internal and hidden, or external and out in the open.[15] It can also be positive or negative, motivational or demotivational, automatic or deliberate, global (a broader all-encompassing framework) or context dependent.[16] Most research has been conducted on positive or negative forms of self-talk.[17] When self-talk is positive, it's constructive and encouraging. When negative, it can be destructive, a form of criticism.

Constructive thinking has been defined as an automatic thought or deliberate strategy that 'facilitates solving problems in everyday life at a minimum cost in stress'.[18] This means that constructive thinking can reduce our experience of stress by helping us interpret stressors in our environment as challenges rather than as threats,[19] something Brian did via his positive self-talk. He saw the pandemic as an opportunity to create a great business culture and forge a new direction. Self-talk can allow us to feel more efficacious, more capable of addressing challenges as we encounter them. Destructive thinking, alternatively, has a high cost in the form of stress relative to its effectiveness.[20] This means it increases our experience of stress as we interpret stressors in the environment as threats, leading us to feel less efficacious, less capable of addressing those threats.

Prior research by Epstein,[21] Spirrison and Gordy[22] and Ginacola and associates[23] has found that constructive thinking brings about certain benefits which include not only diminishing physiological and psychological distress, but also diminishing the likelihood of maladaptive coping such as drug abuse, antisocial behaviour and avoidant coping behaviours and improving cognitive performance. Constructive thinking has been associated with resilience and its counterpart, flexible adaptation,[24] the ability to tailor coping strategies to the stressor at hand, as we discussed earlier.[25]

In response to adversity, constructive thinking is, unsurprisingly, regarded as a positive adaptation strategy that precedes and/or facilitates problem solving and that drives situation-specific responses,[26] whereas destructive thinking is arguably a negative adaptation strategy that might prevent us from developing a resolution.[27] Individuals who engage in positive self-talk and the constructive thinking on which it is based are more likely to be resilient; not only able to manage stress but to resist it as well, as a kind of protective factor. This occurs by reframing a situation or crisis in ways that allows them to think about what they've accomplished despite the event, what they did to cope and how this can help them achieve their greater goals, beyond a crisis.[28]

In some instances, however, it's worth noting that negative self-talk can yield positive results. When we aim to improve a particular skill, like the entrepreneur who is trying to increase their financial literacy or refine their communication skills, engaging in negative self-talk that is corrective and constructive in nature may be an effective strategy.[29] For example, think of a competitive tennis player who might say to themselves and/or to others such as their coach, 'I need to do better and improve my serve'. Self-talk in this situation can lead to more or better drills.

Finally, self-talk has important implications for emotions and behaviours. Take the example of redundancy. If I lose my job, positive self-talk might be especially useful. In this situation, saying to myself, 'I will use my good people skills to ask around and find another rewarding job' and 'I respond well to change' might make me more hopeful about what lies ahead and encourage me to take action. In contrast, negative self-talk such as 'I'm not very good with people and it will make finding a new job much harder for me', and 'Change is difficult for me' is more likely to make me feel bad, anxious, and less willing to act; less likely to take the steps that might be required to find a new job.

When is positive self-talk most effective?

Studies conducted by Van Raalte and colleagues,[30] Calvete and Cardenoso[31] and Karoly and Ruehlman[32] have found that positive self-talk has a positive impact on wellbeing, resilience and stress management, and on reducing depressive symptoms. Negative self-talk, in contrast, is more often associated with depression, anxiety and rumination.[33] Positive self-talk, more so than negative self-talk, is effective in stressful situations like a crisis partly due to its links to healthy functioning.

To illustrate the effectiveness of positive self-talk in a crisis, let's consider natural disasters and especially tornadoes. The United States averages more than 1,000 tornadoes a year. That's more than any other country on the globe.[34] Different ingredients have combined to create fertile conditions for tornadoes in this part of the world, including warm, moist air, an unstable atmosphere and wind at different levels.[35] Between 25 April and 28 April 2011, 360 tornadoes struck the Southeastern United States. This 'super outbreak', as it was referred to, was the largest ever recorded tornado outbreak, killing 348 people and causing a billion dollars in damages to homes, schools, businesses and infrastructure. Public officials and community members have spoken passionately about the devastation created by the tornadoes, the hardship and loss experienced.

Wahl-Alexander and Sinelnikov[36] studied a group of 45 students directly affected by the tornado outbreak who had lost their homes and/or family members. These individuals were asked to participate in an intervention programme at the University of Alabama which was focused on reducing the physiological and psychological stress of crisis victims. One of the main techniques introduced by researchers to accomplish this was positive self-talk. After discussing the technique with the students, the researchers provided scripted examples for them to practice before encouraging them to develop their own examples. The researchers asked them to use examples of positive self-talk such as 'Everything will be okay', 'I'm doing great' and 'I can do this' both with and without prompting. Many of these students started using positive self-talk at home and reported experiencing positive effects, such as feeling calmer and more confident about the future.

Positive self-talk is also regarded to be an effective strategy for individuals employed in high-stress professions. For example, Wetzel and collaborators[37] found that surgeons often use positive self-talk to manage stress while performing surgery, reminding themselves that they are helping their patients and that things could be worse. Likewise, Beaton and colleagues[38] uncovered that positive self-talk had a protective function for firefighters with emergency medical training who were frequently exposed to intense work-related stressors and trauma incidents.

Positive self-talk is a particularly effective strategy for keeping people focused on the present, rather than on the past or distant future.[39] It tends to be aligned with making a realistic assessment of our reality and is likely to be opportunity focused, which involves framing difficulties as challenges rather than threats. Brian was able to do this and to see the pandemic as an opportunity to create not only a strong culture for his business, but also a new direction. Negative self-talk, in contrast, keeps us focused on the past or on the future rather than the present. It involves making a critical and unrealistic assessment of reality and is threat focused.

Building on my own research with entrepreneurs in crisis, I've done some exercises on self-talk with my masters' students, asking them to flip negative statements into positive ones. In one session a student asked me if positive self-talk could sometimes be superficial, to which I responded 'Yes!'. Where positive self-talk is vacuous, not grounded in realistic assessments of ourselves generally or our abilities specifically – for example, stating 'I am the best there ever was or ever will be, and I can get any job I apply for or solve any problem I encounter' – it might be less effective.

Monitoring self-talk

Zooming in on our self-talk, its form and function, can be revealing, as the examples of entrepreneurs featured next would suggest. Sometimes in the past when my daughter would speak about maths it would make me wince. Despite catching on to new concepts quickly, her negative thoughts could, on occasion, get in the way and stop her from trying. It's the one subject that seemed to fuel her anxiety. That made her question her abilities. 'I'm not smart', I heard her say a couple of times. It broke my heart. I tried to remind her that learning something new doesn't mean you have to know how to do it from the outset and that she just didn't know how to do it yet. Another approach was to ask her to think about all the times she persisted and figured it out. Often, we're not aware of how we talk to ourselves. 'I'm not very good at working with others', someone might say playfully, or 'I don't hold up well under pressure'. And even, 'I can't seem to do anything right'. Using the resources at the end of the chapter we can better discern how our self-talk might be setting us up to tackle the challenges ahead or to fall before the first hurdle, and how we can use it more effectively.

The role of self-talk

I observed many instances of positive self-talk in the accounts of entrepreneurs like Brian following the London riots, as well as during and after the COVID-19 pandemic. The examples presented here share similar features, such as how entrepreneurs navigate the crisis by adapting behaviour, accomplishing certain goals, realizing opportunities and thinking about themselves in a favourable light (for example, 'I've proved myself on being caring'; 'I'm quite proud that we managed to do what we did').

The positive self-talk of entrepreneurs in crisis

Camille studied drama and worked as a licensed therapist before starting her own business. Following the pandemic, Camille, the 40-something-year-old owner of a theatre company established more than a decade before, reflected on how, despite having to work from home and managing home-schooling with her children, she had not only kept the business going but had managed to stay in touch with her vulnerable audience:

> I'm sure there were other things that could have been done. But considering my personal situation, I managed to keep my company alive, and my theatre workshop groups alive and be in touch with everyone. I did what I could, considering the situation, and I was lucky not to be too affected. I mean professionally, I'm in a good place.

Camille's reflections suggest that while she was aware of other ways to manage the COVID-19 crisis, she had done quite well, considering the personal and professional difficulties she had encountered. She believed that her actions enabled her to move to a place beyond the crisis.

In contrast, Olivia, a composer and musician in her late 40s, felt she had done all she could to survive during the pandemic when much of her work had dried up. She described how well she had managed in terms of staying both artistically productive and healthy:

> I think I did as good as I could. Yeah, I feel fortunate that I was able to be productive and release some music. I was able to release my piano preludes that came out as an album. I made a little bit of money afterwards, so I did do something that was productive. Even though all the work vanished, it was reassuring that people didn't forget about me, that people were still calling me for things. So, I managed to keep my mental game ... I don't know what else I could've done unless I had just written more music, but feel like I was fortunate and able to use the time well.

Kate, the 50-something-year-old owner of a dance studio in North London, spoke about how her business had suffered during the pandemic and her concerns about having to let her dancers go:

> I've had a lot of conversations in my head about whether or not I can continue, and the only reason I am continuing is because I've promised those dancers work. I will do all I can to give them that work for this year and then I'll see what we can do.

Nevertheless, she went on to remind herself how she had managed to achieve her goal of keeping everyone employed during the pandemic and how she had explored different ways to adapt the work and engage more with the dancers. This was a source of pride:

> I don't normally say things like this, but I'm quite proud that we managed to do what we did, because I felt like

> I was very aware of judging how at times dancers were getting tired of doing the same thing. So, we tried to think of news ways of engaging ... but that also was their lifesaver, to have something consistent. And we didn't stop the whole time. We had classes three days a week and you didn't have to show up ... and then I just kept thinking of ways that we could do things. I went to the board and said, 'Should I spend this money on films?' And they said, 'Yes, absolutely' ... It meant that we could tour in the spring. So, there were some positives.

Two years following the London riots, Anne described the crisis to me as a one-off event driven by deprivation rather than the regular state of affairs in her neighbourhood. Framing the situation in this way enabled her to think about the riots as a challenge to be managed rather than a threat. Reflecting on her bespoke clothing store, she said:

> So, it's better to think that we were here for 20 years before and we didn't have any problems like that, and we weren't ever burgled the same [way] – maybe one odd shoplifting incident. But we had a decent run in as far as you can have a business on High Street. So, you know, it's better to resolve it [as], 'It wasn't personal. It was an opportunity to steal!' It was the poorer people ... what people are willing to do is a very personal decision, and I think that's why we got looted. We have decided to stay here for as long as we have the energy to do so.

Rather than catastrophizing or taking things too personally, Anne made a more realistic assessment of the situation by remembering how things were in the business before the riots and concluding that they as business owners had little trouble in the past or at present. This thinking enabled her to move beyond the crisis, to adapt and create a different way of working in the process:

> That made a difference because we had energy then [to rethink our business model]. We were completely stocked at the time when we were completely looted. ... I think

people are very used to, in this particular society, things being replenishable but if you have a business whereby you're a maker of something, it doesn't function in the same way. It's very, very specific ... [After the riots] these cupboards were even more empty; now they're still relatively empty but we've decided to kind of try and work with them and make them singular kind of samples, but we don't sell anything anymore. Two years on and we don't sell anything [pre-made], because we don't have the space.

When I asked if it was ever an issue, she replied, 'It's an opportunity'. Anne and her business partner Chloe saw the crisis, which wiped out most of their handmade stock, as an opportunity to make clothes to order. This enabled them to better use their time and energy.

The negative self-talk of entrepreneurs in crisis

Negative self-talk was far less commonly observed, but I still show here how it can manifest and the potential implications for entrepreneurs. Positive self-talk can be used in part to undo negative self-talk and associated negative emotions and behaviours, as the example that follows suggests.

Amir worked in the markets selling clothes before opening his North London shop. Passionate about fashion, he felt this is what he was meant to do. And without an education he said he couldn't do anything else. Amir was in his late 40s when we met. He told me about the distress he had experienced seeing his business for the first time after it was looted, vandalized and flooded due to the actions of rioters who had attempted to set fire to the premises, triggering the sprinklers:

> I come and see my shop and I can't believe it. It's like, so hard to explain. Where's my shop? Door broke, fire alarm going on ... Fire in the back. Water leaking. Downstairs, this much water [gestures to his waistline]. And I'm just shaking ... Computer missing. My till is gone. My counter is broke. Ceiling damage and fire. All the stock is gone. All I have is burned. I have this feeling ... My

son says, 'Daddy you are finished'. Ah. I have no words. I was like nothing to say. I'm finished.

Amir saw the crisis as a serious threat to the continuity of his business and he could not see a future for it beyond the riots, telling himself he was 'finished'. Amir went into a 'deep depression' and isolated himself for the next two or three weeks. Following this, however, he was able to recover both personally and professionally from the riots even though his business still had not returned to pre-riot levels two years later. He explained, 'Once I set my mind to something … I just have to do it.' This example of negative self-talk suggests that it can be hasty, focused on framing a crisis as a threat and as more than what can be managed, at least for a time. On reflection, however, Amir decided that restoring the business was something he could do.

What can we do to engage in positive self-talk and constructive thinking more effectively in a crisis?

Self-talk sometimes gets a bad rap. On occasion, self-talk is seen as nothing more than meaningless platitudes, a quick fix or a superficial cure. And depending on how it's used, such references to self-talk may be right. But self-talk does matter, and negative self-talk can be especially problematic.

To engage in self-talk more effectively, we can ask ourselves questions about how we are managing in a crisis and whether we are making realistic assessments of the situation, as indicated in Table 4.1. This can help us discern whether self-talk is positive or negative, and constructive or not. Table 4.2 can serve to monitor self-talk as it arises.

We can practice positive self-talk. Box 4.1 provides some actionable takeaways for building positive self-talk into our lives. In so doing, we can become more aware of the kinds of situations or routines that might get in the way. For example, not giving ourselves enough time and space to reflect on what's happening or how we are responding under the circumstances, jumping from one urgent task to another, can heighten anxiety and exhaustion. It can reduce opportunities for positive self-talk, and possibly allow for more fear-based destructive thinking to settle in.

Table 4.1: Guiding questions for a more positive and constructive self-talk strategy

How am I managing?	• What have I done well in response to the crisis more generally? • What solutions have I identified in response to the crisis more specifically? • What have I/have we achieved during or after the crisis as a result of my actions/our actions?
Am I making a realistic assessment of myself or the situation?	• Am I interpreting difficulties associated with the crisis as challenges as opposed to threats? • Am I able to see the positives in terms of what I have done or set out to do, or am I only able to notice the negatives? • Does the crisis define me or my business or can I see beyond it?

Table 4.2: A self-talk log

Self-talk examples	Is your self-talk positive or negative?	Is it focused on the present?	Does it involve making a realistic assessment about the situation?	What are the implications for how I think and act?

We can also engage in negative self-talk interventions. Negative self-talk can have a negative impact on our wellbeing and our ability to act during a crisis unless it's corrective and constructive. It's been argued that the first step towards limiting negative self-talk is becoming more aware of it and directing attention towards eliminating or reducing its frequency. Different interventions have been proposed for this purpose by Zinsser,[40] Hardy[41] and others, such as asking individuals to keep logbooks to measure the number of negative statements they make over a period of time, providing examples and discussing what triggers them, and an activity that involves moving paper clips from

Figure 4.1: Shifting negative self-talk towards positive self-talk

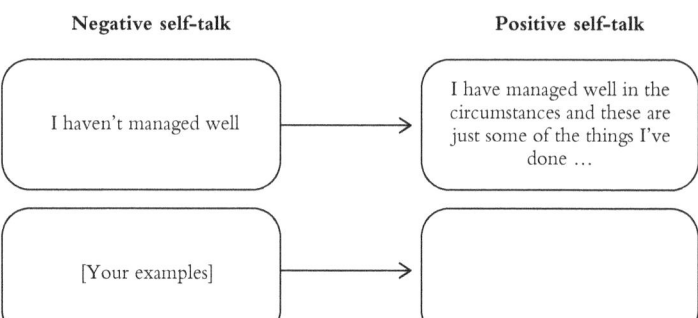

one pocket to another whenever they use a negative self-statement. Once individuals become aware that they are making such statements, reverse listing and thought stopping might be effective. Reverse listing asks individuals to list positive counterstatements for every negative statement, while thought stopping asks them to say a certain word out loud such as 'stop' to interrupt the negative self-talk.[42] In a study with undergraduate kinesiology students, Hardy and collaborators[43] found the logbook intervention to be more effective than the paper clip activity at drawing attention to when and how often negative self-talk was used and its content. Entrepreneurs and others can use reverse listing to shift from negative to positive self-talk. See Figure 4.1 for an example of how this might work and include your own examples too.

As actual or aspiring entrepreneurs, I have asked my students to reflect on their own self-talk around starting up a business. Students often report feeling that they 'don't have enough experience generally' or 'experience in the industry' to be an entrepreneur. When asked how they could spin it, one student suggested saying, 'I need to start somewhere' and that 'I can learn' new things along the way. Similarly, another said that sometimes she felt she couldn't succeed as an entrepreneur because 'industry rivals' were more powerful and experienced than she was. In challenging these thoughts, she reported that she could say to herself instead: 'I can keep up with them'. I reminded her and the others that they could reflect on all the times there was competition and they were successful or stood their ground. A different student was concerned that some people 'won't take you seriously because you're young'. At the same time, in challenging those thoughts, he said, 'In a way people might value you more because you're young' and can offer a 'fresh perspective' and 'provide something new' that 'our generation will value more'.

Finally, although self-talk is usually self-generated, there is some evidence that it might be modifiable and directed by other parties (such as coaches towards athletes), and that these modifications in self-talk can impact performance, as comments made by others are internalized.[44] Meeting often with supportive friends or family, a life coach, mentor or business advisor can be helpful. I have spoken with many entrepreneurs and business professionals over the years in different settings who have testified to the benefits of using mentors or coaches to promote their personal and professional growth. Therefore, in a crisis we may look to others to guide our self-talk.

★★★

As we've learned, positive self-talk is a powerful strategy that helps to manage stress and create stress resistance. In addition to positive self-talk and expectation management, positive reappraisal, the subject of the next chapter, is a thought-focused strategy entrepreneurs used to adjust to a crisis. Like positive self-talk, it emphasizes the value of reflection and reframing.

> **Box 4.1: Actionable takeaways for positive self-talk**
>
> - Observe your self-talk: Catch the things you say to yourself and to others about yourself. Think about how your self-talk might be affecting you and your behaviour. Notice whether the things you say are encouraging and constructive or corrective in nature. If not, revisit.
> - Practice positive self-talk: Make it a point to reflect on what you have achieved and are capable of. This will help you manage stress and to see the challenges ahead as being surmountable.
> - Talk to others: Ask others for their insights into your self-talk and for their support in helping you grow. Talk about how you can frame problems as challenges and spot opportunities.

Chapter summary

- Self-talk is a voice, a dialogue or activity used by individuals for the purpose of self-regulation as a way to provide instructions or reinforcement to oneself.
- Self-talk enables individuals to reflect on their experiences, to develop their self-efficacy – their perceived ability to accomplish certain tasks – and adapt their behaviour.
- Self-talk can be positive or negative. Positive self-talk has been associated with constructive thinking which enables people to see stressors in their environment as challenges rather than as threats, leading them to feel better able to manage them.
- Positive self-talk may be especially useful in a crisis by helping us focus on the present and to make realistic assessments, to see beyond the crisis or to see the crisis as a challenge rather than a threat and to notice the opportunities. It can also help us reflect positively on how we have managed despite the difficulties in order to forge ahead.
- For entrepreneurs in crisis, positive self-talk relates to how they adapt their behaviour, accomplish certain goals or realize opportunities. Positive self-talk is about how they think of themselves and their actions positively.
- In a crisis we can engage in positive self-talk and constructive thinking more effectively by reflecting on how we are managing, assessing the current situation by asking ourselves certain questions, practicing positive self-talk, engaging in negative self-talk interventions and modifying self-talk with support and direction from others.

5

Positive Reappraisal

Marie worked in publishing and marketing for a time but after having a family set her sights on starting her own business. 'I realized that I couldn't carry on doing what I was doing and have a baby,' she said. 'I thought, "alright, I'm going to open this shop, and it's going to be."' Marie opened what soon became a popular children's clothing shop in West London, in the early 2000s.

The day her business was hit by rioters, Marie received a couple of messages including one from the local council to say that the riots might be heading her way. Despite her feelings of disbelief, she contacted neighbouring businesses and, like them, removed items from her store front window, turned off the lights and went home. Later that evening, around 10 pm, she got a call from her alarm company. 'It's such a horrible feeling. It's like if your purse has been nicked and you feel helpless.' Her husband jumped into the car but didn't get as far as the shop. He turned around, according to Marie, because it was complete 'chaos', 'too many people around' and he felt 'unsafe'.

A couple of hours later, a friend rang Marie: 'I'm outside your shop now and it's totally trashed. There's nothing in there. It's just trashed,' he said. Marie set out to investigate but it wasn't long before approaching the shop that she saw 'people streaming everywhere', some of which surrounded her car. 'It was like I was in a dream. A really bizarre and frightening and bewildering dream.' She was stopped from going any further by a police cordon and told to 'go home'. At around 2 am while watching the news, helicopter footage captured a business on fire just a few doors down from hers and she was unable to tell if the fire had spread. 'So that's when my husband

and I just looked at each other and my heart sank.' At some point after 2 am she drifted off to sleep and by 5 am she was awake and set out once again. Her shop had been emptied with some of its contents strewn across a field nearby. All shop fittings, fixtures and windows were broken. Despite her initial upset, wanting to 'throttle somebody' or leave, she had a change of heart and said, 'I'm marketable, I could probably go and get a job'. She explained:

> I think what changed my mind was having, well, it's probably not the deciding factor but, I had so much support, I'll show you in a minute I've got a file that big of messages [she signals a couple of inches with her fingers]. And, I thought, maybe something good could come out of it, if I could get it back? At the time, it felt as if we wouldn't get back up and running at all, but looking back, it was all things that could be fixed. It wasn't as if I was hurt, although I felt threatened on the night when they [the rioters] surrounded my car and all that. But at least it wasn't burned down. Everything can be repaired.

Marie's account shows both an awareness for the possible opportunities that could come from the riots, and a sense of gratitude she hadn't been as badly affected as others, including those who were injured, killed or had their businesses burned down. These thoughts comforted her somewhat and helped diminish some of the negative emotions she was experiencing, such as fear and anger. They also created positive emotions, including a sense of hope for the future.

Marie's example is a reminder of something that has never ceased to amaze me … and that is the tendency of entrepreneurs to report the positives in what is an otherwise difficult period. As in Marie's case, these reports from entrepreneurs usually go something like this: 'Although it has been very challenging in the last few weeks and the business is struggling financially, my team has been amazing', or 'I know we've been luckier than some, so it helps to think about that'. It turns out that reflecting on the upside of adversity is rather common.[1] There is a stream of research dedicated to this manner of coping, which is known as 'positive reappraisal'. Although reappraisal has not been examined in prior entrepreneurship research, it was frequently employed by the entrepreneurs in crisis I engaged with, and, in this chapter, I share some examples of positive reappraisal in particular.

What is reappraisal?

When we have a hurtful argument with a friend but come to see it as a valuable turning point in the relationship, we're engaging in reappraisal. When we get a promotion at work but reflect sometime later on how we're spending less time with family or on the activities we love, this is reappraisal.

Reappraisal involves adjusting our thinking by modifying the meaning we give to a situation and our interpretation of it 'after' we have made an initial evaluation of the situation as being good or bad, as innocuous or harmful.[2] In this sense, reappraisal is a kind of emotion regulation strategy that requires cognitive change. Reappraisal involves altering the emotional significance we attach to a situation, making it seem more or less emotionally significant by changing how we think about the situation or our capacity to manage the demands that the situation imposes and, in turn, how we feel about it.[3] According to James Gross,[4] a psychologist and leading scholar on the topic of emotion regulation, 'a situation typically does not in and of itself generate emotion. Rather, it is the individual's evaluation of that situation that is emotion-generative'.

Reappraisal can take the form of changing how we think about, understand and interpret a situation (reconstrual), or changing our goals to take advantage of an opportunity created by the situation (repurposing).[5] Regarding job loss, the former would involve interpreting the loss as not being that bad, while the latter would be more about seeing it as an opportunity to change our career goals or to pursue a different career, both of which are good examples of positive reappraisal.

Positive reappraisal has been linked to benefit finding and benefit reminding. Benefit finding is about finding value in adversity or growing from adversity.[6] Making new connections with others is an example of something positive that can come from adversity.[7] This might include meeting others who have been affected by the crisis or those who have come forward or are available to help in a supportive capacity. Benefit finding can also comprise thinking about the opportunities that might arise, something noted by Marie in her reflections on the riots; imagining something good might come from all the support she had received in the aftermath. Benefit reminding involves more deliberate and repeated recollections of the benefits, sometimes referred to as counting one's blessings. Marie also felt she was better off than other riot victims, something she was grateful for.

Across a range of adverse situations, positive reappraisal, and its counterparts benefit finding and benefit reminding, have been connected to resilience following adversity, to diminished levels of distress, increased psychological and physical health or the absence of unhealthy functioning, as well as posttraumatic growth, all features of resilience.[8] In a longitudinal study of disaster survivors in three US states, McMillen and co-researchers[9] found that those who reported benefit finding shortly after adversity – a plane crash, tornado or mass shooting – were less likely to experience PTSD three years later and more likely to recover than those who did not. In another study of the devastating flood in the Indian state of Kerala in August 2018 which struck 13 districts, affecting more than 5 million people and killing 440,[10] survivors across three villages were utilizing benefit reminding as a coping strategy, mindful that they were still alive and with their families, unlike others.[11] By considering the experiences of others, as Marie did, these individuals were able to draw attention away from their own painful experiences and comfort themselves.

When is positive reappraisal most effective?

Positive reappraisal might be an especially effective strategy in certain situations, including those that aren't easily defined and that possess a degree of uncertainty which require sensemaking, such as raising a child or experiencing an illness, or navigating a crisis such as a natural disaster or a human-induced crisis like riots. Positive reappraisal is less effective, however, in situations requiring little sensemaking, situations that are defined by observable and certain events,[12] such as turning a year older on your birthday or getting paid on a specific day of the month.

Positive reappraisal can be effective in or following a crisis because it involves attaching positive meaning to an adverse situation.[13] To illustrate, for people living in certain parts of the world, wildfires are a frequent occurrence. During the 'wildfire season' in Australia in 2020, more than 46 million acres of land burned and over a billion animals were affected.[14] In 2023, 45.7 million and 2.6 million acres burned across Canada[15] and the United States respectively.[16] The consequences of wildfires can be devastating and long lasting for those impacted. They pose serious risks to life, personal and commercial properties, public buildings and critical services, causing disruptions.

California is often among the states most badly affected by wildfires in the United States. On 7 January 2025, fires tore through Los Angeles County with the largest blaze taking place in the Palisades, a residential area in the Westside of Los Angeles, between Santa Monica and Malibu. At the time of writing, in excess of 40,000 acres of land had been destroyed, along with 16,000 structures – including homes, schools and businesses. More than two dozen people lost their lives[17] and approximately 30,000 people had to be evacuated from the area, housed in temporary accommodation or with friends and family.[18] Estimated costs of the fires stood at 250 billion.[19]

Just over a decade and a half earlier, the state fell victim to another series of devastating fires. Between 2008 and 2009, three major fires swept across California: the Gap Fire, Tea Fire and Jesusita Fire. Collectively, these three fires burned more than 20,000 acres of land across the state, displaced thousands of individuals, and destroyed or threatened to destroy hundreds of homes, businesses and other commercial properties. Felix and colleagues[20] studied residents of a coastal community in California, including parents and children evacuated from their homes that were either damaged by the three fires (two-thirds) or destroyed (one-third). Residents were asked, 'How stressful has your life been because of the fire?', 'How stressful was the fire right after it happened?' and 'How stressed are you now as a result of the fire?'. Researchers found that positive reappraisal was highly significant across the sample and associated with their resilience. Positive reappraisal involved modifying the meaning of the crisis in order to see the good with the bad, as reflected in statements such as, 'I think I can learn something from the situation' or 'I think that I can become a stronger person as a result of what has happened'.[21] Individuals who adopted positive reappraisal as a coping strategy reported more posttraumatic growth, a feature of resilience as we discussed earlier, and greater overall family health.

Positive reappraisal also tends to be a more effective in less emotionally intense, less stressful situations,[22] or when the emotional intensity of the situation has died down a little, because it requires significant cognitive resources making it a costly short-term strategy but a cost-effective strategy in the long term.[23] For this reason, a bit of a delay between the onset of a crisis event and reappraisal might be expected, once those affected have had an opportunity to reflect, as Marie did a few months after her business was looted and vandalized.

Monitoring reappraisal

It can be helpful to think about when we might be using reappraisal to our benefit or could be. I was listening to Desert Island Discs recently, a popular programme broadcast on BBC radio throughout the UK. It's a show that asks its guests to imagine being stranded on a desert island and the music they would bring that's meaningful to them, along with a book and a luxury item. It's a clever format that compels people to speak about important periods in their lives. This particular episode was with the British comedian, actor and writer Robert Webb. What really stood out for me was how he spoke about his mother who had passed away when he was a teenager, whom he described as his favourite person. For him, getting through the painful experience of her death had encouraged him to think differently about other parts of his life, like applying to Cambridge, and to keep his worries in check. It resonated with my own experiences of loss and, further, how feeling grateful for the time spent with loved ones no longer present has always been a source of comfort for me. Using the prompts and tools I provide later, which draw from the ideas outlined and especially the accounts of entrepreneurs in crisis that follow, you can reflect on your own examples.

The role of positive reappraisal

In my experience, positive reappraisal is one of the most common strategies entrepreneurs in crisis utilize to minimize their distress and be more resilient. It occurs when these individuals shift their thoughts away from something negative and/or redirect them towards something positive or less negative. My research suggests this often involves drawing comparisons between themselves and others who are worse off, or comparing their present and past experiences.

Examples of positive reappraisal centre around four themes or sub-strategies. That is, I identified four different forms of positive reappraisal adopted by entrepreneurs in crisis: (a) other victim-centred framing, (b) other event-centred framing, (c) support-centred framing and (d) growth-centred framing. Benefit finding and/or reminding is present across the different themes, as indicated by the accounts of entrepreneurs in crisis that follow. In each case, entrepreneurs felt that while the crisis was difficult in general or at specific times, they were still able to manage.

Other victim-centred framing: 'We are better off than some crisis victims'

Frequently, positive reappraisal manifests in the tendency of entrepreneurs like Marie to draw comparisons between themselves and other crisis victims whom they perceive as having it much worse. This allows them to downplay the emotional significance of the crisis event, alleviate somewhat their negative emotions and evoke positive emotions in turn.

Following the London riots, not everyone was paid by insurers in full or in a timely fashion. Long delays over financial compensation were usual and well documented. Those who were paid quickly, like Nathan, the owner of a shop selling electrical goods and appliances in East London, felt lucky: 'Our insurance claim was met very quickly … I think we got some initially within sort of six weeks … I think we were very fortunate compared with what I've heard from other sources.' Two years after the riots, when we spoke again, Nathan made a point of discussing how insurers' actions had made him feel less angry and more positive about everything that had transpired.

During the COVID-19 pandemic when businesses selling non-essential goods were ordered to close and people were directed to stay home, positive reappraisal – particularly, feeling better off than some – was a common strategy employed by many of the entrepreneurs I encountered. Three weeks after the first lockdown, Robert, the café owner in Southeast London, wrote in his diary about how his café was doing relative to other businesses negatively impacted:

> We paid everyone, furloughed everyone, and paid all our suppliers so now we're sitting on a bit of cash – nothing's coming in and not much is coming out until next month. It's just a bit of a waiting game as to how long this all

lasts and how long our cash lasts. Now everything's done though it's quite nice. We're not in a particularly stressful position compared to some.

Other entrepreneurs spoke about how they fared better than some during the pandemic, both personally, in terms of their health, and professionally. Olivia, a musician and composer said:

> I feel like I was fortunate, and I was able to use the time well and be productive, and not have my health badly affected, whereas some people – I have one viola player friend, a very professional viola player and he was in a coma for months with COVID-19 … when he finally recovered … he then spent 5 months having to relearn the viola to get his skillset back up again. So, you know, compared to that really it was a walk in the park for me.

Andrew, who was in his mid-50s and ran a restaurant in West London, reported that what got him through the pandemic was feeling grateful for all that he had, for being healthy and able to carry on:

> I just always thank whoever, whatever is up there that I have, you know, a job that pays a cheque, a roof over my head and I can put food on the table. And I actually flew through Wuhan on the 23rd of December 2019. And yeah, I kind of just about escaped it. But yeah, I mean just general gratitude and just happy to be alive and being able to carry on relatively speaking essentially unaffected.

Other event-centred framing: 'The crisis "pales into insignificance" compared to other things'

Some entrepreneurs see a crisis as being less significant than other stressful events they have endured that affected them personally and/or professionally. One entrepreneur I spoke to said that the current crisis had 'paled into insignificance' in contrast to his previous experiences. In these instances, entrepreneurs do not interpret crisis events as being more positive in some way (as with the previous theme), but rather as less negative or problematic than other events they have encountered.

Two years after the riots, when I spoke again to Anthony, who sold seasonal items and decorations in Southwest London, he described himself as being in a better position than other riot victims, even though the shop had been burned down. He also made a point of noting that the riots were less significant to him than other personal hardships he and his family had endured:

> When the shop burned down, I said to my wife … 'Well, no-one got killed. We're still alive. We've still got a house … It's not the end of the world. We'll get back on our feet again. The worst thing that can happen is that we make a bit less money, but our health and everything is still there'. So yes, it was traumatic, but not as traumatic – I've been through much worse in my life, that's all … with major catastrophes and illnesses and things like that, and my wife got breast cancer when she was 40, so we went through a whole period of distress then. My son was seriously ill, and all those things make financial situations less significant … Every time I would come down [to the business] I would just think about how lucky we actually are … compared to the people we're helping in [the country where his charity is based], for instance. Like, we have a nice house and we have a car. Okay, so I'm having to work seven days a week at the moment to keep that on its feet, but I'm capable of working, capable of doing it … I've got food to eat so we're lucky.

By comparing his current situation to his previous hardships and others' experiences of adversity, Anthony reconstrued or reinterpreted how he felt about the riots and the damages the rioters had inflicted on his business. This way of thinking helped him manage his negative emotions and generated positive emotions. For both Marie and Anthony, framing the crisis as less emotionally significant was comforting and enabled them to keep their negative emotions in check by focusing on the bigger picture. It was also a way to ignite their actions and help them persist through difficult times.

Other entrepreneurs drew on previous professional hardships to help them through crises. David was in his early 60s when we met. Since he was a schoolboy, he had lived in the same neighbourhood and worked in the same North London hardware store he eventually took over more than 30 years later. When I visited David in his shop following the London riots, we were frequently interrupted by customer queries and sales. He told me in snatched conversation that the riots wouldn't stop him from working and that his business and his family had been through much worse:

> I intend to retire, that is, when I feel it's time. But that's on my terms. I will retire on my own terms. Not on anybody else's. I'm not going to be driven out by the riots. No. I'll go when I'm ready, not before. Six years ago, there was a big fire. The whole building around me was all burned down and the shop was flooded. We lived in temporary accommodation for 18 months and we worked through it all.

David saw the riots as a 'lesser' crisis, perceiving it to be less damaging and less intense than the fire and subsequent flooding that had severely damaged his business and his home in the back of the shop. His experience during the previous crisis also served as a reminder that he would get through the riots.

Finally, several entrepreneurs reflected on how lucky they were to be running their own businesses and how far they had come in terms of where they had been and what they were doing previously, enabling them to carry on. Alara, the owner of a restaurant in North London, discussed:

> I think the main thing that kept me going during the pandemic is, like I reached a level good enough in my career, I was making a really good wage from a corporate job, but I wasn't really happy and I knew I wanted to do my own thing. So, the first thing that kept me going was the reality that I actually, now, have my own place and I can make all the decisions, the mistakes and everything will be my mistakes, and I can take it. So that kept me going.

Support-centred framing: 'We have received a lot of support during the crisis'

Frequently, crises are regarded by entrepreneurs as a time when they were fortunate to have received a lot of support, or unlucky not to have received enough support, which either diminishes negative emotions and evokes positive emotions, or heightens negative emotions, respectively. In the former case, entrepreneurs often mention receiving significant support from friends, family and other business stakeholders such as staff, suppliers, landlords, other businesses and members of the public/their broader community. Many also repurpose the crisis into an opportunity to make new connections, which is common in cases of posttraumatic growth, a feature of resilience.

A focus on support influences not only how entrepreneurs feel about a crisis per se, but how they feel about their ability to manage the demands it places on them. Following the riots, communities often rallied around business owners, offering them material and emotional support. Nathan noted how people had gone out of their way to say 'hello' or to buy something. One customer had purchased nearly £4000 worth of appliances as a gesture of goodwill. 'I think the riots might have given us a boost in certain respects because it's made people understand what's gone on and want to support us.' Vivek's community had raised nearly £30,000 for him, making him 'feel very good'. Dylan also spoke about all the support he received after his business burned down:

> You know the emotional side of things was immense. Grown men in the shop crying, people coming in and saying what a terrible thing ... These are members of the community. We had a little old lady come in and crotchet that there for us. She came in and said 'I need to buy a bed. I can't afford it at the moment. But I need to do it now because my arthritis is getting bad' ... I mean we've had letters from all over the world. Emails, hundreds and hundreds and hundreds of emails. The website crashed because of the media. When they've seen all of the TV things. It's just, I mean I've not experienced anything like it in my life.

Rick, the 50-something owner of a design agency in Southeast London, encountered hefty financial losses to his business during the pandemic. The business shrunk by 10% and revenue dropped by £1 million. Although Rick noted the considerable financial losses he had incurred, he also described the support he had received from the local council, which he greatly valued:

> As you sort of move back into the, 'Was it so bad?' Well, actually you know what? I think that the council have been amazing … They've given all the businesses breaks on business rates. They've given grants. They've been absolutely stunning … Just rates alone, that probably saved us, on this building, about £88,000 a year. That's a huge amount … Yes, we shrunk down £1 million in turnover, but … we didn't necessarily lose all our profitability.

Rick described the positives and negatives of the crisis on a spectrum, with financial losses at the 'horror end of the spectrum' and support from the council at the positive end. Thanks to the council, Rick's financial losses were not as severe as they could have been. Unprompted, he highlighted other positives during the pandemic as well, like the opportunity to establish new collaborations:

> We work with our clients in a sort of collaborative way. So, they said to us, in quite a few instances, 'What can we do?' or 'We need to reduce the billing this year', which is quite understandable because … there was nobody shopping … We normally work over say a 3-, 4- or 5-year term, and what we agreed in quite a few cases was actually we would reduce the billing for 2020, and at the same time they extended our contract by a year or 2 years, depending on what the deal was … It was probably not a situation you'd particularly welcome, but actually you worked collaboratively to find a good solution for your client and at the same time something that works well for you as a business.

The previous examples show the important role that external stakeholders might play in supporting entrepreneurs through a crisis.

It also can draw entrepreneurs' attention to the value of internal stakeholders such as staff. Two years following the riots, Anthony described the 'great dedication' some of his team members had exhibited towards the business:

> All negative things have a positive side, so experiences are far more valued than anything else. This experience has taught me a lot about people ... with my staff it showed who were the real supporters ... and wanted to stick with me. After the fire riots I did have staff coming in working for nothing to help, you know, just to be there.

Learning which staff members he could count on following the crisis, who his 'real supporters' were, brought Anthony a great deal of comfort during an otherwise difficult time.

Growth-centred framing: 'We are better off than before'

Some entrepreneurs repurpose a crisis into an opportunity for business growth or for personal growth. In these cases, a crisis is deemed meaningful because it has strengthened businesses or themselves. A few entrepreneurs I engaged with were emphatic that their businesses were better off because they had time to improve products, increase sales and/or expand their businesses.

Arjun, the co-founder of an online platform connecting businesses in the hospitality industry, was in his early 30s when we met. He explained that while the first lockdown during the pandemic had posed several challenges for his new business which opened a few months earlier, he also saw it as an opportunity to 'take stock' and make adjustments that eventually made the business stronger:

> When literally everything obviously just shut down, we were still small enough where we were able to effectively pull up the drawbridge, because we didn't have any employees, we needn't worry about furloughing, etc. It was a big frustration because we'd been growing quite nicely to that point ... then suddenly we had this opportunity to take a deep breath, look at what we'd learned over the first few months.

> So, actually, for us it was quite a good opportunity for [business partner] and I to take stock, make some product improvements ... when things started to open up in May or June, we were in a position that we could actually grow stronger.

While the majority of the entrepreneurs I spoke to complained that their businesses had contracted in size and function as result of the London riots, for a handful of these individuals, intense media exposure throughout the ensuing weeks and months drew attention to their businesses, boosting sales in the process. Jack, who was in his mid-50s when we met, had trained as a designer. He worked for some of the big design consultancies and then did freelance design work. A cyclist all his life, he opened a bicycle shop in Central London a year and a half before the riots. Jack said that because of the riots they now had more of a 'presence' and had been able to expand:

> The riot was very good for us. It sounds a terrible thing to say, doesn't it? ... But what happened was more people heard of us. The first two months after the riots were pretty dreadful actually, because we didn't have anything to sell ... they'd taken everything ... and then because we were better known, literally week-on-week sales have gone up ... literally every week's got better since then ... way above normal ... I think it really did give us a kick start and gave us a bigger presence in the bike world and we've opened another store now.

Growth was not restricted to businesses. A few entrepreneurs report that certain crises led to personal growth, that they had been able to improve their skills and professional competence. This was the case for Emma, a freelance artist in her early 40s, who came over to the UK from Japan just over 20 years ago. Although Emma experienced some frustrations during the first lockdown, with the support of government funding she found she was able to repurpose the pandemic into an opportunity to develop her skills as a creative professional:

> I think once they announced – the government – that they're giving us money to survive, I thought that was a great opportunity for me to develop my own skills … When you don't have a job, you feel you are the only one doesn't have a job … But that's the first time [where] I don't have a job and my mate is not having a job either. There's no job to pursue, there's nothing you can do. So, at the same time, it was revelatory. It's like 'Oh God, I can dedicate this time for myself'.

Some entrepreneurs, like Alex, the 40-something-year-old owner of a marketing distribution business in Southeast London helping brands increase their audience and sales through multi-channel campaigns, became more invigorated over the pandemic. Alex said that during the crisis he had 'regained' his 'spark'. When we spoke in the spring of 2021, one year after the first lockdown had been imposed, he declared, 'I'm running it [the business] with the mentality of a start-up but with 20 years of experience.' He also became more passionate about working with young people, not only bringing more of them into the business, but mentoring them as well:

> I remember sitting there and thinking, 'What is the life that you really want to live?' You get a chance to do that, particularly living in this city … and I'm quite lucky I have a house in [part of the UK] which means that I've got a bit of chance to, bit of time to go and sit there with my little cat, ponder, and it was, you know, you forget sometimes that, or I did that I'm in control to choose what I want. I choose what my view, life, will be, you know, and that's probably the biggest choice you have as an entrepreneur. So, it gave me the chance to kind of revaluate and kind of reassess, reenergise, revisit, and actually reignite the passion, you know, and I came back probably far more passionate than anyone expected me to and far more committed to a social endeavour, hence the youngsters, that I hadn't thought about for a long, long time … One of the things they do in [birthplace] which I was very, very glad to have been one of the first people to join, was the role model programme where

we go in to talk to schools and we go and tell these kids, 'Listen, I came from no money, I had no money, my dad was in university with me for heaven's sake! I had no money, whatever I had to do I had to earn but it was that dream, it was that vision that anyone can achieve anything'. And I want to go and tell the youngsters this, and I did that for a period in my life and then when we were in London you forget that, the social kind of disappears, and it kind of reignited that within. How's that for the pandemic?

Other entrepreneurs I interviewed during the COVID-19 pandemic noted that they had become more empathic managers, more concerned for their employees' wellbeing than ever before. The crisis created a lot of unease among employees due to the uncertainty surrounding their health and financial situations. Many entrepreneurs stepped up in response. In these cases, adversity was associated with business growth and/or personal growth for the entrepreneurs.

What can we do to engage in positive reappraisal more effectively in a crisis?

It's not always easy to see the positives, to find any value in adversity. And yet, it's something that most of us have done, at one time or another, intentionally or otherwise. Reframing a crisis in this manner can have powerful effects, as the examples in this chapter show.

To engage in positive reappraisal effectively during a crisis, we can reflect more broadly on the different ways of reconstruing or reinterpreting a crisis event and situations arising from the crisis as opportunities to do things differently. Like the entrepreneurs here, we can also consider whether our professional goals can be changed or repurposed in some way.

We can take the four themes or sub-strategies just highlighted and unpack the focus and perceived emotional significance of each (see Table 5.1). Importantly, we can consciously apply these sub-strategies by asking ourselves questions (refer to Table 5.2) and include our own examples for each of the four themes: other crisis victims, other events, support and growth (Table 5.3). We can also

Table 5.1: The focus and significance of positive reappraisal strategies

Positive reappraisal themes for entrepreneurs in crisis	Main focus	Emotional and perceived significance	Effects
I am better off than some crisis victims.	Other crisis victims, people or businesses, that are faring worse.	The emotional significance of the crisis is downplayed. The crisis is not as emotionally significant for me as it is for some.	Negative emotions diminished; positive emotions evoked.
The crisis 'pales into insignificance' compared to other things I've had going on.	Other events that one has endured or observed that have been more significant.	The emotional significance of the crisis is downplayed. The crisis is not as emotionally significant for me as other things.	Negative emotions diminished; positive emotions evoked.
I have received a lot of support during the crisis.	Support received from others (family, friends, staff, other businesses, members of the public, the community, landlords, insurers, government bodies, funders).	The emotional significance of the crisis is heightened. The crisis is emotionally significant because of the support we have received.	Negative emotions diminished; positive emotions evoked.
I am better off than I was before the crisis.	Business growth or personal growth (for example, developing skills or professional competence).	The emotional significance of the crisis is heightened. The crisis is emotionally significant because of the growth we have experienced.	Negative emotions diminished; positive emotions evoked.

Table 5.2: Guiding questions for positive reappraisal strategies

Other victim-centred questions	• Are there others who are worse off than me in this crisis? • How or in what ways might I be better off than others affected by the crisis?
Other event-centred questions	• What else do I have going on in my life and how does the crisis compare? • How can I balance the crisis against other difficulties I have encountered in my life? • How have I managed other difficulties in my life and come through to the other side?
Support-centred questions	• Who has been supportive of me/my business over the crisis? • In what ways have others supported me/my business over the crisis? • Have I developed any new or meaningful connections during the crisis? • How can I build on these connections going forward?
Growth-centred questions	• Has the crisis made me and/or the business stronger in any way? • Have I made a positive contribution to the recovery of my business during the crisis or others affected by the crisis, such as my community? • Have I developed new interests or forged a new path due to the crisis? • Have I improved my skills and/or professional competence in some way, for example, by learning how to better manage my staff or business during the crisis?

Table 5.3: Positive reappraisal prompts

How my experience compares to others affected	How the event compares to other events I've experienced
• • •	• • •
What support I've received	What personal/professional growth, if any, has come from this
• • •	• • •

make positive reappraisal part of our routine. Box 5.1 includes some actionable takeaways.

The good news about positive reappraisal is that it's not too late to start. As illustrated by my research with entrepreneurs and by prior research as well, even when benefit finding is initiated several weeks or even years after an adverse event, its positive effects can still be felt.[24]

We can actively engage in benefit finding and benefit reminding, key aspects of positive reappraisal. Such exercises might allow us to see crises in ways that would enable us to simultaneously process events and enhance our wellbeing. At the same time, and while existing research doesn't support the assertion that benefit finding or reminding in adversity discounts or denies in any way the negative effects, it's important to say that strategies focused solely on the positive aspects of adversity (whether it be a serious illness, job loss, economic crisis, terrorist attack, operational crisis, or otherwise) could mask its severity and its consequences and be harmful to you in the long run. For this reason, it's recommended that any benefit finding or reminding interventions, including those we initiate ourselves or those directed by others, should focus on both the positive and negative aspects of adverse experiences.[25]

Finally, to engage in positive reappraisal more effectively in a crisis, we can become more aware of the potential interpersonal benefits arising, such as new relationships and support. Other studies have shown that noticing support from others can enable us to move beyond conflicting and sometimes negative feelings about asking for help and seeing it as an expression of care, allowing us to move towards greater acceptance of the negative situation.[26] As hinted at previously, acceptance can also help us process negative emotions, which is important to our overall health and wellbeing.

★★★

We've seen that positive reappraisal, like the previous strategies, requires entrepreneurs to make adjustments to their internal environment, via their attention or how they think. In the next few chapters, we consider the strategies they employed to adjust their external environment.

> **Box 5.1: Actionable takeaways for positive reappraisal**
>
> - Practice positive reappraisal: Regularly reflect on challenging situations and identify any positive aspects or opportunities for growth. Ask yourself questions like, 'What can I learn from this?' or 'How can this make me stronger?'
> - Gratitude journaling: Keep a gratitude journal to note down things you are thankful for each day. This can help shift your focus from the negative to the positive.
> - Seek support: Leverage your social network for emotional support. Sharing your experiences and receiving encouragement from others can help you see the positives more clearly.

Chapter summary

- Reappraisal is a strategy that involves modifying the meaning of a situation, such as a crisis, by reconstruing or repurposing it, and regulating emotions in turn.
- Positive reappraisal and its counterparts, benefit finding and benefit reminding, can help individuals including entrepreneurs adapt to a crisis and be more resilient.
- Entrepreneurs in crisis commonly employ reappraisal and do so in four different ways, each of which has a specific focus – on other crisis victims, other events, support and growth – as well as a certain emotional significance and effect.
- To engage in reappraisal more effectively in a crisis, we can: attempt to reconstrue and repurpose events, reflect on the four themes relating to reappraisal, including the focus and emotional significance of each, ask ourselves questions that might prompt benefit finding and be aware of the potential interpersonal benefits of a crisis.

6

Situation Selection and Modification

Vivek, who was in his late 40s when we met, had moved to London from South Asia. He prided himself on a strong work ethic which he used to start his own shop over a decade before. His busy convenience store, located in an East London neighbourhood, was targeted during the London riots. Vivek set the scene: 'If you put a bomb on the shop, it was like that. With the ceiling down, electric wires hanging there, lights hanging, the counter was completely flat, fridge broken, freezer broken.' Yet, despite the extensive damages, what angered him most were the scattered takeaway boxes, carelessly discarded on what little of the business remained: 'They went out' and came back again to 'eat chicken and chips in the shop'. He explained, 'They had a party inside!'

Vivek described to me the day after the London riots, when his world as he knew it had ended:

> You know that day, you never forget that day. I'm telling you. It's the saddest day in my life. When my dad was passing, I never cried. My dad lived a good life. You know? I didn't cry. He just had, you know, a good death ... heart attack, so, it's a good, you know, death. But this [the riots] is, oh, I cried. I cried. The whole day I cried! I couldn't take it ... I just went home. I didn't step in the shop at all. I couldn't. I couldn't. I couldn't do it. The mess of the shop. It's completely ripped from top to bottom.

Although he didn't really sleep the night after the riots, upon waking the next morning, Vivek was alert. 'What am I going to do next?', he thought. 'I wake up at 5 o'clock and my wife is asking, "There is no shop, why'd you wake up this morning?" And I say, "I have to do a lot of things to do and go".' The newspapers, for one thing, would be there as he didn't get the chance to cancel them the day before. 'My brain is working. What am I going to do? I have a habit like, if anything happens to me, I'm worried, one hour, two hours, and then, I'm always like, "how can I overcome that?" That's me.'

He arrived at the shop by 6 am and could see the newspapers had been delivered. While he still didn't go inside, as doing so would have been too painful, he opened the newspaper bundle and proceeded to sell newspapers on the sidewalk, all morning long.

> Probably my neighbour doesn't know me at home, but [here] everyone knows me. So, I sold the papers and everyone was shocked, 'Yesterday you were crying and you're selling papers this morning. How can you do this?' And I say, 'What else can you do?'

In some cases, and similar to Vivek, we can make small changes to our external environment, adjustments to the situations we encounter, that allow us to manage potential distress or subvert negative emotions altogether, before they arise.[1] At the same time, by seeking out, avoiding or tweaking certain situations, we can encourage and prolong the generation of positive emotions, thereby increasing the likelihood of resilience.[2] These strategies have been referred to as situation selection and situation modification and they can both be effective in a crisis.

To use two additional examples, take a moment to consider the individual who has just received difficult news, a troubling diagnosis. To manage this health crisis and the negative emotions they are likely to be experiencing in turn, which might include painful feelings of fear and anxiety, the individual in question might choose to seek out a friend or to avoid speaking to people who might upset them or situations that create more stress. They might change how often they work, or even where they work. They might decide to spend less time at work and more time in nature.

Next, think about a public relations crisis that has besieged a large family business, wherein one member of the family who holds a top management position is arrested for a major infraction and is sentenced to serve prison time. Imagine that both internal and external stakeholders start abandoning the company in droves. Different people within the family, the CEO and others on the leadership team, might experience distress and decide to avoid attending public functions until the negative publicity dies down or they might do the opposite, showing more visibility and their solidarity. Some might decide to work from home more and refrain from speaking to the press, while others might spend more time at the office or in front of the press than usual. They might spend more time with family and seek out or surround themselves with new allies.

Despite their utility in a crisis, much less is known more broadly about situation selection and situation modification than the other strategies we have discussed so far. Moreover, and despite an absence of studies on how individuals in crisis or entrepreneurs more specifically might utilize these strategies, some of the entrepreneurs in crisis I observed did adjust in this way, by selecting and/or modifying their situation. For this reason, I include a few of their stories here.

What is situation selection?

Situation selection involves taking actions to make it more likely or less likely in future situations that we experience certain emotions. This might involve choosing how to spend our time and with whom. If our desire is to have a good time, we might plan a night out with a group of friends. If it's to mourn a break-up, we might plan to meet with a friend who is good at listening, empathetic.

According to Gross[3] and Sheppes,[4] situation selection takes the form of approaching or avoiding specific people and events. It can also involve approaching or avoiding certain tasks, as we learn later in the chapter, or places, as we saw with Vivek. We might, for instance, decide to avoid certain kinds of gatherings or media forums where a painful experience could be remembered or brought to our attention by others, thereby stirring up negative emotions. For the individual who has lost their job, situation selection might involve avoiding places where they could encounter former work colleagues or unfollowing work-related social media groups. Situation selection might also include putting oneself in places where securing another job is possible or arranging to meet with a mentor or coach to discuss possibilities for the future.

Situation selection is regarded as a particularly proactive emotion regulation strategy. It entails circumventing negative emotions by 'projecting oneself into the future' and considering how certain situations might make us feel and gravitating towards those most likely to lead us to a desired experience.[5] Situation selection, therefore, requires planning and foresight, and the belief that we can manage, at least to some degree, negative situations or feelings 'before' they arise.[6] Situation selection may also require remembering which situations will evoke certain emotions, like how interacting with a specific person will make us feel. For this reason, the perspective of friends, family members, colleagues or advisors can help make this strategy successful.[7] While the term situation can be vague, it is used here to describe an external physical environment.[8]

Situation selection, like distraction, may be considered an avoidance strategy. It requires us to anticipate how we might feel in the future, more proactively identify those feelings, take control of the situation and adjust to the situation to prevent new negative emotions from surfacing. Distraction, on the other hand, does not change how we deal with the situation in the future,[9] and as a strategy may be focused on interrupting or suppressing negative emotions. With situation selection, if we feel that doing something might make us feel better or worse, we might approach or avoid those situations. In Vivek's case, he applied both situation selection and distraction. He avoided going into the shop and selling newspapers served as a distraction.

When is situation selection most effective?

Situation selection might be an effective strategy for those individuals who find it difficult to regulate their emotions otherwise. Situation selection, it seems, is a less cognitively demanding strategy to implement than some of the other strategies we've discussed, such as reappraisal.[10]

As implied, situation selection may be most effective when we have an opportunity to adjust our external environment and are able to plan how we might feel in the future. Similarly, it's more likely to be effective when we make these adjustments before emotions surface.

At the same time, as with Vivek, we can use situation selection to manage negative emotions as they arise.

Finally, situation selection may be a more effective strategy for those who tend to experience especially intense emotions,[11] and who find them difficult to manage. Vivek was distraught by the extensive damages to his business. He knew going inside the shop immediately to investigate the damages more closely would only make him feel worse and so, to limit these negative feelings, even if only a little, he stayed outside and sold newspapers.

Monitoring situation selection

Reflecting on the situations we may have avoided to stop ourselves from feeling bad, or those we sought out to feel good, can be useful, whether it's certain events, interactions, tasks or places. Checking my work email on holiday is something I try to avoid, if I can, and, in my line of work, it is often possible to do, although I know this isn't the case for everyone. And, whenever I have looked at it, it's often something I've regretted. Going to the cinema, alternatively, is always a positive experience, one that makes me happy, and I do when I can. It feels like a treat, especially when I'm tired or my brain is on overload. In contrast, attending big professional events, like conferences, is not always something I feel like doing but when I do, I'm often delighted by the interesting people I meet and, on occasion, the opportunities that can come from such. Similarly, for many people, it can be daunting to attend a big social event and to mingle with those they don't know well or at all. But often, these very same individuals talk about how glad they were that they did go, because they had fun, made new connections, got some work out of it, or had a new experience. These insights can serve as a reminder and a guide for the future. At the end of the chapter, I include a log for capturing how we can approach or avoid certain events, interactions, tasks or place, their implications and how they make you feel, along with other resources.

The role of situation selection

I found that some entrepreneurs in crisis like Vivek approach or avoid certain situations to help them adjust, to diminish the likelihood of experiencing negative emotions or increase the likelihood of eliciting positive emotions. As shown in prior research, this strategy tends to involve reaching out to certain people or putting oneself in certain places or avoiding them altogether. In the case of entrepreneurs, it is also evident in their attempts to seek out or avoid performing certain tasks.

Avoiding situations to diminish negative emotions

During the COVID-19 pandemic many entrepreneurs like Brian and Robert reported that staff anxiety was at an all-time high, prompted in part by fears of being laid off and associated financial insecurity. Especially during the first few weeks of the first lockdown before the furlough scheme to protect salaries was officially announced.

Brian wrote in his weekly diary at the time that working from home had made dealing with staff anxiety easier: 'Because of the decisions around staff, it was an emotional week. Actually, being away from the office and not seeing the people every day made the emotional aspect a touch easier'. In Brian's case, being physically absent from the office and not seeing people throughout the day helped him protect his wellbeing by avoiding emotional contagion from staff members who were concerned about the financial, health, and social implications of the lockdown.

Situation selection is also used by entrepreneurs in crisis to avoid certain tasks that might lead them to experience negative emotions. Robert initially avoided investigating government-backed 'COVID-19 bounce back loans', because the idea of going into debt was 'depressing'. Three weeks into the first lockdown he wrote the following in his diary:

> I've been kind of slack doing too much research into the forms of help because the initial news on the loans is so depressing. I feel morally opposed to forcing good businesses into debt. But the grants, if they materialize, will be a help. Although they still highlight the skewed thinking on all of this.

Attempting to avoid these negative feelings, Robert put off researching such loans for a time. A few weeks later, however, once his situation had stabilized and he was feeling more optimistic about the future and ready to plan for such, he applied and was successful. These examples suggest that situation selection might give entrepreneurs the space to process negative emotions over time.

Approaching situations to increase positive emotions

Entrepreneurs in crisis also seek out situations that enable them to experience positive emotions. Like Daniel, the restaurant owner who, in contrast to Brian, explained why surrounding himself with his team during the early stages of the pandemic made him feel good and helped him move forward, both personally and professionally:

> I am getting energy from them. I'm getting life from them. I had terrible days. My head was in a terrible place and just to see their faces and getting a hug from them was everything to me. They were listening to everything. They were helping me with like brainstorming together. They were in it with me and it, that, made everything amazing. Really is, really, really, I was very lucky with my team.

Likewise for Matteo, the 50-something owner of a deli in Southeast London who struggled at the beginning of the pandemic with past trauma enlivened by the crisis, spending more time at work with his team gave him a lifeline: 'At work I'm feeling fine. I really enjoy working in my office and creating my and my company's future. At home I'm still dealing with my unconscious and it is a fight hard to win.'

Alternatively, for Deepak, the 30-something owner of a small chain of restaurants in Central and Southwest London, being in the countryside and later taking a holiday, kept him going during the 'shitstorm'. When we spoke in early 2021, less than a year after the first lockdown, he said:

> I actually went, spent most of my time at my parents' house in the country so that, I think, is better mentally and physically than being cooped up in my little flat in London. So yeah, that definitely helped and, also, I was

> very lucky that I went on holiday in December last year and I was supposed to go on holiday for two weeks, and then because of lockdown and stuff I ended up not coming back for about two and a half months. So that was very lucky timing and, I mean, I had my laptop with me, so I was still working but that was very, yeah, that kept me going a lot to be honest.

Similarly, Liam, the owner of the consultancy specializing in public sector projects, wrote in his diary in the summer of 2020 that booking a holiday had helped him manage his current and anticipated increase in workload and gave him something to look forward to:

> I am feeling a bit overwhelmed by work requirements, as I can see our workload increasing over the next few months and we are still not back at full capacity … I am very glad I booked a break. A complete rest for two weeks away from my home office will be a big relief.

Much further down the road, beyond the third and final lockdown in the summer of 2021, once the vaccine had been rolled out, Liam decided that he and his team would benefit from returning to a physical working space. He believed that the experience of working together in the same space would help them all get out of the 'rut' the crisis and remote working had created:

> For our staff, there has been a noticeable enthusiasm amongst many to return to some office working. I think for many of them, including me, working at home all the time for the last 16–17 months has become a bit of a rut. So, there is a strong desire for a change of scene, more variety, and social interaction. As a result, we have taken back the full office space we had before March 2020 and, from September, we have decided to extend the space available, because we are now a bigger team.

This quote suggests that Liam wanted to create positive feelings and a more positive working environment for himself and his staff, so he switched to a space he believed would facilitate this. In both cases, Liam put himself in situations where positive emotions were likely to be evoked.

What is situation modification?

Making adjustments to the features of certain situations may also diminish the likelihood that we experience distress in a crisis and corresponding negative emotions, and further increase the likelihood of experiencing positive emotions.[12] This is known as situation modification.

Situation modification is an emotional regulation strategy aimed at changing our external environment in order to tailor its emotional impact.[13] We can modify situations to different extents. In some instances, several aspects of the situation can be modified at the same time, whereas in others, few adjustments to the situation can be made.[14]

For example, you might not be able to change where you work (at home or the office), but you may be able to make small changes to your working environment, like deciding what music to listen to, how to arrange your workspace, when to schedule meetings or take breaks or what to do on your break. For the individual who has lost their job, situation modification might entail still going to an old work hangout but only staying for a short time, sitting in a different part of the venue, or ensuring that they have someone with them or something to do while they're there on their own, diminishing the likelihood of experiencing negative emotions by running into people. It might also include going to a networking event early and chatting to as many people as possible, which can increase positive emotions and the likelihood of positive outcomes, such as landing a new job.

Prior research on situation modification is especially scarce and few previous examples could be found. The insights outlined next might help us think more about how it can be applied to our own lives.

When is situation modification most effective?

Similar to situation selection, situation modification is likely to be more effective where a less cognitively demanding coping strategy would be beneficial and when it's employed early on, before negative emotions have a chance to surface. Nevertheless, it might also have some utility in circumstances where negative emotions are likely to arise, and we might need a little help with managing them. Situation modification is also more likely to be effective when we have some control over manipulating some, but not all, features in our external environment.

Monitoring situation modification

It's also important to track the smaller adjustments we make to our physical environment and their consequences. Often the day before doing a big public speaking engagement, and even the morning of, I feel much more relaxed if I can have some uninterrupted time to reflect on the content. Knowing this about myself, I try not to schedule meetings or take on additional tasks during this time, if I can help it. I've asked for space at home to prepare as well. I'm also reminded of my neighbour who, like some other company executives, has a work phone and a personal phone. By using her work phone at defined times of the day and week, she's able to create clearer boundaries for herself and more balance between work and family. Whether it's re-arranging your work schedule, exercising before or after work or going for a walk on your lunch break, such adjustments can influence how you feel. Using the resources I include at the end of the chapter can help you think about whether these changes are improving the situation or your feelings around it, why/why not and what you can do differently or reinforce.

The role of situation modification

In certain instances, entrepreneurs in crisis make changes to their external physical environment which serve to diminish their negative emotions and/or enhance their positive emotions. Sometimes, as the example that follows suggests, they do both at the same time. In such situations, entrepreneurs appear to be learning how to manage their negative emotions rather than how to prevent them altogether.

While entrepreneurs in crisis may not be able to avoid situations that evoke their negative emotions altogether, I found that they do tend to modify them somewhat. This involves changing how they think about their work environment and adapting their behaviours accordingly. For example, although Brian could not elude staff anxiety entirely during the pandemic, he was able to make certain adjustments that minimized his distress and made him more resilient. That is, when Brian returned to the office, after a brief stint of working at home, he learned to structure his day and his meetings differently, in a way that allowed him to shape the emotions he was experiencing. He explained in his diary how he was faring a month after the first lockdown:

> [I'm] surrounding myself with positive influences and speaking to the right people at the right time is also key. I've found that many of the people I'm speaking to are either up or down based upon their last conversation. For personal energy saving and harvest reasons, planning who I speak to and when has become an important part of the day.

Although Brian could not avoid difficult conversations with his staff, he could decide how to structure his day to ensure that other positive conversations were happening as well. In this way, he was better able to manage the energy exchanges between himself and those around him.

What can we do to engage in situation selection/ modification more effectively in a crisis?

Our external physical environment can be a source of stress or serve to compound our stress. Alternatively, our physical environment can reduce stress and elicit positive emotions in us. Changing it, in turn, can have a profound effect on how we feel, for better or worse. In the former case, we often experience this when we're in outside in nature or when the sun is shining.

To engage in situation selection or situation modification more effectively, we first need to understand whether certain environments, certain events, interactions with others, places or tasks, have the potential to create stress for us or add to an already stressful situation, and whether we can adjust these for the better to minimize distress and corresponding negative emotions or increase the likelihood of

Table 6.1: Guiding questions to help us adjust our situation

How do I feel in certain situations?	• Do situations involving certain people, tasks and environments give me energy or drain me of energy in a crisis? • How can I better organize and manage my interactions with others, tasks and environments in a crisis to maximize my energy or limit how much of my energy is drained? • What features of these situations, if any, can I change? How can I change them?
Can I adjust my immediate work environment for the better?	• Can I change where/when I carry out my work in a crisis? • Can I change how I work in a crisis? How can I change my work? • What features of my work environment have become difficult in a crisis? • How, if at all, can I change the features of my work environment for the better? • How much can I change the features of my work environment?

experiencing positive emotions. Table 6.1 presents a list of questions we can ask ourselves to help us adjust to a potentially stressful situation and strengthen our resilience.

Specific circumstances may arise from a crisis that create additional stress. For entrepreneurs in crisis, I've found this can include workload increases, a tense atmosphere at work, and feeling less connected to internal and/or external stakeholders. As such, we can, for instance, plan when, how and how much time we are devoting to certain tasks, as illustrated in Table 6.2. We might notice that spending a lot of time on a specific crisis-related task can prolong our stress and be counterproductive. At the same time, feeling like we are not focusing enough on certain tasks can create stress. Creating bounded opportunities to approach and deal with certain tasks such as raising capital and contacting regulators may be useful, if you're an entrepreneur.

We should also ensure we're not employing situation selection as a long-term avoidant strategy with the intention of eluding negative emotions entirely. Relatedly, we can find ways to process these negative emotions more effectively, through situation modification

Table 6.2: Using situation selection and modification to diminish crisis-related stress at work

Examples of crisis-related situations that can impact on work	Situation selection	Situation modification
Increased workload: you are compelled to manage the crisis and everyday operations simultaneously.	• Can you seek out those people who can help and delegate tasks to them? • Can you surround yourself with people and ideas within and outside of the business that might help you resolve certain issues? • Can you avoid situations that might add to your workload unnecessarily?	• Can you quantify how much time you will spend on certain tasks? • Can you incorporate short breaks into your working day? • Can you impose boundaries on your time, for instance, by muting certain conversations on your phone even if only for a short period of time or checking emails at certain times of the day?
Tense atmosphere at work	• Can you determine what kinds of situations may be adding to or easing tensions at work and make some adjustments? • Can you decide which meetings are important and necessary to schedule or attend and which ones are not?	• Can you reflect on what time of the day or part of the week makes the most sense for you and your team to have these meetings? • Can you devote some time in the meetings to shifting attention towards the positive or end meetings on a positive note? • Can you place a time limit on how long you discuss certain items in a meeting that might cause conflict or that might be more difficult or challenging to address during a crisis, but require some thought and attention?
Feeling less connected to internal or external stakeholders	• Can you create more situations/opportunities to connect with these individuals? • Can you put yourself in situations where you're interacting more with these individuals?	• Can you connect with these individuals in more meaningful ways?

Table 6.3: A situation monitoring log

Strategy	What is the situation creating stress? Is it an event, interaction, person or task?	Applying the strategy, what would the adjustment look like/what did I adjust?	What would the implications of the adjustment be/what were the implications?	How would the adjustment make me feel/how did the adjustment make me feel?
Situation selection (approach/avoid a certain physical environment or aspect of it)				
Situation modification (tweak the physical environment)				

or otherwise. Scholars have argued that while as an avoidance strategy situation selection can be more problematic long term by hampering learning and leading to more psychopathology and should be employed in the short term as a result, situation modification has the potential to do the opposite: it can encourage learning and decrease psychopathology.[15] Indeed, Brian's use of forced avoidance as a coping strategy was short-lived, lasting only a week. He quickly learned whom to speak to and when; restructuring his day gave him a greater sense of control, positively impacting his wellbeing.

We can also systemically monitor what kinds of adjustments we can make or did make previously, what the implications of these adjustments could be or were, and how the adjustments might feel or did make us feel (see Table 6.3). Engaging with the actionable takeaways in Box 6.1 can make situation selection and modification more familiar, worthwhile strategies for you.

★★★

In short, by making certain adjustments to their external environment, like proactively avoiding a situation, entering into a new situation or modifying an existing one, entrepreneurs like Vivek and Brian were able to minimize their distress in a crisis and strengthen their resilience. In the next couple of chapters, we look at how entrepreneurs utilized resource-based strategies, such as offsetting resource losses and leaning into social support, and the role they played in their resilience.

> **Box 6.1: Actionable takeaways for situation selection and modification**
>
> - Reflect on how you express emotions: Are you someone who experiences intense emotions? Do you find it difficult to regulate your emotions? Are there many things demanding your attention and/or weighing on you at the same time? If your answers to these questions is 'yes', then adjusting your physical environment might be a good strategy for you.
> - Anticipate how you might feel in certain situations: Make a list of the kinds of events, interactions, places or tasks coming up that might create stress for you. To minimize stress, consider whether you can opt out of the situation, do something to change the situation, or you can gravitate towards the situation with the intention of exercising control and learning. Next, make a list of situations that make you feel good or can help you to grow and manifest these.
> - Share your experiences with others: Other people can help you remember what kinds of situations make you feel good or make you feel bad. Sharing your experiences can help you notice your feelings before engaging with certain situations and to process them afterwards.

Chapter summary

- Situation selection and situation modification are emotion regulation strategies that involve making small adjustments to the external physical environment such that negative emotions become less likely and positive emotions become more likely.
- Situation selection and situation modification may be especially useful to those who are able to make adjustments to their

environment, who have a tendency to experience intense emotions and might find it difficult to regulate their emotions otherwise.
- Avoiding certain situations is often more effective as a short-term strategy. In the longer term, we might need to learn other strategies, which can include making small modifications to the existing environment that enable us to better manage and process our emotions, including any negative emotions that might arise.
- Entrepreneurs in crisis engage with situation selection when they actively approach or avoid certain people, places or tasks that add to their stress. Where they can't avoid situations or do so for long, they might revert in some cases to modifying their environment.
- To engage more effectively in situation selection and modification, we can become more aware of the kinds of situations that create stress, reflect on whether we can adjust our environment, and how we might select a new situation or modify an existing one. We can also plan how much time we will devote to certain issues, ask ourselves specific questions to help us adjust to crisis-related situations that may be more commonplace, and ensure we are not employing certain tactics to avoid negative emotions longer term.

7

Offsetting Resource Losses

Mark, the owner of an electronics business in South London, was in his early 60s. During our first meeting following the London riots Mark came across as shy, a little quiet and reserved. When I entered his shop, it was filled with boxes stacked from floor to ceiling, with a couple of television monitors on display to the right-hand side. Mark had worked in the shop for more than 40 years and it was the only job he had ever known. He was employed there as a teenager and then took it over many years later. His plan was to run the business up until his retirement: 'Although,' he said, 'the riots might have been the catalyst to stopping me altogether and I did think, should I or shouldn't I?'

On the night the rioters came, Mark believed his shop was secure, unlikely to be targeted. 'I thought being in the side street here with a shutter, I thought, "I'm going to be alright", so I wasn't particularly worried.' Unfortunately for him, he didn't manage to escape it:

> The shutter had been levered out and damaged. The door glass had been kicked in. There's a, the second window on the right had a big hole in it. So, they kicked that in. They also smashed the other one but there wasn't a hole in it. Everything virtually had gone. All the stock. I mean they'd been out to the back room and all sorts. My neighbours here told me they started around midnight and carried on until 5 o'clock. Cars turning up.

Mark was notified about the damages by a café owner nearby who called him, saying: 'I'm very sorry but your shop's in a bit of a state.'

However, Mark didn't know the full extent of it until the next morning. Walking into the shop with his wife, he couldn't believe his eyes, 'I thought that I was – that the business – was finished.' The shelves had been 'completely cleared'.

Mark described with some frustration the financial difficulties he then faced, especially his struggles around bringing in more stock. He also didn't feel his insurers were quick to assist: 'The insurance company didn't want to help me in that respect, although I had some insurance that would cover loss of customers' TVs. They in effect said, "Get on with it yourself and compensate the best way you can" and that was the hardest time'. He went on, 'The truth is, it was a bit tough for me to smile for a few weeks, and it took a while even to get my sense of humour back.'

Mark was eventually able to replace his lost stock and associated earnings by applying to the High Street Fund, a charity set up by the private sector to help hard-hit small businesses affected by the London riots overcome government bureaucracy by swiftly distributing grants to these businesses in the months that followed. Two years later, when we met again, Mark admitted, 'Probably without that, it would have been quite difficult to carry on.' What he especially appreciated about the funding scheme was that 'you didn't feel like you were begging'.

When he was feeling frustrated by the events, both the damages and aftermath, including his struggles with insurers, what helped Mark most of all was the 'mental support' he received from other business owners in his community. 'The girls in the hairdressers were very sweet,' he said. 'That made a difference at the time, yeah. And if you got really p'd off with things in the early days … go and have a cup of tea with one of them or something like that, and that helped tremendously.'

In a crisis, resources matter. As Mark's story shows, resources can take many forms, including having a job and a business, which were threatened by the London riots, but also access to funding and a network which became an important part of his recovery. The nature and extent of the resources we possess can determine whether we see situations as threatening or not, which shapes in turn how we respond and feel.[1] The ability to get through a crisis, therefore, may depend on resources – on adjusting the balance of resources. I've labelled this as offsetting resource losses.

What are resources?

Resources are those things we value or that help us acquire the things we value.[2] Resources can include a broad range of things, from certain objects we might possess (such as a home or a business, as mentioned), conditions (having a job or qualification), personal characteristics (such as self-efficacy or self-esteem) and sources of energy (time, money, knowledge or even the absence of disease),[3] as well as other material and social or interpersonal assets. As human beings we are motivated to actively acquire and protect the things we value – our resources.

Resources can make our lives easier. Think of two business executives from different companies: one with a big expense account, company medical plan and generous holiday package and one without. Or two lecturers from different universities, one who has teaching assistants, significant admin support and sizable research funding, and the other who doesn't. Or two entrepreneurs in the same industry, one with great connections and access to funding and the other for whom these things are absent. The experiences of these individuals would vary greatly.

Stress tends to occur when we have limited resources. Stress can occur when events such as a crisis exceed or tax our resources,[4] threaten to incur resource losses, or when there is a failure to gain resources despite investment.[5] Without resources, we are more limited. We also might experience difficulties acquiring the things we value and achieving the results we desire.

Resources have an important role to play in creating both negative stress and stress resistance.[6] Resources can act as a buffer. Individuals with resources, such as support networks, a stable income and financial reserves, may be less likely to encounter stressful circumstances that negatively affect their psychological and physical wellbeing, and to be negatively affected by resource losses during stressful situations. Those of us with resources are often more capable of solving problems during periods of stress and likely to acquire additional resources; that is, resources foster the acquisition of other resources. Mark's social network provided him with important emotional support following the riots. Other examples might include having a stable income, which means you are more likely to get a mortgage from a bank than someone without a stable income. If you have a degree or qualifications, you are more likely to get a job in a profession such as law than those without.

If you have good physical health, you may be more likely than those with poor health to join certain athletics clubs and to play specific sports. Those with resources are also more likely to benefit from them in the long term, and to possess resources valued by others.[7]

I've observed first-hand the strong connection between resources and stress resistance among entrepreneurs in crisis. To illustrate, during the COVID-19 pandemic, the furlough scheme initiated by the British government to subsidize up to 80% of employee wages while people were unable to return to work created a strong sense of relief for many entrepreneurs across the UK. Joseph, the pub owner, mentioned multiple times in his weekly diary how the furlough scheme had positively impacted his staff and his ability to lead his team, and had improved his mental state in turn. A few weeks into the crisis he wrote: 'Money to pay furloughed wages finally arrived so paying staff cheered me up'. Just under a year later, drawing attention to the benefits of the scheme once again, Joseph noted: 'All in all, the furlough scheme for PAYE employees[a] has helped them incredibly, unbelievably and it has of course made my role as an employer so much easier – they'd have lost their jobs by now.' Weeks later, and almost exactly a year after the first lockdown had been imposed, he again highlighted how critical the furlough scheme had been for him:

> The one thing the government got right was protecting PAYE employees as to have had to let mine go would have been devastating – they're all deeply valued and even if they now choose to move on I will always be relieved that they have been looked after.

When resources aren't forthcoming or are less than we expect, as we saw with Mark or in an earlier chapter with Sam after the London riots, it can add to our stress, making us less stress resistant. In Sam's

---

[a] Pay as you earn employees (PAYE) are those employees in the UK whom an employer pays a salary to (over a certain threshold) and who may receive a pension from the employer as well. Through the PAYE system, employers collect income taxes and national insurance contributions from an employee's paycheque.

case, receiving compensation so late in the day and much less than he had claimed for, delayed his ability to rebuild his business and prolonged his anxiety.

When is offsetting resource losses most effective?

The balance of resources we maintain in a crisis – that is, balancing the nature and extent of the resources we've lost against the nature and extent of the resources we've accrued – is critical, and our resilience might well depend on it in part. To illustrate the important links between resources and resilience, I turn to some research on human-induced crises, specifically terrorist attacks.

According to the Global Terrorism Index, in 2023 there were more than 3000 terrorism incidents and over 8000 deaths due to terrorism attacks globally, as recorded in 163 countries.[8] Terrorism and the threat of terrorism can have significant economic and political effects, as well as debilitating psychological effects. On the morning of 11 September 2001, 19 terrorists from the Islamist extremist group Al Qaeda hijacked four commercial airplanes, crashing two into the World Trade Center in New York City which collapsed, and one into the Pentagon in Arlington, Virginia. Passengers on the fourth hijacked airplane, upon learning of the other attacks, crashed the plane destined for Washington, DC into an empty field in Western Pennsylvania. Nearly 3,000 people were killed in the attacks, mostly civilians and service workers.[9] As a human-induced crisis, September 11 had significant physical and mental health consequences (PTSD, depression, anxiety), for thousands of residents in New York state, especially those most directly affected, who were living in the vicinity of the attacks or had lost loved ones.[10]

Numerous studies have captured the implications of 9/11. Bonanno and colleagues[11] examined the presence of various resources and resource losses after the 9/11 attacks and implications for stress and resilience, measured as the absence of depression and PTSD symptoms and less substance use. Findings from their survey of 2,752 households in New York state showed that following the 9/11 crisis, people were less likely to be resilient if they had lower levels of interpersonal resources or perceived social support, material losses resulting from the attacks, particularly the loss of income, and less energy resources due to a pre-existing health condition.

The idea that the balance of resources is important for resilience is clearly explained by the conservation of resources (COR) theory developed by Stevan Hobfoll.[12] COR theory suggests that changes in resources reduces or generates stress for us as individuals. It has been applied mainly to studies of stress management,[13] burnout[14] and work-family conflict.[15]

According to the theory, when resources are abundant, our resistance to stress and our resilience are enhanced, and more resources may be forthcoming in the future leading to 'gain spirals'.[16] If we lose our job, for instance, having a wide and supportive social network may not only be comforting to us, but might also expose us to job opportunities. Similarly, if we have significant savings and lose our job, we might invest in retraining and feel less anxious about being out of work for a time. When resources are limited, however, the opposite may be true. That is, when we encounter resource losses, especially suddenly, or do not acquire resources despite investment or use the resources we have available, or we don't endeavour to create new resources, we may experience additional resource losses, stress and vulnerability, and may acquire fewer resources in the future in what has been described as 'loss spirals'.[17] If we lose our job without any financial reserves, few connections and limited psychological resources, we might be more likely to suffer. Actively offsetting resource losses is more likely to be effective in these cases.

Offsetting resource losses is more effective when we can leverage our existing resources, have the possibility of accessing new resources, or value the resources lost. It is also more effective when we can pair certain resource losses with resource gains. COR theory suggests that resource losses are more potent than resource gains: 'a loss is more depleting than a gain is generating'.[18] Not being able to replenish our resources during a period of stress might create more vulnerability and additional periods of stress later, as loss begets loss.[19] Mark noted that had he not received money from the High Street Fund following the riots, it might have been difficult for him to continue.

Monitoring offsetting resource losses

There is a lot we can learn from thinking back to a time when we lost something of value to us or were at risk of doing so – a job, a client, an opportunity, a possession, a loved one, a relationship – and reflecting on what helped us through it. We can also learn from the entrepreneurs outlined, reflecting on their strategies and how we might apply them. And using the tools at the end of the chapter, like the offsetting resources log, we can begin to examine more closely what can help.

The role of offsetting resource losses

Like Mark, entrepreneurs in crisis can experience a range of resource losses. This might include a loss of income, stock, staff and energy, depending partly on the kind of crisis. The entrepreneurs in crisis I worked with were offsetting resource losses in three ways. That is, I identified three different sub-strategies employed by entrepreneurs for offsetting resource losses during or following a crisis, which include: (a) optimizing resources, (b) actively seeking out support and building resources and (c) resource substitution. Offsetting resource losses in a crisis is critical in terms of minimizing the negative effects of a crisis on wellbeing.[20] For the entrepreneurs in my research, this was achieved by taking actions that created positive emotions and reduced stress. I discuss the 'optimize', 'build' and 'substitute' (OBS) strategies next and some obstacles to their implementation or effectiveness.

Optimizing resources

Optimizing resources involves drawing on the resources we have available at the time and uncovering opportunities within our current circumstances.[21] Utilizing space in a new way and developing new skills are common ways that entrepreneurs in crisis optimize their resources.

Kate, the owner of a dance company in North London, explained that COVID-19 regulations prevented her team from performing for audiences indoors during the first few months of the pandemic. As a result, they pursued more site-specific work outdoors to make their performances more accessible to audiences, adapting their creative process accordingly. For Kate, responding to this challenge created intense positive feelings, stimulating her interest and excitement:

> Because of the nature of this last work, these solos, we filmed them in different locations, like a beach, a forest,

a derelict building. So actually, what was interesting is when theatres were starting to do stuff, but not inside, and then were doing stuff outside, we did a series of solos that went around and then we did a whole series of those solos in the V&A museum – so, more like site-specific work – which was really unusual because we're not that kind of company. It was like, 'Oh, look how this can work, and how interesting!'

Re-arranging the workspace during COVID-19 to take advantage of existing resources and generate new resources was also a common practice carried out by several entrepreneurs in the hospitality industry. One restaurant owner, Laura, spoke about how she had turned part of their pandemic related unused space into an Italian food shop, not only creating another revenue stream for her business but supporting local businesses at the same time, including some of her suppliers:

> Our suppliers, they normally import from Italy at least a month or 2 months of stock and we said, 'You know, we've got to help them because they don't supply to supermarkets, they supply to restaurants'. So that was one of our primary things, call them up and say, 'Okay, what dry food stock in cans and jars, in packaging could we sell?' And I also walked into our pantry and pulled out everything that was packaged but it was restaurant size. We said, 'fine, that's okay'. Olive oil was 5 litres not 1 litre. Tomato, the tomato pulp, tomato and risotto was a 1 kilo tin not 250. So we said, 'it doesn't matter'. And we took all the wine we had in stock and we displayed it. Then with our bread supplier, we said, 'we're going to buy bread from you every day and sell it to the locals'. Then we went outside of our own network of suppliers and we contacted, you know, cold called a cookery school in [a borough of London] and said 'okay, now you can't do your cookery classes, let's come up with a product which helps you and we can sell it in our shop'.

In turn, these actions served to boost her mood and create a strong sense of purpose:

> We just kept a very positive, very innovative, very resourceful attitude. We just let our state of mind be let's look forward, let's look positive, you know? Okay this has happened and I think that has really helped us, by not sitting back and being, 'oh my God, how did this happen, why did this happen', you know? We just said, 'Okay, what else can we do?' We've got this retail space, physical space. Okay it's a lockdown. What else can we do? And I think that really helped us. So, I think it's really, it's the business owner's state of mind and not just kind of taking it for granted, 'Oh there's a grant coming, you don't need to do anything.' No, we are focused on what can we use and invest in that business.

Some entrepreneurs in crisis also develop new skills which brings about positive feelings and implications. In the latter case, it can be argued that such a strategy may be connected to posttraumatic growth, which involves reflecting on the potentially positive aspects of adversity, including expanding one's behaviours and skillset. Some entrepreneurs affected by the London riots developed creatively, like Anne who began writing, or Marie and Anthony who honed their public speaking skills. Entrepreneurs affected by the pandemic often described learning new technical skills, including one composer, Steve, who was in his late 40s when we met:

> I was having this amazing period of just the beating the odds, and finding a way to make it work ... I had to learn how to edit, so that all of that could happen. And then I learned how to shoot on my own Canon camera ... So, it was about finding, you know, forcing myself to learn new skills in order to facilitate the creativity.

In these instances, entrepreneurs were finding new ways to work within the confines of the crisis, and this proved to be a great source of interest and satisfaction to them, but also a sense of relief. However, not everyone might be able to optimize their resources in a crisis, as discussed next.

What gets in the way of optimizing resources?

While few barriers to optimizing resources were reported by entrepreneurs in crisis, this strategy might not be adopted by those who are less open or less alert to new opportunities for re-organizing work or developing new skills or who don't look beyond prescribed activities. Our ability to optimize resources might also be affected by structural constraints which could make re-organizing work or home life, or developing new skills, practically difficult for some.

Building resources

Actively seeking out and building resources as a strategy for offsetting resource losses makes entrepreneurs feel more positive about the next steps. Entrepreneurs can invest in financial and social resources. In the former case, Joseph wrote in his diary in early 2021 about how applying for and being approved for an emergency loan during the COVID-19 pandemic had helped him feel more positive during the third lockdown and was important to his business recovery: 'We just got agreed for a new Cbils [coronavirus business interruption loan scheme] which will clear the previous debt and give us the cash to get through to June so financially that keeps us buoyant.'

Entrepreneurs, like Andrew, a restaurant owner in West London, described how they were building connections with others in their industry. As indicated in the following quote, and is evident in the next chapter, this was a critical source of support and comfort for these individuals:

> So much of what the government says is guidance. You know, there's not that much that is mandated as absolutely necessary, and so there's been a huge amount of grey areas. And so certainly interactions with others ... in this part of town I regularly keep in touch with four or five other general managers in the location – what we're doing, how we're doing – and that's a source of support ... The good news is it's kind of just as rubbish for everyone as it is for us.

Some entrepreneurs go a step further to build community. Ariana, also a restaurant owner in West London, went straight from university into starting her own business. She told me that while she was a student she had been fired from two internships and that working for someone else wasn't her 'jam'. Her father was a serial entrepreneur and, as a result, she said, 'I always had the notion of like starting my own company from a young age.' Ariana was in her early 30s when we met. She discussed how in creating so many difficulties for her business, the pandemic also had serious implications for her as individual, 'I've had a lot of stress to deal with in the last like year and a half, like a lot. No, yeah, super stressful, like definite mental health impacts.' To manage this, she developed a support network for herself and other business owners which filled her with a sense of pride:

> I actually started a group, I'd started a group just to like, help out with other smaller operators. So that was quite nice just to like create more of a community ... So, if anyone needed any help on like questions regarding how to apply for certain grants of how to do X, Y and Z, then they were able to ask the questions.

Building a positive sense of community was a highly motivating experience for Malcolm, who was also in his early 30s. Malcolm had worked in hospitality his whole life. He opened his restaurant in North London a couple of years before the pandemic. Before the first lockdown they decided to close and to sell off all their ingredients by setting up an e-commerce site. Sales proliferated and they expanded on the retail side. They managed to keep everyone employed. The chefs did ready meals and the waiters became couriers. Malcolm spoke about the importance of connecting with their patrons:

> I think me personally, you know at the start there was literally nothing else to do, so it was like really good just having this thing of work being so busy. That was great at the start. Then it became more about, we had such a connection with people because we were so positive about everything, our customers were like really loving it. And we were just getting very nice messages all the time people saying like, 'Oh my god like thank you',

you know so that then became the motivator really was just like making people happy. Making people laugh.

What gets in the way of actively seeking out support and building resources?

Despite the benefits of seeking out support and building resources, I discovered that several things can get in the way: (a) not being receptive to support, (b) the support provided may not be enough to offset losses and (c) support may not be forthcoming despite efforts to seek it out.

One of the main reasons entrepreneurs give for not actively seeking out support is that they feel other crisis victims are 'worse off' and therefore more entitled to support. This idea was first raised earlier, in Chapter 5 on positive reappraisal. While feeling others are worse off helps entrepreneurs see the positives in a crisis, it might also prevent them from seeking out the support they need. For example, two months after the first lockdown, Joseph wrote in his diary about being directed by members of his social network to certain support initiatives for 'venues that are struggling' during the pandemic, but said that he wouldn't apply: 'I am sure there are venues in much worse circumstances.' Following the riots, this same feeling initially kept Marie from applying to the High Street Fund, as Mark and some of the others did. With much prompting from others, Marie eventually changed her mind:

> Lots of people got in touch. So, the retail trust got in touch, the riot relief fund got in touch … the High Street fund, which I felt reluctant to – I guess it's sort of my character, not wanting to ask for help and sorting it out myself. And then, in the end just as the closing date [approached] … they said, 'Look, you should do [it]. It's meant for businesses like yours'. So, I did, and I'm just waiting for that, to see if that will be … I think, I just, there were people worse off, I guess.

These examples suggest that sometimes crisis support is available, but entrepreneurs are either not aware of it, not receptive to it or not actively attempting to seek it out. Additional reasons entrepreneurs give for not actively seeking out support is that doing so might drain other resources such as their time. In this case, the costs of acquiring new resources are too high, deemed to be too taxing. For example, after the riots, Anne pointed out that while a lot of people were asking 'What can we do to help?', overseeing their activities increased the demands placed on her and her small team. As a result, she started saying to people, 'This is the kind of help I need, if you can manage it.' This suggests that if support is seen as taxing other resources deemed to be valuable or rendered vulnerable by a crisis (such as time or energy), then it might not be pursued.

A few entrepreneurs described the toll that resource deterioration had taken on their wellbeing as they made desperate efforts to offset financial losses that in the end were not enough. Prior research has found that a crisis can prompt the mobilization of certain resources initially but that after a time, their deterioration is likely, making individuals vulnerable to stress.[22] Two years after the riots, Anthony described the enormous strain he had been under:

> Only looking back at it now do I realize just what a huge stress it's been and how much it has impacted me ... I've lost two years of my life, because I've had no time to do anything. Every waking moment has just been a rescue operation, constantly. The stresses of not having the money to do things, having to raise all the money to fund it all now. We reached the point where ... we'd actually run out of money ... knocking on the bank manager's door and, you know, crawling and licking the soles of his boots to try and get the funding ... I've had to cash in all my other small investments. I've had to cash in my pensions, my endowments, my life policies, everything. I've had to put the lot in 'cause it was a matter of that or go under. So, I've got nothing left ... I've cashed all that in and I've got extra debt.

In some cases, crisis support might be unavailable and attempts to gain support are unsuccessful. William was working with other business owners in the hospitality industry to make it possible for larger small and medium-sized enterprises to qualify for COVID-related government grants, in particular by raising the threshold of the rateable value in a nationwide campaign called 'Raise the Bar'. In his diary, he noted he was working with City Hall to increase emergency support packages for the industry, which was 'not an easy task' but that discussions were 'underway'. Despite his efforts, support from government was not forthcoming.

This example and others suggest that when crisis support is not available, entrepreneurs can experience a great deal of distress. William was excluded from support due to restrictions, making him more vulnerable to the crisis. Collectively or individually, these barriers can prevent entrepreneurs from offsetting losses, making them more vulnerable in a crisis.

Substituting resources

Resource substitution is another way entrepreneurs in crisis work to offset or limit resource losses. Resource substitution occurs when lost resources are replaced and/or compensated for by a different resource that diminishes the distress caused by the initial loss.[23] Resource substitution is likely to be effective when the lost resource can be replaced and the new resource is valued.[24]

In Mark's case, financial and emotional support substituted in part for a loss of stock and delayed compensation from insurers, enabling him to be more resilient, professionally and personally. Similarly, during the third lockdown, William wrote in his diary that funding and especially the emotional support of others was important and encouraged him to continue:

> We did receive support from [the council], from the Mayor's Culture at Risk Fund and Arts Council Funding. However, we have [had over a million pounds] in lost revenue since March and these payments whilst lifesaving do not come anywhere close to the loss of business we have endured. The biggest thing that has kept me going has been the amazing support of loyal customers and our performers and promoters.

Also, like Mark, Jack, the owner of cycling shop in North London, said the High Street Fund had been very helpful after the riots, responding quickly to cover his financial losses. Insurers, in contrast, had not, creating further distress. When we met in 2011 following the riots he told me:

> But we've been very lucky – the High Street Fund. Have you heard of that? Oh my God. We got a payment after a week, an emergency payment of 2000 pounds, and then they came did an interview with us, maybe a month ago now, maybe three weeks, and they said, 'I think you're entitled to some more money', and they gave us 8000 pounds. Another 8000 pounds! And that covered all our loss over turnover, so they've been brilliant. They've been really good. And a lovely guy come around and he was genuine and wasn't trying to catch you out, do you know what I mean? I mean if I hear from my insurance company, I'm going to tell them to fuck off! 'You can keep your money and stick it up your arse'. Cause the amount of hurdles I jumped through, the hours I spent. I had to send them copies of the lease and everything. You know what I mean? It's ludicrous!

Two years later, Jack made a similar comment to me, explaining that while the High Street Fund was very supportive, insurers were not and had instead added to his stress:

> The High Street Fund was good, and there were no strings attached ... It wasn't a lengthy form. Just someone came round, informal chat, said, 'Yeah, we can help you out', and they just put some money in our bank ... Woke up one morning and thought, 'Oh blimey, there's a lot of money in the bank' ... [On the other hand,] the insurance took a year to settle up with us. But they really were a pain in the neck ... casting doubt on everything all the time ... they paid a very small compensation on loss of earnings, but then the High Street Fund pitched in with their bit so we were fine, we didn't lose a penny.

These are examples not only of how resource substitution works, but how it can make a difference. These cases also show that substitute resources can be similar or dissimilar to the original resources lost.

Moreover, they also illustrate how the absence of support to address resource losses can cause much discontent and thwart attempts at recovery and compromise resilience.

What gets in the way of resource substitution?

Resource substitution might be unsuccessful and can potentially lead to negative outcomes if it is partial in nature or if the resources lost are not replaced with resources that are as highly valued.[25] In the example as provided by Jack, money from the High Street Fund made up for the financial losses that were not reimbursed by insurers, and yet, the latter still evoked negative feelings. The burden of the loss and sense of injustice remained two years following the crisis.

What can we do to offset resource losses more effectively in a crisis?

We know that resources are important and can make us more resilient. When we have resources, we perceive situations as being less threatening. We take comfort in knowing that we may be able to cope with what lies ahead. As such, when our resources are limited or taken away suddenly, knowing just what we can do to offset these resource losses becomes critical.

To more effectively offset resource losses in a crisis we can first proactively maintain reservoirs of personal, social and financial/economic resources before a crisis strikes.[26] Building up resource reservoirs enables us to better prepare for future crises and maximize resources should a crisis occur. As an entrepreneur, engaging in crisis training and training focused on enriching social support resources can be helpful prior to or during a crisis.[27]

We can more effectively offset resource losses by identifying situations or opportunities to optimize existing resources. This might be achieved by remaining open to opportunities to reorganize our work or develop new skills. We can more effectively offset resource losses if we not only seek out support but are receptive to support, if that support is forthcoming and sufficient, and when we employ resource substitution, especially when substitute resources are highly valued by us.

To facilitate decision-making, we should consider the questions outlined in Table 7.1 and the barriers that might stand in their way,

Table 7.1: Guiding questions for developing strategies to offset resource losses

Do I have enough resources in my arsenal to manage in the event of a crisis? (e.g. financial reserves, connections, good health)	• Can I do an audit of my reserves? My personal reserves, my financial reserves, my social reserves? What does it reveal? Where am I falling short and how can I begin to address this shortfall? • Can I identify any pre-crisis support or resilience training? • What can I do now to build up my personal resources and my business resources?
Can I engage in resource optimization during a crisis?	• Can I utilize my existing resources in different, more effective ways? • Can I look for new opportunities to channel/utilize my existing resources?
Can I seek out and build resources?	• What forms of support are currently available? Am I entitled to that support? • Do I feel unentitled to the support available to me? Why? Should I challenge these feelings? Who can I identify to serve as a sounding board for these feelings? • What are the costs of seeking out support? Do they outweigh the benefits? Can I get assistance? • Can I identify a new source of supply for the resource? • Are my strategies for building resources having the desired effect? Do I need to change these?
Can resources be replaced entirely or compensated for with new resources?	• Although I have experienced a loss, have I noticed any gains? • Can I identify any resource substitutes? • Is the substitution for the lost resource partial or full? • Do I value the substitute resource equally, more, or less than the lost resource?

as summarized in Table 7.2. We can monitor what we're doing to optimize, build or substitute resources, the implications of this and how it's making us feel, as indicated in Table 7.3. By tracking these actions, we'll have a better idea of what works. See Box 7.1 to see

Table 7.2: The focus of and barriers to strategies for offsetting resource losses

Strategy/Features	Optimize	Build	Substitute
Focus	No new resources are acquired, but existing resources are reconfigured or reorganized.	Acquiring a new resource or adding to an existing resource.	A lost resource is replaced or a new/different resource is acquired that is also valued.
Barriers	Not being alert to opportunities, structural constraints.	Not being receptive to support, support is provided but is insufficient, support is not forthcoming.	Substitution is partial, substitute resources are not as highly valued.

Table 7.3: An offsetting resource losses log

The sub-strategy	What am I doing to make it happen?	What have been the implications?	How is it making me feel?
Optimizing resources			
Building resources			
Substituting resources			

how you can make the OBS strategies and offsetting resource losses part of your routine.

★★★

Working to adjust the balance of resources and offsetting resource losses in a crisis was something entrepreneurs pursued. Support from others played an important role in this process and their resilience. I devote the next chapter to discussing further the value of leaning into social support.

> **Box 7.1: Actionable takeaways for offsetting resource losses**
>
> - Practice optimizing resources: Observe the resources you currently possess. This might include financial, social or material resources, as well as personal resources. Really push yourself to think of all the different ways you can use each resource to extract greater value from such.
> - Look for ways to build resources: Don't wait until you're in a crisis to acquire resources. Start investing in new resources. Investigate that financial lead, work up the courage to make a new connection and take that course. You never know when or how these resources will help you.
> - Seek out resource substitutes: Consider whether your existing resources can be replaced or compensated for by other resources. If they can, what might these substitutes look like? If they can't, think about the steps you can take to make yourself less vulnerable should you lose them.

Chapter summary

- Resources are things we value or that help us acquire things we value.
- When resources are readily available, individuals are more likely to develop stress resistance and resilience, but when resources are limited or lost, negative stress and vulnerability result.
- Resource gains in a crisis are especially important but might be most effective when they offset resource losses which can be especially detrimental.
- A crisis can create certain losses for us or our businesses that impact on us negatively.
- Entrepreneurs in crisis work to offset resource losses in three ways, by: (a) optimizing resources, (b) actively seeking out support and building resources and (c) resource substitution. Each comes with certain obstacles to implementation or effectiveness.

- We can be more effective and better able to adapt to a crisis by regularly taking stock of the resources we have available, particularly during non-crisis periods.
- We can offset resource losses by proactively maintaining our resource reservoirs prior to a crisis and implementing strategies to minimize resource losses, including resource optimization, investment, and substitution, overcoming barriers that might get in the way.

8

Leaning Into Social Support

Kate, who was in her 50s when we met, trained as a dancer from a young age and worked with many of the greats over her long career. Dancing was all she ever wanted to do. After a few injuries and stops and starts, she started her North London dance studio well over a decade ago. When the announcement of the first lockdown on 23 March 2020, was officially made, she felt a deep sense of 'shock and concern' and quickly moved into 'problem-solving mode'. With performances scheduled for April, rehearsals had already begun. To reassure herself she thought, 'It's only going to be a few months' and so 'it just means that we can't do this now and they're going to reschedule'. But this was not to be the case, and over the next year there was much for Kate to figure out and do. At times, it was all a lot to bear and taking a toll on Kate and her energy levels:

> There was so much going on ... we had a huge amount planned. We had a residency, a kind of collective, that was happening, that was reduced. Everything was obviously reduced. Everything was renegotiated. It was like working seven days a week constantly because everything was constantly shifting and changing. So, it was exhausting for me ... It was like the further we got onto it, the more it was like, 'Oh, my God, how will we get, how are we going to survive further down the line?'

Kate's ability to keep up the momentum and stay positive during the pandemic was due partly to the support of her dancers who did Zoom classes for her to keep things ticking over. 'Staying connected' with other dancers further afield also filled her with a strong sense of appreciation and pride:

> I think there's something about the union of the dancers, that there was a, you know, there's a sense of family, of like staying connected, and that erm … and we did achieve, we did achieve a considerable amount, you know, given, given the limitations.

Kate's broader network was also a great source of help. 'I think I relied on them more than usual,' she said. 'Like we reached out to the venues that we normally go to and they, and they tended to be supportive.' There was a lot of 'good will at that point', she explained, within the creative community. 'People were very open to doing, when we looked at venues for costs of filming, lots of people were willing at that point to go, oh, well, yeah, of course.' They were keen to work and, in some cases, 'took a lesser fee' at that time.

Kate had received waves of funding from the Arts Council in the past for this project or that. During the pandemic she applied to them again for emergency funding and was successful. This money proved to be critical to her. 'I mean, without it, [and] without the support of my husband', she said, 'we wouldn't be here'. She stressed: 'the company wouldn't exist'.

Examples like Kate's emphasize the importance of the social context in terms of strengthening or weakening individual resilience in a crisis. As highlighted in Chapter 5 on positive reappraisal, the presence or absence of social support has an important role to play in helping entrepreneurs reframe a crisis, making them feel better or worse about what's happened. That is, crises were often construed by entrepreneurs as times when they were either fortunate enough to have received a lot of support or unlucky not to.

The entrepreneurs in crisis I have connected with over time, some of whom are featured in this book, have often referred to the value of 'leaning' into social support. This was the case for Ava, who described how she was able to manage throughout the pandemic and maintain her creativity because of her network: 'There was more collaboration. I did have a bit of a history of collaborative projects, but I would say [I was] absolutely leaning on these other groups.' While social support is also an important resource (as discussed in several chapters, especially Chapters 5 and 7), it merits more focused attention due to the critical role it can play in adjusting the balance of resources for entrepreneurs and those among us who might find ourselves in a crisis.

What is social support?

Social support encompasses all of the resources provided by our social network, including family members, community members and the state, that help us cope with stress.[1] Social support can take the form of structural support (the extent and frequency of social interactions), functional support (the experience of social interactions being beneficial in some way), emotional support (feeling cared for by others), material support (goods/services that help solve specific problems) and informational support (information or guidance that helps manage problems).[2] High levels of functional support or positive interactions within a social network can enhance individual resilience,[3] promoting certain behaviours such as exercise or emotion regulation that enable us to regulate stress and be more resilient.[4] In contrast, low levels of material support, stemming from, for example, limited funding from public bodies or restrictive conditions attached to funding, can lead to paralysis, increasing our stress and making recovery from a crisis less likely.[5]

This is something I've observed in the accounts of entrepreneurs in crisis. Following the London riots, for instance, Amir was angry and disheartened when his local MP failed to visit him, something he felt was very 'disappointing ... nobody here'. In contrast, Vivek's MP came to his reopening. Moreover, members of Vivek's local community raised several thousand pounds for him, which went towards his business recovery. Anne felt supported by her local council who gave her an emergency loan. She said, 'If it wasn't for the council, to be honest with you, we wouldn't be here.' This is in sharp contrast to Jacob who complained that 'the council were the worst' and provided no support whatsoever. Nathan reported his insurers were helpful and that he received compensation easily and quickly, facilitated by the fact that he had belonged to a retailers' association which assisted. Jack, on the other hand, noted insurers had him jump through 'hurdles' and that it was 'ludicrous', while Mark said insurers told him he should figure things out for himself.

Therefore, where businesses were located and depending on which insurers they were working with, determined in part the amount of support they received.

During the pandemic, there were also issues. Kate was fortunately successful in her funding application with the Arts Council, but this was not the case for everyone who applied. And while local administrations offered more consistent support to business owners during the pandemic as compared to the riots, not everyone was eligible for COVID-19 emergency grants, depending how long their businesses had been registered for and how big those businesses were.

Where emotional support was present during the riots (from locals/customers), or as was Kate's experience during the pandemic (from family, staff and the greater creative community), it gave entrepreneurs a renewed sense of positive energy. But where it was absent or negative, it could be depleting. For instance, following the riots, Jacob said, 'We received quite a lot of support from local people who were very sympathetic and then we also had quite a bit of hostility. "Don't be pathetic, take down the boards [covering structural damages]". It cost me, emotionally.' Similarly, Sofia noted that when they received a small amount of recovery funding, £1200, from the Mayor of London's office for her neighbour bar, not everyone was happy: 'Some customers were complaining, they were saying, "Why should you get money?!" One commented, "Who is paying for that? We should get something as well. We live in this borough"'. Disappointed, Sofia added: 'I just couldn't believe it.'

The social context, it seems, can make a difference in a crisis. Consider the Global Financial Crisis (GFC) of 2008. This crisis saw the collapse of financial markets and the loss of jobs, life savings and homes for many individuals around the world. It was created by a housing market bubble instigated years earlier when banks and other lending institutions began offering low interest rates and low-quality mortgages in the form of subprime loans. Financial institutions, including Lehman Brothers, Merrill Lynch and Morgan Stanley, began seeking out such high-risk investments, creating mortgage-backed securities (bundled mortgages) and collateralized debt obligations. These financial institutions also began lending money to homeowners and servicing those loans, profiting from the transaction fees charged at different stages. When housing prices dropped, many of these financial institutions faced serious losses and bankruptcy, instigating a worldwide recession.[6] The recession led to widespread unemployment, property foreclosures, business closures or struggles.[7]

After the financial crisis, an economic crisis in Spain was triggered by the real estate bubble, the global liquidity freeze, an increase in the price of commodities, food, and energy, and a decrease in national competitiveness.[8] Unemployment in Spain rose significantly between 2008 and 2015, and household consumption fell. Revilla and colleagues[9] studied the role that social resources played in Spain's economic crisis. They examined and compared an urban area (a suburb of Madrid) and a rural area (a part of the La Mancha area of central Spain, south of Madrid). They focused on families from areas that were strongly affected by the crisis. Based on participant observation and in-depth interviews with members of Spanish households, researchers found that drawing emotional and informational support from certain social networks such as community associations made people more resilient to the effects of the crisis. The study also revealed that not all households received public support from their local administrations, placing them at a disadvantage compared to those that did, and forcing them to seek support from charitable organizations instead. This was also the case with some of the entrepreneurs I spoke to during the pandemic and the London riots who reported how the High Street Fund had, luckily for them, stepped in to provide business grants.

When is leaning into social support most effective?

The effectiveness of leaning into social support in a crisis may well depend on the type of support provided, the timing of support and our needs as individuals.[10] It might also depend on the groups to which we belong. Beyond our immediate friendship or family groups, support might come from special interest groups, clubs or sports-related memberships, our schools and for some colleges or universities, religious or neighbourhood associations, or certain professional bodies, societies and forums. In a crisis, a failure to belong to a particular social network and/or social group may limit whether, how and how quickly we recover from a crisis. Certain recovery programmes, for instance, may not benefit those without the right connections or those at the margins of society.[11] This can perpetuate social inequality and make some people more vulnerable and less resilient.

The effectiveness of leaning into social support in a crisis might also depend on whether we can draw support from close or more distal networks. It has been found that connecting with and learning from those who are more distant to us, who are also coping with a crisis in other business, political and local contexts, such as business owners/businesses in other industries, and not over-relying on relationships that are closer and more local in orientation, can expose us to different perspectives on a crisis and a wider range of actions for coping.[12] This might apply to the individual who attends a talk delivered by someone who has experienced a personal loss and makes a connection with them from which they are able to derive certain lessons they can apply to their own lives. Or it might relate to the entrepreneur specializing in the healthcare industry who during a financial crisis reaches out to those working in the design or robotics industries for inspiration.

Research suggests that those of us with social support are likely to gain more resources when confronted with a crisis than those of us without, especially when we possess personal resources in addition that promote stability through a crisis and a capacity to cultivate recovery over time.[13] Individuals with less social support in a crisis are more likely to experience stress.[14]

If we have lost our job, for instance, having access to a wide network of social support that not only includes our immediate social circle, but stretches beyond it to incorporate the broader community, and other formal/informal institutions or networks, can minimize distress. A strong network can provide emotional support, funding, information and the tools necessary to find a new position quickly or transition to a new career. In contrast, those who have lost their jobs but have very limited social support, may be more likely to suffer and be unemployed for longer.

Monitoring leaning into social support

The stories from entrepreneurs in crisis that follow show us why leaning into support can be valuable. It can also be helpful to think more about when and why we lean into support from others, and from whom we can access support, what kind of support we receive and its consequences, like how it makes us feel. After moving from Canada to the United Kingdom many years ago as a student, I created new social networks over time and have often leaned into them for support. When I need support raising my daughter, her dad and I turn to close friends or other parents we've met though her nursery or school. When I need support around teaching or research, I reach out to academic friends or work colleagues. I include several resources further along in the chapter that can help you monitor and enhance your own experiences of leaning into social support in a crisis or otherwise.

The role of social support

For entrepreneurs in crisis, leaning into three forms of social support is not only common but a critical strategy for their business recovery, as well as for them personally, increasing their resilience as individuals: (a) informational support (information or guidance that helps manage problems), (b) material support (goods/services that help solve specific problems) and (c) emotional support (feeling cared for by others). Entrepreneurs like Kate suggest that each of these three forms of social support help them balance resource losses by providing them with reassurance, reducing their negative feelings, and creating a sense that they are not alone, motivating them to carry on.

Informational support: leaning into sources of information or guidance

As emphasized throughout the book, one of the key features of a crisis is uncertainty. Seeking out support from others who can provide information and guidance can help entrepreneurs in crisis reduce uncertainty and associated negative feelings and stress. This support can come from those working in the same industry and geographical context, or from industry outsiders.

In the early stages of the pandemic there was little information about how COVID-19 and the subsequent lockdowns would affect businesses, especially for those working in customer-facing fields such as the hospitality industry. Information and guidance regarding how to navigate the circumstances became essential for entrepreneurs running pubs, restaurants and cafes.

Sebastian, who was originally from South America, had a background in marketing but a passion for food. He started his first restaurant a decade before the pandemic. By the age of 40, he was the owner of several restaurants across London. Sebastian discussed how he was benefitting from connecting with other members of the hospitality industry a month after the first lockdown. He joined social media forums and online calls to expose himself to the perspectives of restaurant owners who had also been affected and what they were doing to manage. He explained: 'A lot of people from the sector [have been] sharing information in a very quick manner … industry leaders [are] shining the path forwards … it has been really reassuring.' He added: 'Knowing we're together in all of this, that there are people campaigning for your same interests, that has been really reassuring.' Sebastian found it comforting to be part of a bigger group of business owners who were undergoing similar experiences, campaigning for their interests and providing information to address what many perceived as gaps and limitations in government support. This alleviated his stress somewhat by making him feel that he was less alone and that help was available.

Even those in other industries can be powerful sources of support and guidance to entrepreneurs in crisis. This quote from Malcolm, another restaurant owner affected by the pandemic, nicely illustrates how connections, in this case, evoked positive emotions:

> Informal advice came from a lot of customers, some of whom work in finance, and have bigger businesses. They are a little bit more knowledgeable about finance and government support and what we should be doing in terms of maximizing … being aware of what options were available to us. So, we've had some like people just kind of having good conversations about, you know, 'Look, did you know you could get this loan if you need it?' or 'Did you apply for this grant?' and stuff like that. And so that was really good.

Material support: leaning into those who can provide goods/services

A crisis can also create certain operational challenges for businesses, placing significant pressures on entrepreneurs and managers who, in turn, become tasked with solving a range of problems. Pursuing support from individuals who can help entrepreneurs resolve specific problems alleviates these pressures and reduces negative feelings. This kind of support can come from different stakeholders within the business or from outside of the business.

In the former case, several entrepreneurs in crisis emphasized to me how their team members rose to the occasion and provided additional practical support to them and their businesses, and how this created positive feelings and made them feel less alone. Adam, the owner of a marketing communications business in Southeast London, explained how his team really showed up for him during the pandemic and how this allayed his concerns somewhat:

> I think as a leader I've done a few things through this crisis. One is I've grown up a little bit … In the run up to this crisis you could see it unfolding. I was very open with them [the staff] saying, 'We've got to work out what's going on'. And the world was just falling apart. In that period, I saw a number of team members stand up. It sounds silly, but you know, we were doing anything for anybody for a period, as you'd expect, just to keep work coming in. And our team members saying, you know, 'Pass me the ball, I'll do it. Pass me the ball. Give it to me, I'll do it'. And watching was very humbling, because one of them had just been promoted. I'll never forget. We were in a period of chaos, and it was a job that nobody would want to do normally. She's like, 'Give it me. I'll do it well and I'm going to find another project out of the back of it. Give it to me'. And it was very humbling to see that they cared – they cared enough about the organization. That made me realize it wasn't me against the world anymore. Perhaps this was an agency. I think COVID's been the best team building event we could ever have, and it's taught me to respect my team a little bit more.

Adam found it moving that his team also 'cared' about the business and were more than willing to help him work through the crisis. He expressed gratitude for the efforts his staff had made and gained a new sense of respect for them. These positive emotions and reflections made Adam feel much better about what he regarded as an otherwise difficult time, what he described as a period of 'chaos' when for him and his business, the 'world was just falling apart'. Like Sebastian, Adam felt less alone in the crisis largely due to the social support he had received from others.

During the riots, a handful of entrepreneurs spoke about how other business owners in their community had provided them with materials and/or space in which to conduct their businesses or as a place for storage. This gesture was especially useful to those whose businesses had burned down. Both following the London riots and during the pandemic, several entrepreneurs disclosed how members of their community had raised money to help them manage their cash flow problems. These efforts provided great relief to these individuals and served to reassure and motivate them.

Emotional support: leaning into those who make you feel cared for

A crisis can be overwhelming and, at times, entrepreneurs might feel like giving up. Feeling cared for by others, including members of one's broader community, can reassure entrepreneurs, giving them a welcome 'boost', and the motivation they might require to carry on. During the London riots, several entrepreneurs described how leaning into emotional support was critical to them and elicited positive emotions, including Nathan, the shop owner selling appliances in East London:

> Afterwards, the response from the local community has been very, very, uplifting – people coming in and saying, you know, how sorry they were, nice words … People you see around all the time … come into the shop and make overtures. It definitely brought a lot of community spirit. Yeah, I think out of bad can come some good, from that point of view. The local hall made a handmade card … the kids and adults. You know, it's not a lot, but … people have gone to the trouble to do it. It just gives you a bit of a boost.

Similarly, Vivek spoke at length about the emotional support he had received from the community and council following the riots and the damages to his convenience store, also in East London:

> They [the local councillor and their assistant] both came and they said, '[The] Council will give you support and we will fix your shop back. Don't worry. Whatever you lost, you lost. But we will help you' ... Then the local people ... created the webpage [to raise money] ... So, everybody wants to help me in a different way. A lot of people come forward and say, 'Oh, look I can do the carpentry. We want to help you fix your shop back'. So, you know, different support from different people. Even, you know, some old woman comes with her pension and give me £150 with her pension ... and she says, 'No, you're not going nowhere. You have to fix [it] back, and I want to come to buy from you because I can't go far. This is my shop, so you have to come back to this shop' ... It makes you feel very, very, comfortable ... The [next] 14 days, we was working very hard. Fifteen of us. All my family. My friends come. We work and clean the shop. The council help us to take the rubbish. The council gave the moral support. They came every single day, and they check with me.

The support Vivek felt filled him with a greater sense of ease and enabled him to be more resilient to the negative effects of the crisis. Vivek's example also shows how social networks can facilitate resource gains in a crisis. As discussed in the previous chapter, they can help us acquire more resources. In such instances, networks may not only provide important psychological resources, but also material resources. A lack of support, alternatively, as we saw in some cases with local councils/government or other groups like insurers, can make us feel more alone. It can even pave the way towards more maladaptive strategies such as rumination and behavioural disengagement, as we will see in the following chapters, making us more vulnerable and less resilient.

What can we do to lean into social support more effectively in a crisis?

We're often told that the secret to a longer, happier, and healthier life is our connections with others, our social networks. They can make us feel like we belong. Bring us new perspectives. They can help move us closer to our goals and build our confidence. Our social networks can also provide us with other valuable resources. At the same time, not everyone is aware of what their networks have to offer or feels comfortable leaning into their connections when the chips are down.

To lean into social support more effectively in a crisis, we can identify the forms of social support we currently have access to – informational, material or emotional – what's missing, and what kinds of support we might need. Moreover, we can determine whether we need that support now or in the future. This specificity might help focus our attention, narrow the search parameters and establish a timeline to acquire support. Additionally, while informational, material and emotional support were especially important to entrepreneurs in crisis, structural support (the extent and frequency of social interactions) and functional support (the experience of social interactions being beneficial in some way) might have a role to play as well.

It can be helpful to identify which networks might be able to provide us with support. For example, emotional support can come from personal networks composed of friends and family, but it might also come from professional networks made up of business partners, staff, and members of the broader community. This might require us to reflect on the nature and extent of current personal and/or professional networks and those networks we have not yet joined with the intention of widening our circle to potentially include, for example, industry associations, local/community associations and professional associations for business owners/managers.

We should also take the time to think about how we can extend our social network both offline and online. In the former case, several entrepreneurs were quick to mention how their community involvement prior to a crisis helped them during and/or after the crisis. Continually building these social ties is therefore important. At the same time, not everyone has an obvious offline community to lean into. Many of us are working online and some might be doing so almost exclusively. Building an online network is equally important. Thinking about the forums in which we might find individuals with similar or complimentary interests, skills and experiences is useful. We can begin to build an online community by creating valuable content for network members, drawing connections between them where possible and empowering members to contribute to discussions. Sebastian spoke about how he was able to connect online with industry leaders in his field, hospitality, at a critical juncture during the pandemic, and the positive implications this had for him.

Few people teaching business studies pass up the chance to discuss with their students the importance of networks and networking. Incorporating network building into assignments, compelling students to connect with practitioners and share what they've learned from them, is something I've always done. I've asked my master's students, for instance, to reflect on the steps they've taken during term time to develop their network of owners/managers, both online and offline. Many students employ the usual tactics of attending more events (professional workshops, innovation seminars and women in business events were just a few of the examples given), creating online profiles where there were none, identifying key figures in their industry and potential advisors and contributing more to online discussions and posing questions. Several have spoken as well about the importance of nurturing connections, following up with them on occasion, online or via email or in-person at events, and sharing their own experiences with their newly established professional communities. One student made the effort to write to all of our visiting speakers, those entrepreneurs I brought into our lectures, not only thanking them for their talks but personalizing their messages to include something the speaker said which included the questions they had posed to the students; a great way to increase their chances of being remembered.

Finally, leaning into social support more effectively can involve reflecting on the benefits we've already derived from current support networks. This might allow us to reframe or reappraise a crisis or stressful situation, helping us feel less alone and more motivated to rely on and expand our social support networks as a result, as we figure out how to tackle the challenges that lie ahead. In each case, we can ask ourselves the questions outlined in Table 8.1. For each form of social support, we can also document what benefits we have attained from accessing this support previously, whether we need this support now and where we might draw it from, what we can do to access this support and what the consequences of receiving the

Table 8.1: Guiding questions for creating a more deliberate strategy for leaning into social support

What forms of social support do I need and what forms do I currently have access to?	• Do I need and do I have access to specific information or guidance that would help me manage this situation or crisis (informational support)? • Do I need and have access to certain goods/services that would help me solve specific problems (material support)? • Do I need and have access to individuals and entities that make me feel cared for (emotional support)?
When might I need social support?	• Do I need the support now or in the medium to longer term? • How soon can I start planning for this support? What can I do to access this support?
Which networks might provide social support?	• Can I draw support from my personal and/or professional networks? • Can I draw support from inside and/or outside my business?
What benefits have I already derived from social support during or after the crisis?	• Has it helped to diminish negative emotions and/or create positive emotions? • Has it helped me see the crisis in a new light? • Has it helped me forge my recovery and plan ahead?

support have been (see Table 8.2). Box 8.1 provides some actions you can take on a more regular basis to lean into social support.

★★★

In short, leaning into social support is another strategy entrepreneurs use to adjust to a crisis, strengthening their resilience. The following chapters take a different turn, focusing instead on those strategies entrepreneurs might adopt that can compromise their resilience and make them more vulnerable, depending on how they're employed and for how long. Taking steps to be aware of these strategies, to minimize their use or guard against their negative effects, is vital.

Table 8.2: Leaning into social support log

Form of support	What benefits, if any, have I derived from accessing this support previously?	Do I need this kind of support now and why? What form might it take?	Where might I find this support/draw this support from?	What can I do to access this support?	What have been the consequences of accessing this support?
Informational support (Sources of information or guidance)					
Material support (Those who can provide goods/services)					
Emotional support (Those who make us feel cared for)					

> **Box 8.1: Actionable takeaways for leaning into social support**
>
> - Practice leaning into social support: Asking for help isn't always easy. Practice reaching out to your personal and professional network on occasion for insights and advice, in good times and bad. This will make it more comfortable for you to lean in when times are challenging.
> - Create a broad support network: Having different people to go to for support gives us options, takes the pressure off any one relationship and, importantly, can offer different perspectives.
> - Be supportive: Be available to provide support to others. Doing so will not only strengthen your social connections and create good will, but give you a boost, making you feel active, purposeful.

Chapter summary

- Social support refers to the support provided by our network.
- Social support has a key role to play in helping us cope with stress.
- Those of us with social support are likely to gain more resources during a crisis than those without, and more likely to be stable and have the capacity to cultivate recovery over time.
- The effectiveness of social support depends on the type of support available, the timing of support, our needs as individuals and the groups to which we belong.
- Entrepreneurs in crisis lean into three forms of social support: (a) informational support (information or guidance that helps manage problems), (b) material support (goods/services that help solve specific problems) and (c) emotional support (feeling cared for by others).
- We can all lean into social support more effectively by identifying where our support comes from, the forms of social support we need or are most likely to need and when, from where we can draw support (personal/professional networks, inside/outside the business, offline/online) and by reflecting on the benefits we've already derived from social support.

PART II

Strategies That Can Compromise Resilience and How to Manage Them

9

Denial

When Vivek and I met for the first time it was a typical late autumn day in London, cool, grey and raining heavily. Sitting in his white van parked just outside of his crowded convenience store, Vivek used the street as a canvas to paint a picture for me of the rioters' movements that night and police cordons. He pointed out a couple of locals who happened to be walking by, one whom CCTV footage captured looting his shop in the early hours after it was destroyed by the rioters, and the other who had given him money in the days following, to help with his recovery. Both were older women.

Vivek was in the shop on Monday 8 August, a day he was quick to describe as 'normal Monday trading'. He said it wasn't until 'Monday afternoon we hear, around 2:30, say 2:00, there's going to be riots in [the borough]. You know local people. The news was spreading already. Tottenham was done on the sixth, seventh, and this was the third day'. By this time, he said people 'knew already' what could happen, and the main street was closing down. 'I thought, "Okay, I go. This is my chance to go home on Monday." So, me and these two', he gestured to a couple of employees, 'was there and my brother was here so we just go, shut the shop, put the shutter down. At 2:30 we left the shop'. Despite the concerns of those around him, Vivek felt different, confident:

> Everything closed nicely and I thought, my feeling, is it's never going to happen on my road. Even if it happens on the High Street. We know the people. The people are not going to do it to you. Even if something happens.

It's not going to happen on my road. I believe it's not going to happen in my shop'.

When I probed as to why he was certain nothing would happen to his business, he explained:

> Because you see, you see, other people are a different way. This shop is so friendly. If you come to my shop and I don't know you and you say, 'Oh I am thirsty, water I just straight away give to you'. That's the way I was born and brought up. If you come and you want food, I'll give you even my food.

Vivek went home. By 4:30 he was informed the rioting had begun. He put on the news:

> So, we are watching. And I said, 'oh they are going on the main street'. And I say, 'ok shit, this is bad'. So, we, I'm watching with my kids and wife and around 7:30 they were showing [his road] and I say, 'Shhhhit. What is happening?' And 7:30 there was, they went up to that point, just further down the road, at the like junction, and the police was stepping back. And I say, 'Why do they push it and why are they coming back [towards the shop]?!' And when the police come back, they start to burn the cars over here. Almost six, seven cars burning up here. And then at 8:30, I see people come and break into my shop. And the [Sky News] helicopter was showing that and I thought, 'Shhhhit. What the hell?! Nooo!'

The next morning, upon seeing what was left of his business, he cried. 'And then,' he said, 'I had to call the shutter people.' But before doing so he stopped suddenly and reflected:

> Just one minute, I thought, 'I'm not going to do it. You know, retail again. No more retail, no more [borough]. This is the end of you.' You just feel thrown out into the street. Because this is your livelihood and just feel, you

know, everything's gone! And I just went home. I didn't step into the shop at all. I just looked from outside.

In some cases, learning about a crisis can coincide with protective thoughts that tune out the warning signals. Such protective thoughts might take the form of 'It won't happen to me' or 'It won't be that bad'. Thoughts like these that are comforting in the moment, have the potential to intensify negative emotions after the event, making us more vulnerable and, potentially, less resilient.

What is denial?

A crisis can take place suddenly with little warning. Sometimes, however, there are warning signals from the environment that a crisis is imminent or on the horizon. In these cases, we might disregard the signals because we believe the probability of it happening to us is low, as in Vivek's case. We might also miss signals because their strength is weak, because we are convinced that others will step in and address the signals, or because we lack previous experience.

Denial is an early-stage defence mechanism directed towards potentially painful stimuli originating from the outside world.[1] Denial can be useful to us by serving to reduce our discomfort, limiting in turn certain negative thoughts, feelings or impulses.[2] At the same time, denial can be problematic, delaying those thoughts, feelings and actions that can prepare us mentally for a crisis or help us respond so we can recover efficiently from a crisis, or be more resilient to its effects.

Denial can set in before an adverse event or afterwards. Take the example of losing a job. In this situation, while losing our job can occur without any kind of warning whatsoever, which can be an especially painful experience, there may have been signs that our employer was struggling or that we've over-estimated our role in the business to the extent that we believed the likelihood of our dismissal to be low. In the latter case, following job loss we might avoid reflecting on the personal, social and economic implications, or the effort required to land a new job.

Denial may be reinforced by certain aspects of the environment, including the culture. This could include the culture within certain families, communities or businesses. When, for instance, businesses have been successful in the past, this might be taken as a sign that all is well and that organizational practices are competent and able to withstand any challenge.[3] This is known as the 'success-breeds-failure syndrome'.[4] Research carried out by Argenti,[5] Kets de Vries and Miller[6] suggests that business owners and managers who are more susceptible to the syndrome may be those who are complacent, negligent, overly ambitious, or even, in some cases, arrogant. Those most susceptible to the syndrome might also work in organizational cultures that condition members to focus on the positive and have mantras such as 'we are successful' or 'we have good safety records' which can do more harm than good. Those of us who hold on to positive emotions and seek to reduce the likelihood of experiencing negative emotions at all costs, even though our negative emotions might be signalling something is wrong and worth addressing, may also be at risk.

A stark example of the success-breeds-failure syndrome is the collapse of Baring Brothers and Co. Ltd, a long-established merchant banking business operating from the City of London that was founded back in 1762 and was forced to stop trading in 1995. The Barings story is a cautionary tale of how the actions of one individual, 28-year-old General Manager and key trader Nick Leeson, took down the entire bank due to his high stakes trading practices; practices which were later determined to have been unauthorized and to have involved the concealment of trading positions. The fact that Leeson was able to engage in these practices at all was attributed to his earlier successes and previous behaviours that were regarded as risk averse. Investigations into the collapse suggest, however, that even after signs that the bank's financial performance was declining and losses were mounting, actions were not taken by senior officials to ensure more stringent controls; this, combined with a tradition of making structural and systems-related changes within the bank over the longer term rather than taking the short-term actions necessary, was a recipe for disaster. In the end, the bank incurred significant losses estimated at over one billion pounds.[7]

Monitoring denial

Can you remember a time when you actively held protective thoughts and may have been in denial? Being conscious of the consequences of denial, and how protective thoughts make us feel in the moment or further down the road, can help us reflect more on their utility, regardless of how big or small they might be. I currently have a bad tooth. I'd rather not think about finding the time to go to the dentist, the work involved to fix it and, of course, the cost. So, I've pushed it to the back of my mind. And I've avoided eating certain foods on that side which makes it ache. Knowing my tooth won't likely get better on its own and could get worse, causing me more discomfort and making it more difficult to fix longer term, is the realization I am coming to. I incorporate activities at the end of the chapter that you can work through to help protect you from the negative effects of denial.

The role of denial

For the entrepreneurs I've worked with, instances of denial have been mostly short term and have often related to thinking they've been spared from a looming crisis. As with previous research, while such thoughts provide them with some comfort initially, they can also increase their distress later.

Similar to Vivek, on day three of the riots that swept across London, Marie was emailed by her local business development agency and again by the Council to say something was afoot:

> It was Monday the eighth of August, and I was here. My husband picked the kids up from school, somebody was actually sick that day, so I was, luckily, I was here … I was doing something and then I noticed an email come through at half 5 … from the council as well, saying that 'According to intelligence, something was going to happen in [the borough where her business was situated]'. And they just reminded all businesses to be vigilant, perhaps remove all expensive things from the window … I'd seen what happened in Tottenham, but I just thought, 'Have they really got the right place? Why would anyone come here?'

Despite feelings of disbelief regarding their warnings, Marie still made an effort to connect with some of the other local businesses nearby to see what they made of the situation:

> I emailed a couple of my neighbours, shopkeepers, and said 'Did you see this email?' And [one shop keeper] he said, 'Oh yeah. I might pop down and take something out of the window, but nobody will get into our glass'. I just thought, 'Well, I might as well do what I can'. So, I made sure – we normally have window lights, so I switched those off, and we have a couple of designer buggies just on display and I moved those down to my office, and I locked the stair gate. And then I kind of left.

Vivek and Marie were aware of rioting elsewhere in London, yet neither believed their businesses would be affected. This sentiment was shared among many other entrepreneurs I spoke to as well in the aftermath, including Victor who was in his 80s, the owner of a longstanding barber shop operating in North London. Victor was away when the rioting began but received a call from his nephew who was trying to encourage him to return to London. Victor reassured him: 'They won't touch my place!' Dylan, who owned the furniture store in South London was told around 5 o'clock something would likely happen in his neighbourhood. They put the shutters up but 'we didn't take it that seriously', he said. Similarly, Jacob said on the day, the stories got more 'severe' but 'I was pretty comfortable about all of it, I was quite dismissive about it. I didn't really appreciate what was going on. I locked up the shop, felt quite safe, got an alarm, got shutters, I felt comfortable.'

Many business owners were certain the police would intervene, like Anne and Chloe who assumed their clothing business would be fine. They received a call from a customer around closing time who said, 'Look, there's trouble happening, there's something coming' and 'it's coming to your side, get out'. But Chloe mentioned they weren't worried at the time. 'We are thinking we are secure. The police will come.' Anne added, 'We have a security company. The police station is down the road. The fire department is here. So, we'll be ok, let's hope.' She explained what they did next:

> So, we go home. We're watching the news, glued to the news. Our worst part of the evening is watching. One of the shops we had actually been patronizing for years, is on fire. The whole building is burning, people are

leaving, we don't know whether looters have gone in there, you can't tell. The news camera is just fixed so we think, 'Oh my goodness, it's terrible, the trouble seems to be principally on that road'. So, later on, by the time we get to 11, we're looking at scenes from all over the country, then we see our part of the road. We see a police van seemingly, two near our shop, so, but we couldn't see anything happening. So, I'm on Facebook, I'm on every news channel going, and then I get a message on Facebook just after midnight, saying, 'you need to check your shop, because it looks like it's been raided'. So, of course, your heart, panic, there's nothing you can do. I spent the night trying to get the police, trying to call the security company, trying to and you know the police's advice is 'go at your own risk' (they say in unison). Go at your own risk. 'Can you tell me anything?' 'I can't tell you anything.' So, by the time we do get here we get here around 6 am on the Tuesday. Our door is wide open. It's been wide open all night. Everything is broken, the mannequins strewn across the floor. The police were around. They're guarding Ladbrokes [the betting shop], they're guarding the sports shop, but there's no one here guarding any small business. And among the businesses here, we were really the only independent shop, except the pharmacy, but the pharmacy's a chain. And the money shop. Big, big, companies! So, we're thinking, and it's no solace to me that anybody should be attacked but you're thinking, 'Why us?'. It's such a small business. Why us?

A sense of denial was also present during the COVID-19 pandemic between 2020 and 2023. One notable example came from a London business owner I coordinated a webinar series with to assist small businesses during the first lockdown. During the series we covered a range of issues from preparing for a crisis and containing a crisis, to decision-making in times of uncertainty, flexibility and improvisation, and how during a crisis we might reflect on the role of empathy, rethink our values, and work to protect our wellbeing. In our first session together, he informed me that in January of 2020, his chief financial officer (CFO) had stormed around the corner of his office warning him of the impending crisis: '"Have you seen what's going on in China?!" ... [He] started talking to me about the epidemic as it was and how worried they should be.' He commented in earnest, 'I've got to be honest, but I didn't believe him. I said, "I'm really pleased you're worried about it, but I really think the WHO and the British government will have this".' He went on to explain that because his CFO had seen the challenges early and started planning for it, they were able to formulate contingencies. However, he did not consider the implications of the pandemic for staff until sometime thereafter:

> But for me, the broader side of the business, the people side of it, it didn't really hit us until that week leading up to the fact that we were probably going to go into lockdown. Then someone got coronavirus and we had to shut down. But really post-impact, lockdown, that's when we really started to impact our work. Two to three weeks into it, businesses started to stop and re-evaluate, rethink how they work.

Many business owners, and members of the public more broadly, didn't imagine at the start of the pandemic that it would last as long as it did. This included Kate, who recalled: 'I remember thinking at the time, "Oh, it'll only be a few months"'. Speaking about the company's cancelled performances she thought, 'It just means that we can't do this now and they're going to reschedule it or whatever'. She continued, 'It was shocking but I didn't, I just didn't think it would be that long'.

Those expecting to be affected by a crisis could prepare more mentally, like Anthony:

> The word gets around in the business community, you know? So, we all knew it was going to happen. Basically, we all locked up and went home. We watched the news and we saw reports in the evening. The riots were kicking off. There was no police around. Thousands of rioters just breaking into the stores. There was a report that our store had been broken in to. They rang me that the intruder alarm had gone off.

Anthony added, 'Yah, you know, there's nothing you can do about it. I certainly wasn't going to risk my life, or the lives of my staff, to try and protect the place.' Feeling at the time, 'I'm insured, what the hell. And that was it.' He proceeded to take action: 'I spoke to my broker and arranged to get the shop boarded up the morning.' What he didn't anticipate, however, was what came next: 'Then I got a panic-stricken phone call from a very good friend of mine, "The shop's on fire, the shop's on fire!"'

While these examples refer mostly to denial at the onset of a crisis, denial can also apply to the duration of a crisis, as was evident in Kate's case during the pandemic, and to thoughts about how much a crisis has impacted us personally, our businesses or our community. Denial can relate to how much damage was done, as we saw with Anthony who did not anticipate his business would be set on fire in the riots, and the resources and steps it might take to recover. In each case, the longer-term implications of denial for individuals and/or their businesses is often problematic.

What can we do to protect ourselves more effectively from denial in a crisis?

There are those who might argue that denial can, at least on occasion, be harmless or even helpful in terms of reducing discomfort when we don't have the energy or capacity to cope, especially if it's employed in the short term. But as we've seen here, denial can hurt. It can create bad feelings. It can make us more vulnerable over time. As such, we can better protect ourselves from the negative effects of denial, stay more alert to the possibility of a crisis and be in a stronger position to read the signals of an impending or evolving crisis, by adopting what I refer to as the four Cs of denial busting: (a) checking and challenging what's working, (b) checking in with others, (c) checking vitals and (d) checking in with prior experiences. Prompts in Tables 9.1 and 9.2 can guide us. Box 9.1 also includes actions you can perform on a regular basis to better protect yourself.

Research has shown that concerns about a crisis are often driven by the actual occurrence of a crisis.[8] Extrapolating from this, many of us might fail to prepare ourselves for a crisis because we simply do not anticipate it. Therefore, one thing we can do to protect ourselves from denial is to check and challenge what's working, and to maintain a

Table 9.1: Guiding questions to protect yourself from denial

Is denial being used as a coping strategy?	• Am I attuned to sudden or key changes in my environment (internal/external business environment)? • Am I being too complacent about my current situation? • When a negative situation or crisis arises, do I have tendency to avoid thinking about it or do I think that I won't be affected?
How can I protect myself and my business from denial or manage it?	• Can I take steps to be less complacent and challenge what's working? • Can I talk to other people to get a different perspective on the issue? Have I checked in recently with others (e.g. internal/external stakeholders)? • Am I regularly checking my vitals (e.g. personal vitals, business vitals) to monitor how I'm/we're doing and how I'm feeling? Is there anything I can or should be doing differently? • Is this experience similar to prior experiences I've had? What was my thinking previously, what actions helped me persevere, and what steps might I take now to help me move forward?

Table 9.2: The 4 Cs of denial busting

Denial busting strategies	What did I discover?	What can I do differently?	What did I learn from taking action and from their consequences?
Checking and challenging what's working			
Checking in with others			
Checking vitals			
Checking in with prior experiences			

healthy sense of wariness regarding stability, routine and complacency.[9] This will enable us to be more vigilant, more accepting of potential problems which may include those in the internal and external business environment, and to be more aware of possible resource deficiencies at the personal level as well as the organizational level.

We can further protect ourselves from denial and read the signals of a crisis by checking in with others, as Marie did. For most of us this might involve speaking with friends, family, work colleagues and peers. Checking in with others can help us process what's happening, make the unreal real, and encourage us to take certain actions, or potentially, to dismiss concerns. Checking in with others can also prompt communal coping, which can be especially helpful during a crisis. Communal coping occurs when both the appraisal of a situation and the actions taken to resolve problems occur within social relationships.[10] In this way it's different from more general forms of social support that incorporate emotional support, financial support or information and advice.

Entrepreneurs and other business leaders more specifically can check in with their team. Encouraging internal stakeholders such as employees to report vulnerabilities and mistakes and to speak up when they see potential problems can aid this process. This requires, in part, establishing a no-blame culture which revolves around promoting greater openness and transparency in the organization.[11] Such a culture can be created by meeting periodically with teams to raise potential concerns, keeping lines of communication open and discussing possible responses to a potential crisis or problems, including how they might be executed and who would be responsible. Checking in with external stakeholders is also important. During both the London riots and the COVID-19 pandemic, some entrepreneurs were discussing the evolving situation with other business owners in their industries, customers and community members, insurers, local councils, and looking to the media to fully comprehend the state of affairs.

We can better protect ourselves from denial related to the damages wrought by a crisis and begin to reflect on the path to recovery by 'checking vitals'. Checking vitals is about monitoring our own personal functioning, and whether, how, and why our physical and mental wellbeing has deteriorated, for example, in the form of lower energy levels. Catching this sooner than later is important. In a medical sense, think of the vitals of seriously injured individuals: their breathing and heart rate. Emergency workers tend to check the vitals of such individuals often at first and less frequently over time as they recover. However, we should be cautious about stepping back too soon. For the entrepreneur or business leader, checking vitals might also include business functioning, that is, looking for any damages associated with financial, human, physical or operational aspects and detecting further risks to the business which might manifest as declining work, sales and reserves. During the pandemic, the entrepreneurs I spoke to were monitoring staff morale and wellbeing, threats to their financial security and changing work practices. Monitor business vitals closely following the onset of a crisis and fairly regularly thereafter, particularly in the face of new changes or challenges.

Finally, I've found that entrepreneurs who have previously experienced major setbacks in their business operations (such as an external shock, fire, or burglary) or personal lives (such as a troubling medical diagnosis or the loss of a loved one), are more likely to be alert to a crisis. With such experience we may be more likely to take precautionary steps, act quickly during a crisis, and maintain a quiet confidence that we can recover. We might benefit from reflecting on our thinking during that time, what actions helped us persevere, and what steps might help move us forward.

★★★

While we are unlikely to catch every crisis before it happens or reduce its negative effects entirely, being mindful of protective thinking and engaging in denial busting strategies can help us better prepare, minimize the blow of crisis and even facilitate our recovery from a crisis. Rumination can also compromise resilience, depending on the form it takes, and we turn to this next.

Box 9.1: Actionable takeaways for protecting yourself against denial

- Examine denial: If you think you might be in denial about a particular challenge, consider what purpose these thoughts might be serving for you and if they're intended for the short or long term. Denial over the long term is more likely to be problematic and to interfere with your goals.

- Challenge your thinking: Reflect on the beliefs or mantras in your life, at home or at work, that could be getting in your way when it comes to noticing certain challenges or dealing with them.
- Practice hearing hard things: Whether it's someone disagreeing with you or raising a problem at work, see it as an opportunity to gain a different and potentially valuable perspective.

Chapter summary

- Denial is a defence mechanism employed to tune out negative thoughts or feelings associated with a painful stressor, which might include signs of a crisis and its effects.
- Denial is an avoidant strategy that can make us slower or less likely to react to a crisis, more vulnerable to its effects.
- Denial is more likely to occur when signals associated with a stressful situation such as a crisis are weak, and when there has been a history of success.
- For entrepreneurs in crisis, denial often manifests in the thoughts they have about the onset of a crisis but can also relate to thoughts they hold about the duration of a crisis and its effects.
- We can limit the possibility of denial and/or seek to manage its potentially negative effects by continually checking and challenging what's working, checking in with other stakeholders, checking vitals, and checking in with prior experiences.

10

Rumination

Two years on from the London riots, Amir spoke about his persistent concerns and anger. He felt let down in the aftermath of the riots by the lack of support. 'I worry about the insurance, I worry about the Government,' he said. As discussed, his clothing business in North London had been seriously vandalized, looted and flooded when rioters attempted to set fire to it. His local councillor, Member of Parliament (MP) and insurers were not as helpful as he believed they could have been, adding to his stress. 'Come on,' he said, 'you pay so much [business] rates, you know? ... My local council could have helped us further.' Following the riots, he had 'no money to start with' and it took six months for him to be compensated. This was a difficult time: 'I'm down so much mentally, I'm just, it affected me mentally.' The inaction of his local MP continued to irritate him:

> I was really disappointed ... we vote for them, right?! Who's on our side? So, you find out it's all bullshit. Nothing. Nothing. Nobody here! The local MP could have come later to us. Fine, they can't come to visit everybody, but [at the] end of the day they could write, 'Okay sorry. We know what happened'. They don't give a shit! ... What's the MP for? This is bad!

While only a few explicit examples of rumination in the accounts of entrepreneurs in crisis really captured my attention, it is an important topic to consider here for two key reasons. First, because the actual number of instances of rumination may be higher. Rumination can be kept hidden unless probed directly. And second because, as with Amir, rumination can be a consequence of a crisis which can, whether hidden or more out in the open, heighten negative feelings like anger, fear and anxiety in crisis victims,[1] and have a negative impact on resilience.[2]

What is rumination?

Like distraction, rumination as a strategy allows us to shift our focus in order to change our emotional experience. However, unlike distraction, which involves shifting attention away from negative thoughts and emotions, rumination shifts attention towards them, focusing instead on one's depressive symptoms.[3] This was the case with Amir following the London riots. With rumination, research by Martin and Tesser,[4] Wade and colleagues,[5] Nolen-Hoeksema and Morrow[6] has shown that negative thoughts and feelings are generated and prolonged, and not necessarily directed towards problem resolution. Rather, they are fixated on the problem,[7] and may not provide any relief as a result.[8] Rumination can, therefore, lead to indecision and interfere with instrumental behaviour,[9] meaning it can prevent us from taking actions to achieve a certain goal.

For instance, if you lose your job, rumination might stop you from taking the steps required to find a new job by focusing your attention on your hurt feelings instead and by replaying events that led to your dismissal over again. Rumination can also impair concentration and reduce your sensitivity to changing contingencies and context.[10] Although the threat may no longer be present – for example, if you have lost your old job due to the recession but since then the economic climate has improved and you have found a new position – rumination can keep the threat alive.

Regarding the effects of rumination, a meta-analysis[a] on the topic has revealed a strong connection between rumination and posttraumatic stress syndrome (PTSS).[11] Studies of survivors of road traffic accidents[12] or fires[13] have shown that rumination after a crisis can also predict posttraumatic stress syndrome far into the future. In the latter case, on the night of 7 April 1990, a fire broke out on

---

[a] A systematic assessment of the results of several studies on the same topic.

the Scandinavian Star ferry which was transporting passengers and vehicles from Oslo, Norway to Frederikshavn, Denmark. At the time of writing this book, the source of the fire, initially believed to be arson, had yet to be verified and an investigation into the events of that night was ongoing. Among other things, officials were investigating claims that certain safety precautions had not been taken to ensure the adequacy of fire doors and fire exits, sprinklers and alarm systems, and that the training of crew members had been inadequate, all of which may have led to the rapid spread of the fire, tragically killing 159 of the 482 passengers.[14]

Nearly three decades later, Birkeland, Blix and Thoresen[15] carried out a study of 321 survivors, many of whom were in the deadliest areas of the ferry during the fire, and the bereaved who had lost loved ones to the fire. Researchers were interested in understanding whether these individuals engaged in rumination. They measured rumination using a four-item rumination coping scale, asking participants whether they agreed/disagreed with statements such as, 'I dwell upon the feelings the situation has evoked in me' and 'I want to understand why I feel the way I do about what I have experienced'. The self-reported measures indicated the presence of rumination and PTSS in these individuals. Moreover, the researchers found that high levels of perceived social support protected victims of the ferry disaster against the negative effects of a ruminative coping style and PTSS.

Social support can protect us against the negative effects of rumination by offering an empathetic ear but also an alternative perspective, among other things. At the same time, by prolonging distress, it has been found by Kemp and colleagues,[16] as well as Nolen-Hoeksema and Morrow,[17] that rumination can lead to poor relational outcomes as well as poor psychological outcomes. Social support, it seems, may be eroded by the tendency of those who ruminate to continually talk about their loss and its meaning, even long after the event.[18]

Some degree of rumination after a loss is regarded as a natural response.[19] However, rumination can become problematic depending on the form it takes and with what it interferes. Rumination is especially problematic when it is focused on higher level causes and meanings surrounding an event, such as thinking 'Why me?' or 'What does this mean for my life?' as opposed to lower-level details and emotional reactions like, 'How can I intervene to solve this problem?'.[20] Rumination is also problematic when it is intrusive and vague rather than deliberate.[21] In the former case, for the person who has lost their job, rumination might take the form of thinking, 'Why does this kind of stuff always happen to me?', rather than finding ways to address the situation. Using rumination more deliberately might entail thinking about how to upskill or how to go about finding new work, deciding who best to speak to about career opportunities, and where to start looking.

Monitoring rumination

Have you ever fixated on certain negative thoughts and emotions, replaying them in your mind long after a threat they were connected to diminished? What purpose did this serve? How did it make you feel? Later in the chapter I provide questions and exercises that might help you unpack these thoughts and emotions, work through and transform them, and protect you somewhat from the negative effects of rumination; particularly that which is higher level, vague and intrusive.

The role of rumination

For entrepreneurs like Amir who find themselves in a crisis, rumination can have long-term negative effects on wellbeing, creating and prolonging negative emotions. Rumination can take the form of repeatedly going over events, thinking about why a crisis has occurred, why it has happened to me, or what could have been done differently. Someone who ruminates might wonder whether they should have purchased a different kind of insurance cover or what would have happened if they had acted sooner, had more reserves, had taken a different approach to recovery or received more help. Rumination can involve reflecting continuously on the negative implications of a crisis, the professional and personal losses, and the psychological or physical effects.

While there were only a few observable instances of rumination in my research, when rumination did manifest, the effects were especially negative, particularly where ruminative thoughts were vague rather than deliberate and not focused on problem solving.

In one particularly notable case, Jacob had told me shortly after the London riots about the extreme measures he had taken to protect his high-end clothing store on the night it was looted. As soon as Jacob was alerted by a concerned neighbour over the phone that his business was being broken into, he drove to his shop and stood outside all night long with a crowbar and his dog. 'I did what I had to do', he said. He explained to me the rationale behind his bold yet risky actions:

> I did it without thinking. I got dressed, went in my car, and come to protect my business and my future, 'cause there's lots of things in here – not just stock-wise – that belong to me, that I would never be able to replace. So, you know, this is, I spend more time here than I do at home.

When I asked if the rioters had cleaned him out completely, he quickly replied: 'No.' In the end, only one side of the shop room floor had been looted which he said was because 'I got here. I put all the lights on'. Unfortunately, however, insurers were making things difficult for him as a result:

> I said to the insurers … 'You know, I've saved you paying me a lot of money. I could have just let it [happen] … like a lot of people did … I put my life at risk. I could have been attacked. I could have been anything. So, now you're penny pinching me? So, I'll know next time'.

Two years following the riots, when Jacob and I met again, these events were on his mind. He explained how he had many negative thoughts about the crisis still and regretted his actions to stop the rioters, actions which he felt made it more difficult to obtain compensation from insurers: 'I wish I'd never even come and attended and let my business have a total loss. And then I would have had complete compensation.' A lack of support from insurers and the council, along with the damages to his business and the additional work this had created, had taken a significant toll on him:

> You felt very isolated after everything settled down with advice and help. It just wasn't there. It just frittered away.

> It literally was forgotten about quite quickly ... you're left to your own devices. Okay, we run our own business anyway, but you know it's, it was a hard thing to ... I mean personally back home was affected because my frame of mind was – I became quite an angry, negative person for what took place. I was frustrated that, you know, here we are, we've done nothing wrong and we've been a victim of this mindless act that's took place, so.

When I followed up and asked him if the events surrounding the riots had affected him personally, he replied:

> Yeah. Very, very much so, and it's always done. I have lots of regrets thinking, you know, when we had the warning should I have made greater provisions to protect the business? But I just didn't think it would happen!

Jacob's example shows how rumination can negatively impact an entrepreneur's wellbeing and personal relationships. Dwelling on and replaying events surrounding the riots made him an 'angry, negative person' and left him feeling frustrated, as he felt he had done nothing wrong.

Where rumination is focused more on problem solving, its negative effects over time are lessened. Anne, whose handmade formal wear had been cleared out by rioters (minus the items she had placed in her car or hid moments before), shared her worries about being looted again and the routines she had devised in response to manage. Two years on, she told me why she still resorted to hiding clothes within the shop at the end of every workday, especially during the bridal season:

> The content of the shop is the important thing. So, you know, people think if this [the riots] happened again what would you do? ... You know how you kind of do a damage control situation whereby you've kind of chosen five items that you would save ... in a fire? ... I've done that ... I still [hide our stock] ... It's bad, but ... Hiding things is the difference between me coming and finding them and not finding them.

What can we do to protect ourselves more effectively from rumination in a crisis?

Rumination might be comforting at times. It might feel good on occasion or like it's helping. But often, and depending on its form, rumination can create stress and generate negative feelings. Rumination can prevent us from finding solutions to our problems, the source of our distress, and stop us from taking action to resolve them. This can make us more vulnerable and less resilient, in turn. Finding ways to protect ourselves from the negative effects of rumination is, therefore, crucial.

We can do so first by seeking out support. Social support has been shown to be an effective rumination intervention.[22] Social support can serve to mitigate psychological distress for individuals who engage in maladaptive forms of rumination which are higher level and vague. Turning to friends and family, work colleagues, and others working in our industry for advice and guidance can be enormously beneficial. At the same time, and as noted, rumination can be difficult for our relationships and bringing our awareness to this possibility is important.

A mindfulness practice can be another effective strategy for alleviating the negative effects of rumination by encouraging us to notice our thoughts and emotions without judgement or without becoming absorbed by them, helping us gain control over our attention.[23] Nolen-Hoeksema and co-researchers[24] have argued that mindfulness practices can be immensely useful in that they help challenge the validity of ruminative thoughts and separate individuals from their thoughts. Such mindfulness practices might include, but are not limited to, meditation, focusing on our breathing or on our bodies or the sounds arounds us, and bringing our attention to the moment.

Additional therapies have been shown to be effective against rumination as well. Cognitive behavioural therapy (CBT), for example, can teach us different tactics to deal with rumination, and interpersonal therapy can help us understand our relationships and relational problems better and any kind of interpersonal conflict that might result from rumination.[25] A medical practitioner would be best placed to work with you to address what kind of therapy, if any, might be most useful.

We can also protect ourselves from the harmful effects of rumination by employing distraction. Research suggests that neutral or positive distractions such as exercise or socializing in the short term, followed by reappraisal, problem solving or other kinds of behavioural interventions that help us change or improve our environments, can also be effective strategies to limit rumination.[26] This might involve going for a walk or working some place new. Positive reappraisal, and the reframing it entails, can also help us think about the source of our rumination in a new light.

Finally, other interventions that might be helpful in dealing with rumination include allocating a specific time each day to worrying, rather than allowing worries to surface randomly. For example, we might set aside 30–60 minutes in the early afternoon to focus on our worries, so they don't interfere with our sleep at night or other activities throughout the day.[27] Also, it's advisable to move away from vague concerns such as 'Why did this happen to me?' towards more specific concerns such as 'What can I do going forward to begin to address this?'. Following up on more specific concerns with concrete actions is key. Tables 10.1, 10.2 and Figure 10.1 will guide you.

Table 10.1: Guiding questions to protect yourself from rumination

Is rumination being used as a coping strategy?	• Am I fixating on a stressor or problem? Has the immediate threat dissipated? Is this fixation negatively impacting my wellbeing? Is it impairing my concentration or ability to act?
	• Am I focused on something that is specific and deliberate, or more general, vague, hard to define?
	• Am I focused on, or able to focus on, how to solve the problem, which might include a crisis?
	• Am I able to come up with a plan of action to resolve the problem(s) at hand?
How can I protect myself and my business from rumination or manage it?	• If I am ruminating, can I seek out support or advice from my social network?
	• If I am ruminating, can I adopt a mindfulness practice?
	• If I am ruminating, might it be useful to seek out other forms of support such as therapy?
	• If I am ruminating, can I employ some form of distraction in the short term?
	• If I am ruminating, can I allocate a limited amount of time during the day to worry?
	• If I am ruminating, can I move away from more vague concerns towards more specific ones?

Table 10.2: A rumination log

Rumination examples	Are my concerns specific or vague?	What actions can I take?	What actions did I take?	How did taking action make me think and feel about the issue?

Figure 10.1: Shifting from vague concerns to more specific concerns

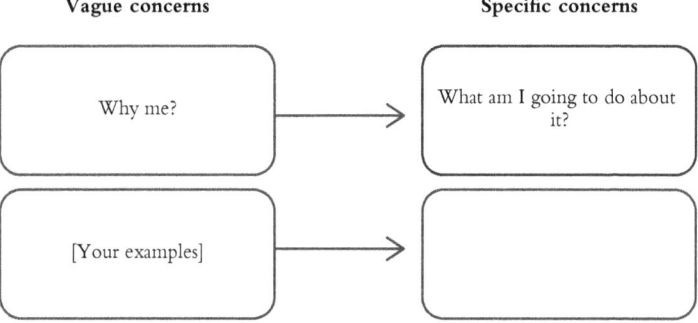

Box 10.1 further provides some actions you can perform to protect yourself from rumination.

★★★

Rumination as a strategy is, for the most part, problematic when it is higher level and vague, and not deliberate in execution or focused on problem solving. Taking steps to minimize this maladaptive form of rumination is important. Coming up in the subsequent chapter we discuss behavioural disengagement, our final strategy, which like rumination is about where we direct our attention. As we'll see, like denial and rumination, behavioural disengagement can compromise the resilience of entrepreneurs and make them more vulnerable, especially when it's employed longer term.

> **Box 10.1: Actionable takeaways for protecting yourself against rumination**
>
> - Identify the triggers: Keep notes on the possible triggers of your rumination, on where you are, who you're with and what you're doing at the time when you ruminate. Now consider the circumstances in which you're not ruminating. Reflect on what you can learn in each case.
> - Define the problem: Try to identify the specific problem or challenge you are fixating on. Unpack each one. How would you describe it? What are its features? This is something you can do on your own or with others. The more specific and clearer the problem, the easier it will be to outline the steps you need to take to address it and manage the negative emotions associated.
> - Be solution focused: Direct your attention and energy towards resolving the problem. When you notice your attention shifting back to the stressor, and away from the solution, stop yourself. If it's not a problem that you can resolve, consider letting go. Seek out support.

Chapter summary

- Rumination is an emotion regulation strategy that shifts attention towards negative thoughts and emotions which, in our case, may be associated with a crisis, prolonging these negative thoughts and emotions, and rarely providing relief as a result.
- Rumination may be more likely to occur when our anticipated progress on goals may be thwarted and social support is limited, among other things.
- Rumination can impair decision-making and the kind of instrumental behaviour that might be necessary to guide us through a crisis.
- For entrepreneurs in crisis, when rumination is focused on past grievances or hardships, about which little can be done, it can have negative implications for their wellbeing.
- We might be able to limit the possibility of rumination and/or manage its potentially negative effects by seeking out social support, engaging in different forms of distraction, mindfulness and certain kinds of therapies, specifying worry time, and making rumination less vague and intrusive, more focused on specific and deliberate concerns or actions.

11

Behavioural Disengagement

Mark wasn't too concerned about the possibility of more riots in his future. 'It's a waste of time worrying about that', he told me. 'Probably, we'll close the door if it does, but it's not something that I waste a lot of energy worrying about.' He reflected:

> I don't care about the business so much as I used to ... working six days a week here. I dropped it down to five and a half. But if I get an excuse to go over there and have a cup of coffee and lock the door, I'll do it, whereas before I wouldn't.

When I asked why that might be the case, he said, 'I can't give you a reason. It's just I want to be here, but I don't want to be here. I can't think of any other way of putting it.' He elaborated:

> Whereas before you might perhaps argue with a customer, I can't be bothered with any of it. And I would err on the side of, you know, if they want a refund just give it to them and get rid of them, rather than if it's, even if it's not my fault. But I [sighs], I hold my ground, but I wouldn't go over the top. It's just not worth it.

In certain situations, as with Mark, a crisis can leave us disengaged, not only psychologically but also behaviourally. We might react by reducing or even withdrawing our efforts which may cause problems down the road, especially if prolonged. Think of the individual who is undergoing a health crisis who might not seek advice from doctors or family, or the manager in an organizational crisis who might do little to investigate the cause of the crisis or to implement changes. In these cases, we might disengage because we lack the ability to cope otherwise with the negative thoughts and emotions that might arise. While such a strategy might sound appealing in part, if employed long term it can stop us from fully processing events, potentially distancing us from things that bring us meaning, and even hurt us, making us worse off. And, in time, we might become more vulnerable and less resilient to the difficulties we may encounter.

As with rumination, there weren't many observed examples of disengagement across the accounts of entrepreneurs in crisis. While this is good news generally, cases like Mark's shine a light on the possibility of employing such a response and its implications, which can have mixed effects.

What is behavioural disengagement?

Put simply, behavioural disengagement is about withdrawing effort or ceasing to act. After arguing with a work colleague, it might entail missing the next project meeting, abstaining from a work-related social event, or not responding to certain emails. Behavioural disengagement is an avoidant coping strategy[1] that might be used when we don't feel like we have the coping resources we need to deal effectively with a particular stressor, including a crisis.[2] Behavioural disengagement strategies work by directing our attention and our actions away from a stressor and its associated negative emotions.[3] Like other avoidant strategies, including denial and in some cases distraction and rumination, behavioural disengagement has little impact on the stressor in question.[4]

While both distraction and behavioural disengagement can be adopted as avoidant coping strategies, the former can also inform the latter. Distraction, as noted earlier, can be a positive strategy for regulating emotions, especially if it is healthy and used as a form of temporary relief. When used as a permanent form of avoidance, however, it can be unhealthy and suppress negative emotions associated with a stressor. To illustrate, despite being mostly a positive distraction, socializing with our friends could also be a negative distraction, depending on why, when and how often it is employed. For example, if I text or call a friend or go out with friends whenever

I don't feel like working, with the intention of avoiding work, it could stop me from completing some of the things I need to do. While healthy forms of distraction can direct our attention away from a stressful situation and towards activities that produce positive emotions, they can also allow for better behavioural engagement later on.[5] Negative forms of distraction however, such as substance abuse, can prolong disengagement. It is also the case that whereas distraction is about doing something different to stop focusing on the stressor, disengagement is more about withdrawing effort that might be used to manage the stressor. Whether behavioural disengagement does more harm than good, therefore, depends on the form it takes and its duration. As a long-term avoidant strategy, behavioural disengagement may be linked to distress.

For the individual who has lost their job, behavioural disengagement can have serious implications. It might involve withdrawing from activities that could land you a new job, such as attending certain professional events and engaging in networking opportunities, or abstaining from activities like searching internet job boards, speaking to recruiters and updating your CV. It might entail staying home more and doing nothing, negatively impacting your wellbeing.

Previous research suggests that behavioural disengagement may go hand in hand with other avoidant or maladaptive coping strategies like denial, or even substance abuse; strategies where there is limited perceived control over addressing the stressor in question.[6] And although behavioural disengagement can have a deleterious effect on resilience,[7] it has commanded less attention than other strategies, often being studied alongside them rather than independently.

For example, Foster[8] examined the relationship between trauma, coping strategies, and anxiety symptoms in 915 undergraduate students at an American university. She administered questionnaires to participants which included self-report measures based on 28 items from the Brief-COPE inventory. Students were required to use a Likert scale to indicate to what extent they agreed or disagreed with certain statements indicative of engagement, including: 'I've been getting emotional support from others', 'I've been giving up trying to deal with it' and 'I've been taking action to try to make the situation better'. The study found that behavioural disengagement, along with denial and substance abuse, were positively associated with reported anxiety symptoms.

Similarly, a questionnaire study of 586 adults living in Portugal during the COVID-19 pandemic found that behavioural disengagement, denial and substance abuse were common avoidant strategies utilized by these individuals, albeit adopted less often than more positive strategies such as active coping and positive reappraisal.[9] The study also found that behavioural disengagement was a predictor of poor psychological health, anxiety and depression.

Monitoring behavioural disengagement

Can you think of a time when you withdrew effort from managing a difficult situation? For how long did you withdraw and why? What were the implications? Periodically I've noticed people taking a break from social media. A 'social media detox', they call it. Some people do it quietly while others make an official announcement. Often, they do so because they feel social media is too demanding and/or there isn't enough time to engage with a platform effectively. On occasion though, it can have to do with a controversial or misconstrued post and dealing with internet trolls. In these instances, disengaging might offer a welcome pause and allow things to die down. At the same time, this strategy might not address the issue or allow them to pursue their greater goal of disseminating their thoughts and work to a broader network. There are several resources at the end of this chapter – question prompts, a reengagement log and actionable takeaways – that you can work through, in turn, to protect yourself from the negative effects of behavioural disengagement.

The role of behavioural disengagement

Our understanding of behavioural disengagement as a strategy during a crisis, and as it relates to entrepreneurs, is limited. My research suggests that entrepreneurs who disengage during a crisis tend to do so when they feel their mental health is threatened and when they believe their efforts will make little difference to outcomes. My findings also show that behavioural disengagement may carry certain benefits for some in the short term by alleviating feelings of anxiety. If not managed carefully, it could lead entrepreneurs to find less meaning in their work in the long term. It might also encourage these individuals to believe that what they do to improve the situation does not matter and that they have little to no control, creating a vicious cycle. At the same time, depending on how much entrepreneurs disengage, such a strategy could create a better balance between work and other activities, including more leisure and family time when deliberately employed.

On a positive note, there were very few instances of behavioural disengagement in my research with entrepreneurs. Where it was observed, disengagement was mostly temporary, and its negative effects on their crisis response and wellbeing were, therefore, limited. Temporary disengagement, or withdrawing effort in the short term, was sometimes seen as helpful and as giving entrepreneurs the space they needed to regroup. I use a couple of familiar examples next.

Mark, for one, shared with me that, early on in the aftermath of the London riots, he felt compelled to disengage, hoping things would sort themselves out:

> The insurance company gave me an initial payment of £3000 and they've gone quiet now. I'm not in the right frame of mind to chase them up, to be honest. I don't want to do that. I'll just leave them to it. To be honest, I nearly cracked up over it all – chasing people and trying to get things done … In the end, for my peace of mind if you like, I decided not to go down that route. I'm sure it will work itself out in the end. It might just take a bit longer perhaps. I can't be on the phone every other day saying, 'Where's my money? Where's this? Where's that?' It was just getting too much. I couldn't do it. Perhaps if I was younger, I might be a bit more aggressive about the whole lot. But you know, it's not exactly how I imagined I'd end my working life, is to have these kinds of problems.

Mark explained that by disengaging from this aspect of his recovery, from pursuing compensation from insurers, he was able to diminish his anxiety and protect his peace of mind for a time. In the short term this was a helpful strategy, but if Mark was to continue down this path longer term it might prove problematic if he was to give up completely and refuse to follow up with his claim. Taking some space, in this case, allowed him to work out his insurance at a later date. Likewise, and as noted earlier, Amir briefly disengaged from his clothing business following the riots and all the noise and attention around it for a few weeks, isolating himself and becoming 'depressed' for a time. Shortly thereafter, however, he was able to reengage and to carry on personally and professionally.

Disengagement in the longer term can make entrepreneurs less emotionally attached to their businesses. This was eventually the case with Mark, as discussed at the start of the chapter. Vivek too became more detached. Disappointed and upset about the riots and the damages to his shop, Vivek spoke about withdrawing his labour and decoupling his emotions from his business:

> I love my shop. We laugh. We have fun. We argue. We fight ... These are your people. This is what you do. So, I feel very proud to say it is part of the community. So, why should I ... work for it, and ... 11 years afterwards, [end up] empty handed? We're not making a million pounds. We're just day to day activities. Since 2003, seven years, we didn't even go on holiday. My little girl says, 'Daddy, we have a shop. We have money. We have a passport. Why don't we get on an airplane?' I say, 'Okay darling. From next year, every single year, we go on holiday'. I told her, 'Baby, I promise'. I even use credit card. We will go ... It's just, you know, it changes a lot of things in your life ... this is going to be large.

Two years later, when we spoke again, Vivek said he was going on holiday more with his family and spending more time with them and less time at the business because the crisis taught him that nothing lasts and it's important to enjoy your life:

> You feel like, okay, you're comfortable. You're doing okay. You make enough money to live so your life is okay. But once this happened, you feel like 'What I'm gonna do next day? ... How am I going to pay this? How am I going to do this? How am I going to build?' It's like one day your head was just black – you don't what to do next ... So that is the biggest [thing learned] ... it's

nothing gonna last ... just keep, you know, doing what you do and enjoy yourself.

These examples highlight the complexity of behavioural disengagement as a strategy for managing a crisis, and the pros and cons. For Vivek, there were some advantages to disengagement.

What can we do to protect ourselves more effectively from prolonged behavioural disengagement in a crisis?

We all want to unplug, disengage at times. Sometimes we just want to leave a problem to one side. But if we withdraw for too long, it can increase rather than diminish our stress, making us more vulnerable and less resilient. Protecting ourselves from prolonged behavioural disengagement is key.

To do so, we can begin by asking ourselves questions, like those noted in Table 11.1. Working through the actionable takeaways presented in Box 11.1 will also help keep us on track. The entrepreneurs I studied stopped engaging when they felt like they could exert very little control in a crisis[10] and when they wanted to protect their mental health in the process. However, behavioural disengagement can, in some cases, lead to worse mental health over time. Entrepreneurs and others might benefit, therefore, from taking steps to regain their sense of control. This might be facilitated by utilizing strategies such as 'active confronting' and by developing 'reassuring thoughts'.[11]

Active confronting is about directly and consciously facing a specific stressor, engaging with a stressor head on rather than disengaging with it. This might involve thinking about whether to remove the stressor altogether, if that's a possibility, reducing the negative effects of the stressor, or accepting the stressor. So, practically speaking, if a lack of funding is the main problem you face, active confronting might entail considering additional sources of finance, saving money or working with less. William's pub and live performance venue was forced to close during the pandemic for several months. He did not qualify for a COVID-19 grant and was later compelled to operate under very strict conditions in accordance with government regulations for hospitality. He complained over many diary entries how the government's decision-making was 'frustrating', 'devastating', 'crazy',

Table 11.1: Guiding questions to protect yourself from prolonged behavioural disengagement

Is behavioural disengagement being used as a coping strategy?	• Do I feel there is little I can do about a stressful situation or crisis? Do I feel overwhelmed, not in control and unable to cope? • Have I noticed myself exerting less effort to deal with the situation or crisis or am I withdrawing my effort altogether? Has this withdrawal been temporary or longer term?
How can I protect myself and my business from behavioural disengagement or manage it?	• What challenges stemming from the situation or crisis am I currently dealing with specifically and what are some of ways in which I can resolve them? • Do I have the resources I need to cope with this situation or crisis? If so, can I draw on these resources? If not, can I acquire the necessary resources? • What about this situation or crisis have I been managing well? Am I better off than some?

'difficult' and 'negative'. At the same time, he was very focused on diminishing the negative financial implications for his business by lobbying for more financial support, sourcing funding from different government bodies or arms of government, independently fundraising and generating wider public support in the media. He was also focused on reducing the negative social implications for his customers and performers through regular social media posts and online streaming events.

Developing reassuring thoughts can also help. To reassure ourselves we can reflect on what we've managed to do or have achieved thus far, which involves positive self-talk. We might think about how during a crisis we helped others or resolved certain challenges within our businesses, like finding a new client or source of income, keeping customers engaged, retaining staff, identifying a new supplier or improving our website or venue. Nearly a year and a half after the first lockdown, William told me: 'Despite the pressures applied to the business we remain debt free. We did not take any government loans. We kept control of our finances'. This reassurance might further come from putting things in perspective, reflecting on how the situation isn't that bad or could be worse, or the ways in which we might be better off than some, which relates to positive reappraisal. William said that he and his partner had 'certainly found it challenging, but we are both safe and stronger'.

We can also protect ourselves against prolonged disengagement by engaging in 'active planning'. Devising a concrete strategy and clear steps to tackle the issue can enhance our perceptions of control.[12] In Mark's case, active planning might involve contacting parties who can help, such as the local council or MP, which some but not all entrepreneurs found to be supportive after the riots. It might also entail prompting insurers at specified intervals. For Vivek, it might include planning downtime on weekdays or holiday periods to stop feeling like a more permanent form of disengagement from work is necessary. William appealed to his council to provide support, raised money and created a continuous events programme. More broadly, if the problem we face is how to continue delivering a product or service without a venue, one that is no longer affordable or has been damaged during a crisis, then we might consider setting up in a less permanent location (for example, a pop-up or kiosk), selling online or selling through other partners, businesses or organizations, as some businesses do.

Table 11.2 can help us monitor how we're using these strategies and their effectiveness.

★★★

Table 11.2: A reengagement log

Stressor examples	Active confronting (directly and consciously engaging with a stressor)	Reassuring thoughts (reflecting on what you've achieved, keeping perspective)	Active planning (developing a strategy, a plan and steps for addressing the stressor)	How did actions to reengage with the stressor make me think or feel?

In short, behavioural disengagement can be problematic, especially when employed longer term. Taking steps to regain a sense of perceived control might limit its harmful effects. In the concluding chapter, I consolidate the lessons we've learned throughout the different chapters. I highlight the steps you can take for carrying out your own resilience work and for strengthening your resilience.

> **Box 11.1: Actionable takeaways for protecting yourself against behavioural disengagement**
>
> - Practice positive disengagement: Be intentional about disengaging. Regularly taking breaks, getting enough rest, being creative and doing other things, even if only briefly, will help you maintain energy levels and stop you from feeling there's no other option but to withdraw. Practice will also give you permission, even in a crisis, to view these other behaviours positively.
> - Focus on the present and on what you can control: When you're feeling overwhelmed, make a list of things you can and cannot control. Break it down and create smaller actionable steps. Directing your attention to what you can control will help you reduce uncertainty.
> - Reflect on your goals and values: Think about what you're trying to achieve and what's important to you. Is disengaging in the short term bringing you closer to your goals and is it aligned with your values? What about longer term? If it is, then it might be time to make a move and do something else. If not, take steps to reengage.

Chapter summary

- Behavioural disengagement is a coping strategy that directs attention and behaviour away from a stressor, such as a crisis, and associated negative emotions.
- Behavioural disengagement is more likely when one's coping resources and perceived control over a stressful situation, such as a crisis, is deemed to be limited.
- In the short term, behavioural disengagement might not be harmful and can provide some relief, but if employed longer term it has the potential to increase our distress.

- For entrepreneurs in crisis, behavioural disengagement as a strategy can have mixed results. On the one hand, it can reduce anxiety and shift thoughts and activities to other worthwhile things. On the other hand, it can exacerbate feelings of having little control and serve to distance entrepreneurs from those things they previously valued.
- We can limit the possibility of employing behavioural disengagement in a crisis and/or seek to manage its potentially negative effects by engaging in active confronting, developing reassuring thoughts and through active planning.

PART III

Conclusions

12

The Resilience Work We Can All Do

At the start of the book, I described Sofia's experience of the London riots. Through her story and the stories of other entrepreneurs, the purpose of the book has been to understand more about resilience as a process and to show that, like a muscle or a capability, resilience is something we can develop.

Based on insights from the interviews and weekly diaries of entrepreneurs in crisis, and the different studies I've presented, we've learned that the resilient entrepreneur is the individual who brings their awareness to how they think, feel, and act. It's the individual who adjusts accordingly and in specific ways, including those ways outlined across the different chapters.

Until now, the resilient entrepreneur has been an elusive concept, either overlooked, sidelined by research favouring organizational resilience or tied to certain personality traits. Personality traits, while important, only tell us part of the story.

The resilient entrepreneur engages in 'resilience work': the work we undertake to adjust our attention, thinking, situation and/or resources in ways to reduce the stress created by adversity or minimize the likelihood of its occurrence. Figure 12.1 captures these elements of resilience work. When the strategies involved in resilience work are applied consciously and actively, they serve as practices that assist individuals in difficult periods.

Distraction, expectation management, positive self-talk, positive reappraisal, situation selection and modification, offsetting

Figure 12.1: Resilience work

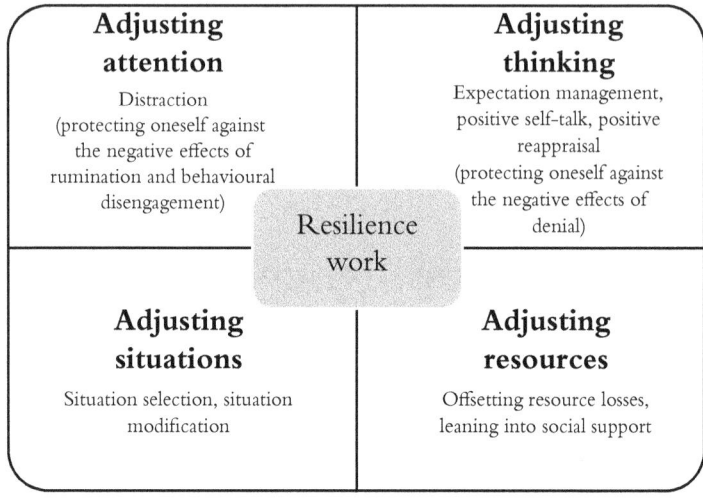

resource losses and leaning into social support, are all strategies that can enhance resilience. Denial, rumination and behavioural disengagement are strategies that can be useful to a limited extent but run the risk of compromising resilience and increasing vulnerability. Steps should be taken, as a result, to protect ourselves from the potentially negative effects of the latter group of strategies. This includes engaging in denial busting practices, ensuring rumination is managed or more deliberate in nature and that disengagement is temporary.

What lessons on resilience work we can take away from the resilient entrepreneur?

There are six key lessons we can all learn from the resilient entrepreneur. Reflecting on these lessons that follow can help you navigate your own crisis and prepare better for the next crisis. We can define a crisis, once again, as any adverse event that has the potential to create significant stress for the individual, overwhelm their ability to cope and disrupt their wellbeing. A crisis can be objectively big, or smaller and more personal in nature. The book has provided examples of both.

Lesson 1: Resilience work necessitates making adjustments

During or following a crisis, we need to adjust. We have learned from entrepreneurs in crisis that to minimize distress and be more resilient, adjustments can be made to: (a) the mental attention we devote to a crisis (attention-led adjustments), (b) the thoughts we hold about a crisis (thought-led adjustments), (c) the situations or features of situations in or around a crisis (situation-led adjustments) and (d) the resources we have available for a crisis (resource-led adjustments).

Attention-led adjustments are about where we direct our attention in a crisis. This can include redirecting our attention away from a crisis or our response to the crisis to other activities such as exercise or social events, which can give us the mental and emotional space we need to gain perspective and approach the crisis as something that can be managed. This is something Anthony did when, in response to the London riots which burned down his business, he temporarily directed his attention to his charity which brought him a lot of joy and purpose.

Thought-led adjustments are about shifting our beliefs or expectations about a crisis or certain aspects of a crisis. They can alter our views about how well we are managing in a crisis or alter the meaning we attach to a crisis. An entrepreneur might expect, for instance, to receive funding in a crisis or for the negative effects of a crisis on their business to be resolved quickly. Such positive expectation management can serve to diminish anxiety initially but also stop us from taking the kind of action that can prepare us if, for instance, funding is not forthcoming or the crisis does not end quickly. For these reasons, tempering positive expectations with low expectations might be useful, compelling us to think more about alternative sources of funding or the longer-term effects of a crisis, helping us minimize the anxiety experienced in the long run.

While thought-led adjustments and attention-led adjustments might appear similar at first glance, they do differ. That is, while thinking-led adjustments can include altering our thoughts about funding (for example, I believe that I will/will not receive funding), attention-led adjustments might alter how much mental attention we devote to funding or the situation around it (for example, thinking more/less about funding). In each case, whether the strategy is attention-led, thought-led, situation-led or resource-led, it will have implications for our cognitions, emotions and behaviours.

When we engage in expectation management, for instance, the focus is on our cognitions, our thought processes, but expectation management also has implications for the emotions we experience and our behaviours. For example, Sam believed that he would receive compensation relatively quickly following the London riots. This made him feel better in the medium term. When the money came much later and was far less than he expected, he felt worse and his plans for rebuilding were delayed. When we use distraction, we are attending to the non-emotional aspects of a crisis or to events or activities outside of the crisis, which in turn shifts our emotions and behaviours. Further, when we engage in the distraction, this can involve certain actions like watching a film or making dinner. Thus, distraction can help to shift our attention in the short term.

Lesson 2: Resilience work requires adjusting the environment

In a crisis we can adjust our internal environment, what goes on inside our heads. We can also adjust our external environment, what goes on around us. Attention-led and thought-led strategies tend to fall into the former camp, while situation- and resource-led strategies often come under the latter (with some exceptions as certain personal resources might be more internal in nature). This gives us some alternatives as to how we can work towards resilience and maintain healthy functioning in or following a crisis, as well as insights into the resilience work needed.

Whether we adjust our internal environment, external environment or both, depends. Some of us might be more prone to experiencing intense emotions and be less able to manage our emotions. For these individuals, situation-led strategies (that is, situation selection and modification) and resource-led strategies (that is, offsetting resource losses and leaning into social support) might be more attractive options and yield better results initially. In some instances, distraction might involve adjusting both our internal and external environment, adjusting the latter to achieve the former. For example, going for a walk might distract us from work but it can also help us process events and achieve some clarity.

It is also likely that even in cases where adjusting the external environment is important and can have positive effects, for example in the case of building up resources like financial or social support, this strategy might require some internal work as well, such as feeling deserving of such support. In some instances, it might also be the case that adjusting our external environment is not possible or is difficult to do so because we have limited control over where we work and how (for example, working arrangements might not be flexible). Similarly, it might be difficult where the adjustment is not immediate and takes time to manifest, as is the case in offsetting resource losses.

Lesson 3: Resilience work is about acceptance and working through negative emotions

We learned that when entrepreneurs in crisis employ strategies of denial, rumination, and behavioural disengagement, resilience might be compromised and such strategies can make them more vulnerable in the long term. Nevertheless, some strategies linked to resilience, including those identified from the accounts of entrepreneurs in crisis, may be healthier than others. In some cases, distraction and situation selection have in common the desire to elude a negative emotional experience and for this reason may be regarded as avoidant coping strategies.[1] Research suggests that avoidant coping strategies are less effective at reducing distress than those strategies based on acceptance.[2]

Acceptance-based coping strategies are grounded in openness, mindfulness and a willingness to embrace negative experiences, and, unlike avoidant strategies, they often involve deliberate actions to heighten contact with, or remove barriers to, positive experiences.[3] Acceptance has been linked to positive outcomes, including improved mental health, wellbeing and personal effectiveness in clinical and workplace studies.[4] Acceptance is about being able to identify our feelings, bringing our awareness to them; expressing rather them suppressing them.[5]

With the exception of avoidance-based distraction with a capital 'D' and, in some cases, situation selection, all of the strategies linked to resilience that we have discussed are underpinned by acceptance. That is, while there were challenges ensuing from the crisis and negative emotions associated with the crisis, these negative emotions were still acknowledged by entrepreneurs, as was the need to process them. At the same time, for my entrepreneurs in crisis, the decision to accept or avoid these emotions was not necessarily a conscious one. By drawing awareness to the different strategies and their intended benefits, a more conscious application of them may not only be optimal but also possible. This is not to suggest, however, that avoidant coping strategies should be dismissed altogether but rather we should ensure that they are deliberately applied in the short term, which can be useful.

Lesson 4: Resilience work can create relief in a crisis via different mechanisms

The strategies we use to adjust in a crisis can provide us with some relief via different mechanisms – that is, either by navigating uncertainty, making realistic assessments, changing or modifying the meaning we attribute to the crisis, offsetting resource losses with gains, acquiring or leveraging social support and by interrupting or subverting negative emotions.

To illustrate, expectation management provides relief by helping us navigate uncertainty. For entrepreneurs in crisis, uncertainty may relate to whether or when the crisis will end or reoccur, when they will get back on their feet or when they will receive support. Expectation management can also allow us to deal with potentially negative outcomes. For example, coming to grips with the notion that the crisis may not end for some time or is likely to reoccur in the future, that I won't get back on my feet in the same way as before and I won't receive support at all or for some time. By expecting that a crisis might go on for some time, as in the case of the pandemic, we can feel more in control and exert more control over what comes next, like the entrepreneurs here.

Positive self-talk, alternatively, provides relief by making realistic assessments of the present, seeing potential opportunities in a crisis and by making us feel more efficacious; in turn, able to manage a crisis. For example, early on in the first lockdown in the pandemic, Brian reflected on his positive performance as the CEO of his company, feeling that he had proved himself to be a caring leader, able to build a great culture and rise to the challenges the crisis imposed on his business and team. In this way, Brian was able to alleviate some of the stress he may have felt regarding the new demands the crisis was imposing on him and his business and seeing them as a way to make positive changes in the business. Positive reappraisal provides relief by changing the meanings we associate with a crisis to become more positive. I found that this occurred when entrepreneurs in crisis reflected on other crisis victims, other events in their lives, the support they had received or growth attained over or following a crisis.

Relief can also be provided by acquiring or leveraging resources, or by offsetting resource losses with gains. In the latter case, resource substitution was one way in which entrepreneurs were able to offset or limit their losses. Mark, who was affected by the London riots, was able to partly replace his loss of stock and the limited support provided by insurers with money from the High Street Fund, an independent charity. He also had the support of other business owners in his community with whom he connected frequently, which he said really helped.

Alternatively, some strategies can provide relief by interrupting our negative emotions or by subverting negative emotions before they occur. This was the case with distraction, situation selection and situation modification. For example, after the first lockdown during the pandemic, Liam spoke about how taking a holiday brought him some comfort and, further, gave him the strength to carry on, to manage his rising workload. Through these different mechanisms some relief from negative stress was created, enabling entrepreneurs in crisis to regain a sense of control and minimize their negative emotions, replacing them in some cases with positive emotions.

Lesson 5: Resilience work can help manage stress in a crisis and create stress resistance

Some of the strategies involved in resilience work carry more benefits than others, by either reducing stress and/or providing stress resistance. We learned that where entrepreneurs in crisis feel they can manage a situation, stress is reduced. Where they can apply how they've managed to other situations, to other aspects of the crisis or beyond, they can create a kind of stress resistance, which can serve as a protective factor. This might be especially valuable in a crisis.

Positive self-talk, offsetting resource losses and leaning into social support can serve not only to help us manage stress, but can also enhance our stress resistance. Positive self-talk, for example, enables us to engage in problem solving by interpreting a stressor, in this case a crisis, as a challenge rather than a threat. At the same time, positive self-talk can provide stress resistance when, as a form of constructive thinking, it can be applied beyond a crisis and when it helps us achieve our greater goals.[6] Offsetting resource losses and leaning into social support can also reduce stress by creating positive emotions that, in turn, diminish or replace negative emotions. These strategies can further create stress resistance in that, by using new or existing resources, we are able to acquire further resources, emphasising the link between resource gains and resilience.[7] As we learned, when we have resources (for example, material support, emotional support), we are less likely to be negatively affected by adverse events and to experience physical and mental distress, and more likely to problem solve and acquire more resources if, and when, needed.

Following the London riots, Mark and Jack spoke about how money from the High Street Fund helped them counter some of the negative emotions they felt towards insurers. Although those negative feelings didn't dissipate entirely, they were lessened. Similarly, Mark's prior connection with other local business owners protected him somewhat from the stresses imposed by insurers following the London riots. Dylan, Anthony and Vivek not only received emotional support from members of their communities after the riots, including other business owners, but also material support in the form of storage space, materials and/or fundraising.

Lesson 6: Acceptance-based strategies are more effective long term than avoidance-based ones

There are differences in terms of how effective the strategies might be over time. Consistent with previous research, the research presented in this book shows that distraction and situation selection are more effective short term, better at disrupting negative emotions. However, neither strategy when used as a form of avoidance appears to evade or help to process negative emotions altogether, which may remain, following an intervention. As such, distraction and situation selection strategies in these circumstances offer a temporary reprieve but should not be relied on long term and combined with other strategies.

During the pandemic, Joseph's distraction strategies (for example, smoking weed or watching television) initially offered him a break from his negative emotions but ultimately showed that avoidance does not help to alleviate such emotions for the long term. Similarly, as the situation changed and Brian had to go back into work, he could no longer avoid the stress instigated by some anxious staff members who were concerned about financial security and health risks, making this strategy limited in duration. He soon discovered another strategy, situation modification, which was more effective longer term and involved carefully scheduling when he met with certain individuals throughout the day. In this way he was still experiencing negative emotions but learning to process and consciously counter these with positive emotions brought about by different members of staff.

The benefits of expectation management can also be short term or more enduring than distraction and, in some cases, situation selection, more effective in the medium-term, as the examples above would suggest. This might vary somewhat according to the length of the waiting period, the expectation strategy selected and when it is applied. The remaining strategies may be effective longer term. This might be because they require continual practice. For example, building personal, economic and social resources can help entrepreneurs navigate through a crisis and experience less stress in the process. Similarly, positive self-talk is not something you do once to be effective, as a one-off intervention, nor is positive reappraisal. Both strategies necessitate sensemaking, reflection, and time to cultivate. These features are also, in part, what makes these strategies protective factors and forms of stress resistance.

Choosing the right strategy for you

So, when and how can you apply these strategies to your own life and start doing your own resilience work? A crisis can have a long trajectory. Years later, the psychological, physical and practical effects of a crisis might continue. For this reason, it's important to begin thinking about the different strategies available to you early on and seeing them not as those strategies you employ only once or only during or immediately following a crisis, but as something you can practice and utilize over time. Monitoring the effectiveness of these strategies is also critical. This involves some reflection. Ask yourself, how am I applying the strategies? Are they working? It's further the case that you can use more than one strategy at a time or at different times, depending on when and where you need

Table 12.1: Resilience work checklist

Nature of the adjustment	Distraction	Expectation management	Positive self-talk	Positive reappraisal	Situation selection	Situation modification	Offsetting resource losses	Leaning into social support
Adjust my thoughts		•	•	•				
Adjust my attention	•							
Adjust my situation					•	•		
Adjust my resources							•	•
Change my internal environment	•	•		•			•	•
Change my external environment					•	•	•	•
Manage stress	•	•	•	•	•	•	•	•
Create stress resistance	•		•					
Avoid a stressor	•				•			
Accept and process a stressor	•	•	•	•		•		•
Do something that might be effective short term	•	•			•			
Do something that might be effective longer term			•	•		•	•	•

Table 12.2: Resilience work strategy overview and application

Strategy	Some examples	When is it effective?	How long is it effective?	How can I apply it?
Distraction	Socializing, cooking, exercising, playing a game, learning a new skill	At tense junctures, when the distraction is more cognitively demanding/absorbing, when it is introduced before the stressor has been fully appraised, when it is combined with an attitude of acceptance, when it's applied short term.	Mostly short term	
Expectation management	Thinking you may succeed here but if you don't your plan is to …	When uncertainty is high and control is low, when waiting for important or difficult news, when it is applied at the beginning or end of a waiting period, when optimism is cautious in the case of positive expectations.	Depends on the length of the waiting period, but mostly short or medium term	
Positive self-talk	Thinking you are prepared, you can manage, you are especially good at …	When encountering stressful situations or working in a particularly stressful profession/job, when assessments of the situation/stressor are realistic and focused on the present.	Short, medium and longer term	

(continued)

Table 12.2: Resilience work strategy overview and application (continued)

Strategy	Some examples	When is it effective?	How long is it effective?	How can I apply it?
Positive reappraisal	Thinking/reframing along the lines of …. You're better off than others affected, this event is not as problematic as other things you've encountered, you feel supported, you've grown personally or professionally from this.	When there is uncertainty, when situations are not easily defined and some sensemaking is required, sometime after the onset of a crisis, when it's applied longer term.	Longer term	
Situation selection	Going out with friends or avoiding a particular social encounter, attending an uplifting event or avoiding a difficult situation, engaging in an interesting or enjoyable task or setting a task aside.	Before negative emotions surface, when adjustments to the situation can be made, when you can consider and plan how you might feel in the future, when you're the kind of person that might find it difficult to regulate your emotions, when you experience intense emotions.	Mostly short term	

Table 12.2: Resilience work strategy overview and application (continued)

Strategy	Some examples	When is it effective?	How long is it effective?	How can I apply it?
Situation modification	Incorporating more breaks into your day, doing something nice before and/or after difficult meetings, events, encounters.	Before negative emotions surface, when a less cognitively demanding strategy is preferred, when you have some control over manipulating the features of the external environment.	Short, medium and longer term, depending on the situation	
Offsetting resource losses	Developing new skills or connections, using emotional support to compensate for other kind of losses such as financial losses.	When resources are limited or lost quickly, when there is an openness and a need for acquiring new resources, when lost resources can be replaced or substituted.	Medium to longer term	
Leaning into social support	Asking for or embracing support from your team, your family and friends, your professional network and members of your industry, and your community.	When you need information or guidance, when you need access to goods and services or help resolving material concerns, when you need emotional support, reassurance and the motivation to carry on.	Short, medium and longer term	

them. This gives you different options in a crisis for strengthening your resilience.

Brian, for instance, adjusted both his thinking and his situation during the COVID-19 pandemic. In the former case, he was cautiously optimistic about his expectations for the future. He was employing positive self-talk to interpret the changes to his business as challenges rather than threats, reminding himself he was able to manage. By adjusting his situation, where he worked after the first lockdown, he was able to regulate his emotions by selecting whether to interact with certain individuals. Later he focused more on when he held certain meetings and with whom.

The next step is to think about what's needed to implement the different strategies. Ask yourself, what adjustments can I make? What do those adjustments look like, practically speaking? What kind of stress relief does each offer? How long might it be effective? Tables 12.1 and 12.2 provide a condensed overview of the strategies entrepreneurs used to build resilience.

In short, you don't have to adopt all these strategies at once. You can road test a few, depending on your needs, preferences, and the situation at hand, and see which work for you.

Final words

As human beings, encountering a crisis seems inevitable. Along these lines we are often told in life, 'It's not what happens to you, but how you react to it that matters' or 'What doesn't kill me makes me stronger'. But knowing just what to do in the face of adversity to move us towards a position of strength, how to be resilient, isn't always clear. Through the research, examples and strategies discussed across the chapters, I hope this book has succeeded in providing some enlightenment.

APPENDIX A

Additional Commentary on the Implications of the Research

For entrepreneurs and business leaders

As I was reflecting on the implications of the research and findings presented throughout the book for entrepreneurs and other business leaders, three immediately came to mind. The first is that a crisis for your business can significantly impact you. Your energy, your resources and your identity are often entwined with that of your business, especially those of you who are small business owners. This knowledge underscores the need to safeguard your health during a crisis and not to focus on the health of the business alone. The pandemic in recent years demonstrated that a crisis can endure and do so with no clear end-date in sight, while the London riots showed us that the aftermath of a crisis can be difficult, and its effects long lasting.

A second implication is that, as an entrepreneur or a business leader, you would benefit from reviewing the different kinds of strategies available to you that might help reduce stress and the negative emotions you may be experiencing, how these strategies might be employed and what role they might play in terms of enabling you to become more resilient. Some of the strategies we've covered within the book you can initiate on your own and will require you to make a small investment of your time and effort (for example, positive self-talk, distraction). Some strategies will mean working more closely with others (for example, institutions, staff, customers) and will demand a greater investment of your time and effort (like offsetting resource losses).

A third implication is that you should be mindful of your choices and those strategies you may be using that can make you more vulnerable and less resilient. Denial, for one, can delay certain emotions or actions that could help you respond to a crisis. Behavioural disengagement can create an emotional detachment between you and your business, especially if prolonged. Thus, the book outlines how you can turn towards strategies that may assist and protect you and away from those that do not.

For stakeholders who work with entrepreneurs and business leaders

The resilience of entrepreneurs in crisis and how entrepreneurs work to build resilience is not solely dependent on what entrepreneurs do alone. Far from it. Instead, resilience may also depend on the actions of different stakeholders; internal stakeholders such as staff, or external stakeholders such as lenders, investors, landlords, suppliers, customers, community members and the like. As such, the research presented throughout this book additionally shines a light on the different kinds of support entrepreneurs require in a crisis, and some of the ways you as a stakeholder might be able to help.

The support of staff and community members might have a vital role to play in terms of helping entrepreneurs reappraise a crisis, and/ or by helping them to offset some of the losses their businesses have experienced, creating positive emotions in turn which can serve to reassure and comfort these individuals, ultimately supporting them to carry on. For staff working with entrepreneurs in crisis this might involve your patience, compassion and, as we've learned, sometimes stepping up and going beyond traditional job roles. For community members, including other business owners, this might include emotional support, creating business opportunities including opportunities for collaboration, practical support and material support. For other kinds of external stakeholders, it might include providing financial support or even financial relief. Check in with entrepreneurs who might be struggling to ascertain what kind of support, if any, would be most helpful to them to ensure that any help you provide is both needed and wanted.

Another implication of the research and findings presented within the book for you as stakeholders is that you may need to collaborate with entrepreneurs to create new working arrangements prior to, during or after a crisis. This might include looking into ways you can protect the business and the supply chain from potential threats. It might involve modifying the workspace or re-arranging meetings. In turn, these things can serve to reduce the burden on the entrepreneur.

Finally, business advisors, coaches and mentors can familiarize themselves with different tools to support entrepreneurs who might be struggling. This includes working with the guidance, question prompts and exercises within the book; encouraging entrepreneurs to utilize these and to reflect on their effectiveness over time.

For policy makers

Stories from the different entrepreneurs featured suggest that certain institutions not only influence business recovery and survival in a crisis but help safeguard the wellbeing of entrepreneurs. As such, the first implication of the research and findings presented in this book for you as a policy maker is that you have a critical role to play in terms of expediting support and reducing wait times and bureaucracy when and where possible. Policies should minimize rather than add to the uncertainty of a crisis, and alleviate rather than elevate the strain on entrepreneurs and business leaders. In the UK, the COVID-19 pandemic and London riots highlighted mixed examples of government support.

In the case of COVID-19, the furlough scheme, which was designed to protect jobs and saw the government paying 80% of employees' wages for hours they were unable to work, was helpful to the vast majority of businesses. However, decisions made to implement or extend the furlough scheme were often imposed at the last minute, as were changes in COVID-19 regulations, adding to the stress of entrepreneurs and other business leaders, especially those working in customer-facing sectors like hospitality. Some entrepreneurs I spoke to also complained that grant providers were not always responsive to queries, creating delays in the application process. COVID-19 recovery loans were found to be efficient in their delivery, although not available to all businesses.

In the case of the London riots, financial compensation from insurers and the Riot Damages Act of 1886 which again authorized payments from the police fund to individuals whose properties were affected by rioting (later replaced by The Riot Compensation Act of 2016) took up to two years in some cases to be made, according to the reports of some entrepreneurs. In addition, after the riots, not all councils followed similar strategies in terms of providing financial or practical support to businesses, or even advice, creating more stress for some. It may be that in the UK some lessons were learned from the London riots and applied to the COVID-19 pandemic. Continuing down this trajectory, we must learn from the pandemic and responses to such in different parts of the world, and what was done effectively and what was not.

As policy makers, you should consider the trade-offs of different support schemes over time. For example, some entrepreneurs were concerned about paying back COVID-19 recovery loans while the economy had yet to recover. Others said that while grants were appreciated, their tax bills rose.

As policy makers, and depending on the scale of the crisis, you can create crisis packs or set up hotlines to help entrepreneurs and business leaders through a crisis. As policy makers you can also work with mental health organizations, including charities to ensure that the kind of support you provide is aligned not only with the needs of businesses, but with the individuals running those businesses as well. Moreover, working with these organizations, as policy makers you can design interventions that provide additional mentoring or coaching for individual entrepreneurs, or entrepreneurs running certain kinds of businesses, or within certain communities or sectors who might be particularly vulnerable to a crisis, to support them through a major crisis or even a more minor one. For example, during the pandemic, entrepreneurs working in the hospitality, tourism, leisure and the arts and cultural industries, were quite negatively affected. Specific interventions can be drafted to help entrepreneurs in crisis offset resource losses and lean into social support, or to encourage entrepreneurs to implement other strategies discussed within the book.

Finally, we've learned that your presence as policy makers is important in a crisis. Reaching out to struggling entrepreneurs, making them feel heard and valued can make a difference.

For family and friends

We've learned throughout the book that our networks can serve as healthy forms of distraction, play a role in terms of how we might reframe a difficult situation to uncover its value, as in positive reappraisal, help us remember which situations make us feel good and which make us feel bad, support us, substitute for lost resources or even protect us from denial and rumination. The family and friends of entrepreneurs have an especially important role to play in strengthening resilience.

As a family member or friend, a key implication of the research and findings presented in the book is that you should work together with entrepreneurs to identify the kinds of strategies they may be using already to adjust to a crisis, what may or may not be working and why, and consider what these individuals can do to minimize the distress they may be experiencing. As family and friends, you can more fully appreciate, from the examples provided in the book, the kind of involvement that may be required to implement certain strategies that support resilience and be mindful of those strategies that might make entrepreneurs more vulnerable and less resilient. As family and friends, you can also better understand the nature and level of strain entrepreneurs may be under and may be experiencing, and the additional support they may require from you in turn. Finally, and as discussed, many of the strategies featured in the book might benefit from your input.

APPENDIX B

Additional Commentary for Studying Entrepreneurs in Crisis and Resilience

I also wanted to include some final thoughts for those who might be interested in further researching entrepreneurs in crisis and resilience, discussing ways in which research could be extended.

The contributions of this research

At the time of writing, I see the contributions of the research undertaken and presented in this book as being three-fold, which include: (a) identifying strategies that enable entrepreneurs in a crisis to strengthen their resilience and consolidating these into different kinds of adjustments that comprise resilience work, (b) introducing concepts from other fields to the areas of crisis management and entrepreneurship and (c) consolidating some of the existing research on the topic of individual resilience and adversity and extending it with new stories and insights from entrepreneurs in crisis.

Identifying strategies that enable entrepreneurs in a crisis to strengthen their resilience and consolidating these into different kinds of adjustments that comprise resilience work
For entrepreneurs in crisis, the road to recovery can be a lonely one. A crisis can be especially difficult for entrepreneurs and take its toll on their wellbeing. The research presented in this book aims in part to

flag to these individuals some of the strategies that their counterparts have employed and with some degree of success to minimize the stresses involved in managing a crisis.

Prior research on entrepreneurship and crisis management tends to focus mostly on organizational-level responses to a crisis and is written up in academic journals, many of which are inaccessible to those it affects, practically or otherwise. The research presented across the book is unique in that it is concerned with what entrepreneurs and business leaders can do to be more resilient during, following or even in anticipation of a crisis. It frames these strategies or adjustments to thoughts, feelings and behaviours as being attention-led, thought-led, situation-led and resource-led and collectively refers to them as resilience work. It provides entrepreneurs and business leaders with a number of ways in which they can initiate and apply strategies. It also notes that some strategies may be more effective than others.

Introducing concepts from other fields to the areas of crisis management and entrepreneurship

The importance of resources to entrepreneurs and their businesses, especially in times of crisis, is something frequently discussed in the entrepreneurship literature by myself,[1] Elina Meliou[2] and others. Resources feature heavily in two of the strategies adopted by the entrepreneurs in crisis I studied: offsetting resource losses, and leaning into social support. Much less well understood to those who study entrepreneurship or crisis management, however, is the role that other factors play in building resilience, namely those that make up the remaining contents of this book, including expectation management, positive self-talk or different forms of emotion regulation, namely distraction, positive reappraisal, situation selection and situation modification. Many of these concepts and some of the strategies that stem from such, have been developed and tested in the field of psychology. Some have also featured within sports, medicine and health studies more broadly.

While emotion regulation has been examined within the field of entrepreneurship around topics such as new venture survival, new venture teams, business failure and performance by the likes of De Cock, Denoo and Clarysse,[3] Fang He,[4] Li,[5] Sirén[6] and all their collaborators, its application to the study of resilience and crisis management was, at the time of writing this book, very limited. It is interesting to note that while all strategies were intended to minimize negative emotions and reduce stress, only four of the eight are documented forms of emotion regulation – that is, positive reappraisal, distraction, situation selection and situation modification. I also found only a handful of studies that examined the application and effects of certain strategies such as positive reappraisal and distraction in a crisis, and no studies that examined situation selection and situation modification in a crisis. Thus, the current research on entrepreneurs in crisis aims to expand our understanding of these concepts and provide a deeper appreciation of their implications.

Consolidating research on the topic of individual resilience and adversity and extending it

For the purposes of this book, I have drawn from a wide range of examples outside of entrepreneurship to understand more about the linkages between individual resilience and adversity, from studies on crisis workers to individuals dealing with personal crises such as illness or, more so, environmental crises such as natural disasters. From these studies we have learned that the strategies featured in this book to strengthen resilience can have positive effects and make individuals more resilient when dealing with adversity. For example, a high level of social support has been linked to the 'absence' of depression, PTSD and substance abuse, often used as proxies for resilience following a crisis.[7] Distraction as a short-term strategy and positive reappraisal as a long-term strategy have both been linked to better psychological health and wellbeing in a crisis, as well as posttraumatic growth, also a feature of resilience, in studies carried out by Wlodarczyk[8] and Felix.[9] Positive self-talk has been found to help individuals affected by a crisis feel more confident about managing what comes next.[10] More optimistic expectation management has also been shown to be associated with lower levels of distress during a period of waiting for news, but distress might still be high at the beginning and end.[11] Situation selection can stop negative emotions from arising, while situation modification has been associated with learning and lower levels of psychopathology.[12]

The empirical research on entrepreneurs in crisis featured in the book adds to this body of work suggesting that, according to the accounts and experiences of the individuals involved, the strategies entrepreneurs employed minimized distress in the short, medium or long term and allowed them to carry on. In some cases, these entrepreneurs were able to continue with their work because of the reassurance and further motivation they received. In other cases, the strategies allowed them to focus on what was most important or interrupted and reduced negative emotions.

Future research

For academics, it is my hope that the research and findings presented in this book have opened up new avenues for exploration, either independently or altogether. Research on expectation management, positive self-talk/constructive thinking and the different forms of emotion regulation highlighted in the book (that is, positive reappraisal, distraction, situation selection and modification), have been, until now, largely unexplored as they relate to entrepreneurs in crisis and within the field of entrepreneurship more broadly. With the exception of positive self-talk/constructive thinking, research on crisis management has also not explored these areas in much detail. Therefore, future research might ask what factors make positive reappraisal in a crisis more or less likely (for example, age/gender/background of the entrepreneur, extent of damages and so on)? Are certain kinds of entrepreneurs or businesses more or less likely to use acceptance strategies, approach or avoidance strategies in a crisis? How effective is mentoring during and following a crisis in terms of being able to generate constructive thinking and positive reappraisal in the entrepreneurs or business leaders affected?

In the latter case, regarding entrepreneurship research more broadly, future studies might examine how expectation management impacts on those entrepreneurs who seek out funding or are awaiting funding decisions, or whether positive self-talk/constructive thinking can help entrepreneurs manage certain challenges, different forms of rejection or their own feelings and behaviours at different stages of business development, from start-up to growth. Future research might consider, in addition, whether distraction and situation modification can allow entrepreneurs to better balance their workloads or the daily stresses they might encounter, and how or in what ways might this manifest. Future research might further explore how entrepreneurs within or outside of crisis situations manage a number of uncertainties at the same time and how this shapes expectation management, and associated feelings and behaviours.

There is also room to explore other strategies that might enable entrepreneurs to be more resilient in a crisis, those that did not constitute the focus of this book but that might be no less important. This might include, but is not limited to, how quickly entrepreneurs in crisis act. The strategies highlighted in this book, while valuable and useful to some, are by no means exhaustive.

Finally, future research should examine further the recommendations proposed at the end of Chapters 2–11 as possible interventions for entrepreneurs in crisis.

Notes

Introduction

1. Stokes, D., Wilson, N. and Mador, M. (2010) *Entrepreneurship*, Boston: Cengage Learning.
2. Pearson, C.M. and Clair, J.A. (1998) 'Reframing crisis management', *Academy of Management Review*, 23: 59–76.
3. Auerbach, S. and Kilmann, P. (1997) 'Crisis intervention: A review of outcome research', *Psychological Bulletin*, 84: 1189–1217.
4. Everly, Jr., G.S. and Mitchell, J.T. (1999) *Critical Incident Stress Management (CISM): A New Era and Standard of Care in Crisis Intervention* (2nd Ed.), Ellicott City, MD: Chevron.
5. Shepherd, D.A. and Williams, T. (2020) 'Entrepreneurship responding to adversity: Equilibrating adverse events and disequilibrating persistent adversity', *Organization Theory*, 1(4): 1–25.
6. Harms, P.D., Credé, M., Tynan, M., Leon, M. and Jeung, W. (2017) 'Leadership and stress: A meta-analytic review', *The Leadership Quarterly*, 28(1): 178–194.
7. OECD. (2002) *Small Business and Entrepreneurship*, OECD Economic Surveys: Russian Federation, February: 74–103.
8. Reading the Riots (2012) Reading the riots: Investigating England's summer of disorder. The Guardian and the London School of Economics and Political Science, pp 1–40. http://eprints.lse.ac.uk/46297/1/Reading%20the%20riots(published).pdf.
9. Bridges, L. (2012) 'Four days in August: The UK riots', *Race Class*, 54(1): 1–12.
10. Scott, E. (2020) COVID-19 local alert levels: Three-tier system for England, House of Lords Library UK Parliament [online] 13 October, Available from: https://lordslibrary.parliament.uk/covid-19-local-alert-levels-three-tier-system-for-england/ [Accessed 2 April 2024].
11. Federation of Small Businesses (2023) UK Small Business Statistics, Federation of Small Businesses [online] 8 June, Available from:

https://www.fsb.org.uk/uk-small-business-statistics.html [Accessed 21 June 2024].
12. Smallbone, D., Deakins, D., Battisti, M. and Kitching, J. (2012) 'Small business responses to a major economic downturn: Empirical perspectives from New Zealand and the United Kingdom', *International Small Business Journal*, 30 (7): 754–777.
13. Korber, S. and McNaughton, R.B. (2018) 'Resilience and entrepreneurship: A systematic literature review', *International Journal of Entrepreneurial Behaviour & Research*, 24(7): 1129–1154.
14. Thorgren, S. and Williams, T.A. (2020) 'Staying alive during an unfolding crisis: How SMEs ward off impending disaster', *Journal of Business Venturing Insights*, 14, e00187.
15. Fekete, A., Hufschmidt, G. and Kruse, S. (2014) 'Benefits and challenges of resilience and vulnerability for disaster risk management', *International Journal of Disaster Risk Science*, 5(1): 3–20.
16. Bullough, A. and Renko, M. (2013) 'Entrepreneurial resilience during challenging times', *Business Horizons*, 56(3): 343–350.
17. De Vries, H. and Shields, M. (2006) 'Towards a theory of entrepreneurial resilience: A case study analysis of New Zealand SME owner operators', *New Zealand Journal of Applied Business Research*, 5(1): 33–43.
18. World Economic Forum (2023) Global Risks Report 2023, World Economic Forum [online] 11 January, Available from: https://www.weforum.org/publications/global-risks-report-2023/ [Accessed February 2024].

Chapter 1

1. Bonanno, G.A. (2004) 'Loss, trauma, and human resilience: have we underestimated the human capacity to thrive after extremely aversive events?' *American Psychologist*, 59(1): 20–28.
2. Bonanno, G.A., Papa, A. and O'Neill, K. (2001) 'Loss and human resilience', *Applied and Preventive Psychology*, 10(3): 193–206.
3. Bonanno, G.A. (2004) 'Loss, trauma, and human resilience: have we underestimated the human capacity to thrive after extremely aversive events?' *American Psychologist*, 59(1): 20–28.
4. Mancini, A.D. and Bonanno, G.A. (2009) 'Predictors and parameters of resilience to loss: Toward an individual differences model', *Journal of Personality*, 77(6): 1805–1832.
5. Fletcher, D. and Sarkar, M. (2013) 'Psychological resilience', *European Psychologist*, 18: 12–23.
6. Warchal, J.R. and Graham, L.B. (2011) 'Promoting positive adaptation in adult survivors of natural disasters', *Adultspan Journal*, 10(1): 34–51.

7 Bonanno, G.A., Wortman, C.B. and Nesse, R.M. (2004) 'Prospective patterns of resilience and maladjustment during widowhood', *Psychology and Aging*, 19(2): 260–271.
8 Bonanno, G.A. (2004) 'Loss, trauma, and human resilience: have we underestimated the human capacity to thrive after extremely aversive events?' *American Psychologist*, 59(1): 20–28.
9 Carruthers, C. and Hood, C.D. (2004) 'The power of the positive: Leisure and well-being', *Therapeutic Recreation Journal*, 38(2): 225–245.
10 Bonanno, G.A., Papa, A. and O'Neill, K. (2001) 'Loss and human resilience', *Applied and Preventive Psychology*, 10(3): 193–206.
11 Fredrickson, B.L. and Levenson, R.W. (1998) 'Positive emotions speed recovery from the cardiovascular sequelae of negative emotions', *Cognition & Emotion*, 12(2): 191–220.
12 Keltner, D. and Bonanno, G.A. (1997) 'A study of laughter and dissociation: Distinct correlates of laughter and smiling during bereavement', *Journal of Personality and Social Psychology*, 73(4): 687–702.
13 Lazarus, R.S. (1991) 'Progress on a cognitive-motivational-relational theory of emotion', *American Psychologist*, 46(8): 819–834.
14 Fredrickson B. (2001) 'The role of positive emotions in positive psychology: The broaden-and-build theory of positive emotions', *American Psychologist*, 56: 218–226.
15 Shih, F.J., Turale, S., Lin, Y.S., Gau, M.L., Kao, C.C., Yang, C.Y. and Liao, Y.C. (2009) 'Surviving a life-threatening crisis: Taiwan's nurse leaders' reflections and difficulties fighting the SARS epidemic', *Journal of Clinical Nursing*, 18(24): 3391–3400.
16 Tedeschi, R.G. and Calhoun, L.G. (1996) 'The posttraumatic growth inventory: Measuring the positive legacy of trauma', *Journal of Traumatic Stress*, 9: 455–471.
17 Westphal, M. and Bonanno, G.A. (2007) 'Posttraumatic growth and resilience to trauma: Different sides of the same coin or different coins?' *Applied Psychology*, 56(3): 417–427.
18 Foa, E.B., Hembree, E.A. and Rothbaum, B.O. (2007) *Prolonged Exposure Therapy for PTSD: Emotional Processing of Traumatic Experiences*. New York, NY: Oxford University Press.
19 Goldmann, E. and Galea, S. (2014) 'Mental health consequences of disasters', *Annual Review of Public Health*, 35: 169–183.
20 Foa, E.B., Stein, D.J. and McFarlane, A.C. (2006). 'Symptomatology and psychopathology of mental health problems after disaster', *Journal of Clinical Psychiatry*, 67(Suppl 2): 15–25.
21 Goldmann, E. and Galea, S. (2014) 'Mental health consequences of disasters', *Annual Review of Public Health*, 35: 169–183.

[22] Goldmann, E. and Galea, S. (2014) 'Mental health consequences of disasters', *Annual Review of Public Health*, 35: 169–183.

[23] Norris, F.H., Friedman, M.J., Watson, P.J., Byrne, C.M., Diaz, E. and Kaniasty, K. (2002) '60,000 disaster victims speak: Part I. An empirical review of the empirical literature, 1981—2001', *Psychiatry*, 65(3): 207–239.

[24] Norris, F.H., Tracy, M. and Galea, S. (2009) 'Looking for resilience: Understanding the longitudinal trajectories of responses to stress', *Social Science & Medicine*, 68(12): 2190–2198.

[25] Garmezy, N. (1991) 'Resilience in children's adaptation to negative life events and stressed environments', *Pediatric Annals*, 20(9): 459–466.

[26] Rutter, M. (1990) 'Psychosocial resilience and protective mechanisms', in J. Rolf, A.S. Masten, D. Cicchetti, K.H. Nuechterlein and S. Weintraub (eds), *Risk and Protective Factors in the Development of Psychopathology*, New York: Cambridge University Press, pp 181–214.

[27] Werner, E.E. and Smith, R.S. (1992) *Overcoming the Odds: High Risk Children from Birth to Adulthood*, Ithaca, NY: Cornell University Press.

[28] Rutter, M. (1985) 'Resilience in the face of adversity: Protective factors and resistance to psychiatric disorder', *The British Journal of Psychiatry*, 147(6): 598–611.

[29] Luthar, S.S., Cicchetti, D. and Becker, B. (2000) 'The construct of resilience: A critical evaluation and guidelines for future work', *Child Development*, 71(3): 543–562.

[30] Maunder, R.G., Lancee, W.J., Balderson, K.E., Bennett, J.P., Borgundvaag, B., Evans, S. et al (2006) 'Long-term psychological and occupational effects of providing hospital healthcare during SARS outbreak', *Emerging Infectious Diseases*, 12(12): 1924–1932.

[31] Gabriel, R., Ferrando, L., Cortón, E.S., Mingote, C., García-Camba, E., Liria, A.F. and Galea, S. (2007) 'Psychopathological consequences after a terrorist attack: An epidemiological study among victims, the general population, and police officers', *European Psychiatry*, 22(6): 339–346.

[32] Detyugina, T. and Molitor, D. (2018) 'Does when you die depend on where you live? Evidence from Hurricane Katrina', National Bureau and Economic Research Working Paper Series 24822 [online] 12 June, Available from: https://www.nber.org/bah/2018no4/mortality-impacts-hurricane-katrina [Accessed 3 January 2024].

[33] Tak, S., Driscoll, R., Bernard, B. and West, C. (2007) 'Depressive symptoms among firefighters and related factors after the response to Hurricane Katrina', *Journal of Urban Health*, 84: 153–161.

[34] Trout, D., Nimgade, A., Mueller, C., Hall, R. and Earnest, G.S. (2002) 'Health effects and occupational exposures among office

workers near the World Trade Center disaster site', *Journal of Occupational and Environmental Medicine*, 44(7): 601–605.
35 Luthar, S.S. and Cicchetti, D. (2000) 'The construct of resilience: Implications for interventions and social policies', *Development and Psychopathology*, 12(4): 857–885.
36 Masten, A.S., Best, K.M. and Garmezy, N. (1990) 'Resilience and development: Contributions from the study of children who overcome adversity', *Development and Psychopathology*, 2(4): 425–444.
37 Parks, V., Slack, T., Ramchand, R., Drakeford, L., Finucane, M.L. and Lee, M.R. (2020) 'Fishing households, social support, and depression after the Deepwater Horizon oil spill', *Rural Sociology*, 85(2): 495–518.
38 Bonanno, G.A. (2005) 'Resilience in the face of potential trauma', *Current Directions in Psychological Science*, 14(3): 135–138.
39 Cheng, C. (2001) 'Assessing coping flexibility in real-life and laboratory settings: A multimethod approach', *Journal of Personality and Social Psychology*: 80(5): 814–833.
40 Bonanno, G.A. (2004) 'Loss, trauma, and human resilience: have we underestimated the human capacity to thrive after extremely aversive events?' *American Psychologist*, 59(1): 20–28.
41 Bonanno, G.A. (2004) 'Loss, trauma, and human resilience: have we underestimated the human capacity to thrive after extremely aversive events?' *American Psychologist*, 59(1): 20–28.
42 Tugade, M.M. and Fredrickson, B.L. (2004) 'Resilient individuals use positive emotions to bounce back from negative emotional experiences', *Journal of Personality and Social Psychology*, 86(2): 320–333.
43 Rutter, M. (1985) 'Resilience in the face of adversity: Protective factors and resistance to psychiatric disorder', *The British Journal of Psychiatry*, 147(6): 598–611.
44 Westphal, M. and Bonanno, G.A. (2007) 'Posttraumatic growth and resilience to trauma: Different sides of the same coin or different coins?' *Applied Psychology*, 56(3): 417–427.
45 Gu, Q. and Day, C. (2007) 'Teachers resilience: A necessary condition for effectiveness', *Teaching and Teacher Education*, 23(8): 1302–1316.
46 Kidd, S. and Shahar, G. (2008) 'Resilience in homeless youth: The key role of self-esteem', *American Journal of Orthopsychiatry*, 78(2): 163–172.
47 Rajan, A.M., Srikrishna, G. and Romate, J. (2018) 'Resilience and locus of control of parents having a child with intellectual disability', *Journal of Developmental and Physical Disabilities*, 30: 297–306.
48 Leana, C.R. and Feldman, D.C. (1994) 'The psychology of job loss', *Research in Personnel and Human Resources Management*, 12: 271–302.

49 Oshio, A., Taku, K., Hirano, M. and Saeed, G. (2018) 'Resilience and big five personality traits: A meta-analysis', *Personality and Individual Differences*, 127: 54–60.

50 Moran, P.B. and Eckenrode, J. (1992) 'Protective personality characteristics among adolescent victims of maltreatment', *Child Abuse & Neglect*, 16(5): 743–754.

51 Bonanno, G.A., Wortman, C.B., Lehman, D.R., Tweed, R.G., Haring, M., Sonnega, J. and Nesse, R.M. (2002) 'Resilience to loss and chronic grief: A prospective study from preloss to 18-months post loss', *Journal of Personality and Social Psychology*, 83(5): 1150–1164.

52 Walsh, F. (1998) *Strengthening Family Resilience*, New York: Guilford Press.

53 Masten, A.S. (2012) 'Resilience in children: Vintage Rutter and beyond', in P.C. Quinn and A. Slater (eds) *Developmental Psychology: Revisiting the Classic Studies*, London: SAGE, pp 204–221.

54 Van Breda, A.D. (2018) 'Resilience of vulnerable students transitioning into a South African university', *Higher Education*, 75: 1109–1124.

55 Richardson, G.E. (2002) 'The metatheory of resilience and resiliency', *Journal of Clinical Psychology*, 58(3): 307–321.

56 Richardson, G.E., Neiger, B., Jensen, S. and Kumpfer, K. (1990) 'The resiliency model', *Health Education*, 21: 33–39.

57 Norris, F. and Wind, L. (2009) 'The experience of disaster: Trauma, loss, adversities, and community effects', in Y. Neria, S. Galea, and F. Norris (eds) *Mental Health and Disasters*, Cambridge: Cambridge University Press, pp 29–44.

58 Bonanno, G.A. and Diminich, E.D. (2013) 'Annual research review: Positive adjustment to adversity – trajectories of minimal-impact resilience and emergent resilience', *Journal of Child Psychology and Psychiatry*, 54(4): 378–401.

59 Van Breda, A.D. (2018) 'Resilience of vulnerable students transitioning into a South African university', *Higher Education*, 75: 1109–1124.

60 Egeland, B., Carlson, E. and Sroufe, L.A. (1993) 'Resilience as process', *Development and Psychopathology*, 5(4): 517–528.

61 Healy, M. (2014) 'The resilient child: Can your child bounce back from failure?' Psychology Today, [online] 10 July, Available from: https://www.psychologytoday.com/gb/blog/creative-development/201407/the-resilient-child [Accessed July 2023].

62 Egeland, B., Carlson, E. and Sroufe, L.A. (1993) 'Resilience as process', *Development and Psychopathology*, 5(4): 517–528.

63 Southwick, F.S., Martini, B.L., Charney, D.S. and Southwick, S.M. (2017) 'Leadership and resilience', in J. Marques and S. Dhiman (eds) *Leadership Today: Practices for Personal and Professional Performance*, New York: Springer, pp 315–333.

[64] Gross, J.J. (1998) 'The emerging field of emotion regulation: An integrative review', *Review of General Psychology*, 2(3): 271–299.
[65] Luthar, S.S., Cicchetti, D. and Becker, B. (2000) 'The construct of resilience: A critical evaluation and guidelines for future work', *Child Development*, 71(3): 543–562.
[66] Luthar, S.S. and Cicchetti, D. (2000) 'The construct of resilience: Implications for interventions and social policies', *Development and Psychopathology*, 12(4): 857–885.
[67] Schinke, R.J., Peterson, C. and Couture, R. (2004) 'A protocol for teaching resilience to high performance athletes', *Journal of Excellence*, 9: 9–18.
[68] Van Breda, A.D. (2018) 'Resilience of vulnerable students transitioning into a South African university', *Higher Education*, 75: 1109–1124.
[69] Hartmann, S., Backmann, J., Newman, A., Brykman, K.M. and Pidduck, R.J. (2022) 'Psychological resilience of entrepreneurs: A review and agenda for future research', *Journal of Small Business Management*, 60(5): 1041–1079.
[70] Korber, S., and McNaughton, R.B. (2018) 'Resilience and entrepreneurship: A systematic literature review,' *International Journal of Entrepreneurial Behaviour & Research*, 24(7): 1129–115.
[71] Hartmann, S., Backmann, J., Newman, A., Brykman, K.M. and Pidduck, R.J. (2022) 'Psychological resilience of entrepreneurs: A review and agenda for future research', *Journal of Small Business Management*, 60(5): 1041–1079.
[72] Doern, R. (2016) 'Entrepreneurship and crisis management: The experiences of small businesses during the London 2011 riots', *International Small Business Journal*, 34(3): 276–302.
[73] Stephens, S., Cunningham, I. and Kabir, Y. (2021) 'Female entrepreneurs in a time of crisis: evidence from Ireland', *International Journal of Gender and Entrepreneurship*, 13(2): 106–120.
[74] Hayward, M.L., Forster, W.R., Sarasvathy, S.D. and Fredrickson, B.L. (2010) 'Beyond hubris: How highly confident entrepreneurs rebound to venture again', *Journal of Business Venturing*, 25(6): 569–578.
[75] Hartmann, S., Backmann, J., Newman, A., Brykman, K.M. and Pidduck, R.J. (2022) 'Psychological resilience of entrepreneurs: A review and agenda for future research', *Journal of Small Business Management*, 60(5): 1041–1079.
[76] Bullough, A. and Renko, M. (2013) 'Entrepreneurial resilience during challenging times', *Business Horizons*, 56(3): 343–350.
[77] Stephan, U., Zbierowski, P., Pérez-Luño, A., Wach, D., Wiklund, J., Alba Cabañas, M. et al (2023) 'Act or wait-and-see? Adversity, agility,

and entrepreneur wellbeing across countries during the COVID-19 pandemic', *Entrepreneurship Theory and Practice*, 47(3): 682–723.

Chapter 2

1. Thiruchselvam, R., Blechert, J., Sheppes, G., Rydstrom, A., Gross, J.J. (2011) 'The temporal dynamics of emotion regulation: An EEG study of distraction and reappraisal', *Biological Psychology*, 87(1): 84–92.
2. Derryberry, D. and Rothbart, M.K. (1988) 'Arousal, affect, and attention as components of temperament', *Journal of Personality and Social Psychology*, 55: 958–966.
3. Gross, J.J. (1999) 'Emotion regulation: Past, present, future', *Cognition and Emotion*, 13: 551–573.
4. Kay, S.A. (2016) 'Emotion regulation and resilience: Overlooked connections', *Industrial and Organizational Psychology*, 9(2): 411–415.
5. Van Dillen, L.F. and Koole, S.L. (2007) 'Clearing the mind: A working memory model of distraction from negative mood', *Emotion*, 7: 715–723.
6. Strick, M., Holland, R.W., van Baaren, R.B. and van Knippenberg, A. (2009) 'Finding comfort in a joke: Consolatory effects of humor through cognitive distraction', *Emotion*, 9(4): 574–578.
7. Strick, M., Holland, R.W., van Baaren, R.B. and van Knippenberg, A. (2009) 'Finding comfort in a joke: Consolatory effects of humor through cognitive distraction', *Emotion*, 9(4): 574–578.
8. Pallardy, R. and Rafferty, J.P. (2010) 'Chile earthquake of 2010', *Encyclopaedia Britannica*, [online] 27 February, Available from: www.britannica.com/event/Chile-earthquake-of-2010 [Accessed July 2024].
9. Arbour, M., Murray, K., Arriet, F., Moraga, C. and Vega, M.C. (2011) 'Lessons from the Chilean earthquake: How a human rights framework facilitates disaster response', *Health and Human Rights*, 13: 62.
10. Wlodarczyk, A., Basabe, N., Páez, D., Amutio, A., García, F.E., Reyes, C. and Villagrán, L. (2016) 'Positive effects of communal coping in the aftermath of a collective trauma: The case of the 2010 Chilean earthquake', *European Journal of Education and Psychology*, 9(1): 9–19.
11. Sheppes, G. (2020) 'Transcending the "good & bad" and "here & now" in emotion regulation: Costs and benefits of strategies across regulatory stages', *Advances in Experimental Social Psychology*, 61: 185–236.
12. Gross, J.J. (1998) 'Antecedent- and response-focused emotion regulation: Divergent consequences for experience, expression, and physiology', *Journal of Personality and Social Psychology*, 74: 224–237.

13. Sheppes, G. and Levin, Z. (2013) 'Emotion regulation choice: Selecting between cognitive regulation strategies to control emotion', *Frontiers in Human Neuroscience*, 7: 179.
14. Wolgast, M. and Lundh, L.G. (2017) 'Is distraction an adaptive or maladaptive strategy for emotion regulation? A person-oriented approach', *Journal of Psychopathology and Behavioral Assessment*, 39(1): 117–127.
15. Wolgast, M. and Lundh, L.G. (2017) 'Is distraction an adaptive or maladaptive strategy for emotion regulation? A person-oriented approach', *Journal of Psychopathology and Behavioral Assessment*, 39(1): 117–127.
16. Morrow, J. and Nolen-Hoeksema, S. (1990) 'Effects of responses to depression on the remediation of depressive affect', *Journal of Personality and Social Psychology*, 58: 519–527.
17. Park, R.J., Goodyer, I.M. and Teasdale, J.D. (2004) 'Effects of induced rumination and distraction on mood and overgeneral autobiographical memory in adolescent major depressive disorder and controls', *Journal of Child Psychology and Psychiatry*, 45: 996–1006.
18. Troy, A.S. and Mauss, I.B. (2011) 'Resilience in the face of stress: emotion regulation as a protective factor', in S.M. Southwick, B.T. Litz, D.S. Charney and M.J. Friedman (eds) *Resilience and Mental Health: Challenges Across the Lifespan*, Cambridge, UK: Cambridge University Press, pp 30–44.
19. Felsten, G. (2002) 'Minor stressors and depressed mood: Reactivity is more strongly correlated than total stress', *Stress and Health*, 18: 75–81.
20. Kross, E. and Ayduk, O. (2008) 'Facilitating adaptive emotional analysis: Distinguishing distanced-analysis of depressive experiences from immersed-analysis and distraction', *Personality and Social Psychology Bulletin*, 34: 924–938.
21. Troy, A.S. and Mauss, I.B. (2011) 'Resilience in the face of stress: Emotion regulation as a protective factor', *Resilience and Mental health: Challenges Across the Lifespan*, 1(2): 30–44.

Chapter 3

1. Renn, O. (2008) *Risk Governance: Coping with Uncertainty in a Complex World*, London: Earthscan.
2. Smith, P. (2023) 'Death toll hits 11,000 in Libyan city destroyed by floods', *NBS News*, [online] 24 September, Available from: https://www.nbcnews.com/news/world/libya-floods-death-toll-derna-rcna105001 [Accessed 10 June 2024].

³ Gov.uk (2014) 'UK floods 2014: Government response and recovery' *Gov.uk*, [online] 14 February, Available from: https://www.gov.uk/government/news/uk-floods-2014–government-response [Accessed 11 June 2024].
⁴ Sweeny, K., Reynolds, C., Falkenstein, A., Andrews, S.E. and Dooley, M.D. (2016) 'Two definitions of waiting well', *Emotion*, 16: 129–143.
⁵ Haan, P., Peichl, A., Schrenker, A., Weizsacker, G. and Winter, J. (2022) 'Expectation management of policy leaders: evidence from COVID-19', *Journal of Public Economics*, 209: 104659.
⁶ Howell, J.L. and Sweeny, K. (2020) 'Health behavior during periods of stressful uncertainty: Associations with emotions, cognitions, and expectation management', *Psychology & Health*, 35(2): 1–21.
⁷ Lebel, S., Jakubovits, G., Rosberger, Z., Loiselle, C., Seguin, C., Cornaz, C. et al (2003) 'Waiting for a breast biopsy. Psychosocial consequences and coping strategies', *Journal of Psychosomatic Research*, 55: 437–443.
⁸ Sweeny, K. (2012) 'Tips for waiting well', *Social & Personality Psychology Compass*, 6: 258–269.
⁹ Sweeny, K., Reynolds, C., Falkenstein, A., Andrews, S.E. and Dooley, M.D. (2016) 'Two definitions of waiting well', *Emotion*, 16: 129–143.
¹⁰ Knapp, S., Wilson, M. and Sweeny, K. (2021) 'The role of two emotion regulation tendencies across two waiting periods', *Motivation and Emotion*, 45(2): 211–220.
¹¹ Sweeny, K., Andrews, S.E., Nelson, S.K. and Robbins, M.L. (2015) 'Waiting for a baby: Navigating uncertainty in recollections of trying to conceive', *Social Science & Medicine*, 141: 123–132.
¹² Falkenstein, A., Dooley, M.D. and Sweeny, K. (2020) 'Waiting for health news', in K. Sweeny, M.L. Robbins and L.M. Cohen (eds) *The Wiley Encyclopedia of Health Psychology*, London: William Wiley & Sons Ltd., pp 781–788.
¹³ Wilson, M., Rankin, K., Ludi, D. and Sweeny, K. (2022) 'Emotional, cognitive, and physical well-being during the wait for breast biopsy results', *Psychology & Health*, 1–20.
¹⁴ Wilson, M., Rankin, K., Ludi, D. and Sweeny, K. (2022) 'Emotional, cognitive, and physical well-being during the wait for breast biopsy results', *Psychology & Health*, 1–20.
¹⁵ Sweeny, K. and Howell, J.L. (2017) 'Bracing Later and Coping Better: Benefits of Mindfulness During a Stressful Waiting Period', *Personality and Social Psychology Bulletin*, 43(10): 1399–1414.
¹⁶ Howell, J.L. and Sweeny, K. (2020) 'Health behavior during periods of stressful uncertainty: associations with emotions, cognitions, and expectation management', *Psychology & Health*, 35(10): 1163–1183.

[17] Wilson, M., Rankin, K., Ludi, D. and Sweeny, K. (2022) 'Emotional, cognitive, and physical well-being during the wait for breast biopsy results', *Psychology & Health*, 1–20.
[18] Sweeny, K. (2012) 'Tips for waiting well', *Social & Personality Psychology Compass*, 6: 258–269.
[19] Sweeny, K. and Shepperd, J.A. (2010) 'The costs of optimism and the benefits of pessimism', *Emotion*, 10(5): 750–753.
[20] Sweeny, K. (2012) 'Tips for waiting well', *Social & Personality Psychology Compass*, 6: 258–269.
[21] Sweeny, K. (2012) 'Tips for waiting well', *Social & Personality Psychology Compass*, 6: 258–269.

Chapter 4

[1] Theodorakis, Y., Weinberg, R., Natsis, P., Douma, I. and Kazakas, P. (2000) 'The effects of motivational versus Instructional self-talk on improving motor performance', *The Sport Psychologist*, 14(3): 253–271.
[2] Diaz, R.M. (1992) 'Methodological concerns with private speech', in R.M. Diaz and L.E. Berk (eds) *Private Speech: From Social Interactions to Self-Regulation*, Hillsdale, NJ: Lawrence Erlbaum.
[3] Hackfort, D. and Schwenkmezger, P. (1993) 'Anxiety', in R.N. Singer, M. Murphey and L.K. Tennant (eds), *Handbook of Research on Sport Psychology*, New York: MacMillan, pp 328–364.
[4] Bandura, A. (1986) *Social Foundations of Thought and Action: A Social Cognitive Theory*, Englewood Cliffs, NJ: Prentice Hall.
[5] Hardy, J., Gammage, K. and Hall, C.R. (2001) 'A descriptive study of athlete self-talk', *The Sport Psychologist*, 15(3): 306–318.
[6] Hardy, J. (2006) 'Speaking clearly: A critical review of the self-talk literature', *Psychology of Sport and Exercise*, 7: 81–97.
[7] Hardy, J., Roberts, R. and Hardy, L. (2009) 'Awareness and Motivation to Change Negative Self-Talk', *The Sport Psychologist*, 23: 435–450.
[8] Van Raalte, J.L., Brewer, B.W., Lewis, B.P., Linder, D.E., Wildman, G. and Kozimor, J. (1995) 'Cork! The effects of positive and negative self-talk on dart throwing performance', *Journal of Sport Behavior*, 18: 50–57.
[9] Hamilton, R.A., Scott, D. and MacDougall, M.P. (2007) 'Assessing the effectiveness of self-talk interventions on endurance performance', *Journal of Applied Sport Psychology*, 19: 226–239.
[10] Rogelberg, S.G., Justice, L., Braddy, P.W., Paustian-Underdahl, S.C., Heggestad, E., Shanock, L. et al (2013) 'The executive mind: Leader self-talk, effectiveness, and strain', *Journal of Managerial Psychology*, 28(2): 183–201.

[11] Swanson, H.L. and Kozleski, E.B. (1985). 'Self-talk and handicapped children's academic needs: Applications of cognitive behavior modification', *Techniques: A Journal for Remedial Education and Counseling*, 1: 367–379.

[12] Wetzel, C., Kneebone, R.L., Woloshynowych, M., Nestel, D., Moorthy, K. Kidd, J. et al (2006) 'The effects of stress on surgical performance', *American Journal of Surgery*, 191: 5–10.

[13] Beaton, R., Murphy, S., Williamson, C., Pike, K. and Corneil, W. (1999) 'Coping responses and posttraumatic stress symptomatology in urban fire service personnel', *Journal of Traumatic Stress*, 12: 293–307.

[14] Vernberg E.M., Hambrick, E.P., Cho, B. and Hendrickson, M.L. (2016) 'Positive psychology and disaster: Mental health strategies for working with children and adolescents', *Journal of Clinical Psychology*, 72(12): 1333–1347.

[15] Hardy, J. (2006) 'Speaking clearly: A critical review of the self-talk literature', *Psychology of Sport and Exercise*, 7: 81–97.

[16] Reyes, Z.B. (2016) *Self-talk and resilience: Impact of Performance in 6 Undergraduates*, Thesis: San Francisco State University.

[17] Moran, P.A. (1996) *The Psychology of Concentration in Sport Performance*, East Sussex, UK: Psychology Press Publishers.

[18] Epstein, S. (1998) *Constructive Thinking: The Key to Emotional Intelligence*, Westport, CT: Praeger Publishers.

[19] Evers, W.J., Tomic, W. and Brouwers, A. (2005) 'Constructive thinking and burnout among secondary school teachers', *Social Psychology of Education*, 8: 425–439.

[20] Epstein, S. (1990) 'Cognitive-experiential self-theory', in L.A. Pervin (ed.) *Handbook of Personality: Theory and Research*, New York: Guilford, pp 165–191.

[21] Epstein, S. (1992) 'Coping ability, negative self-evaluation, and overgeneralization: Experiment and theory', *Journal of Personality and Social Psychology*, 62(5): 826–836.

[22] Spirrison, C.L. and Gordy, C.C. (1993) 'The constructive thinking inventory and detecting errors in proofreading', *Perceptual and Motor Skills*, 76(2): 631–634.

[23] Giancola, P.R., Shoal, G.D. and Mezzich, A.C. (2001) 'Constructive thinking, executive functioning, antisocial behavior, and drug use involvement in adolescent females with a substance use disorder', *Experimental and Clinical Psychopharmacology*, 9(2): 215–227.

[24] Werner, E.E. (1984) 'Resilient children', *Young Children*, 40: 68–72.

[25] Westphal, M. and Bonanno, G.A. (2007). 'Posttraumatic growth and resilience to trauma: Different sides of the same coin or different coins?' *Applied Psychology: An International Review*, 56: 417–427.

26 Moore, P.J., Chrabaszcz, J.S., Peterson, R.A., Rohrbeck, C.A., Roemer, E.C. and Mercurio, A.E. (2014) 'Psychological resilience: the impact of affectivity and coping on state anxiety and positive emotions during and after the Washington, DC sniper killings', *Anxiety Stress Coping*, 27: 138–155.

27 Mallak, L.A. (1998). 'Measuring resilience in health care provider organizations', *Health Manpower Management*, 24: 148–152.

28 Meichenbaum, D. (2017) 'Resilience and posttraumatic growth: A constructive narrative perspective', in D. Meichenbaum, *The Evolution of Cognitive Behavior Therapy*, London: Routledge, pp 157–171.

29 J. Hardy, Gammage, K. and Hall, C.R. (2001) 'A descriptive study of athlete self-talk', *The Sport Psychologist*, 15(3): 306–318.

30 Van Raalte, J.L., Brewer, B.W., Lewis, B.P., Linder, D.E., Wildman, G. and Kozimor, J. (1995) 'Cork! The effects of positive and negative self-talk on dart throwing performance', *Journal of Sport Behavior*, 18: 50–57.

31 Calvete, E. and Cardenoso, O. (2002) 'Self-talk in adolescents: Dimensions, states of mind, and psychological maladjustment', *Cognitive Research and Therapy*, 26: 473–485.

32 Karoly, P. and Ruehlman, L.S. (2006). 'Psychological "resilience" and its correlates in chronic pain: Findings from a national community sample', *Pain*, 123: 90–97.

33 Nolen-Hoeksema, S., Parker, L.E. and Larson, J. (1994) 'Ruminative coping with depressed mood following loss', *Journal of Personality and Social Psychology*, 67: 92–104.

34 CNN (2024) 'Tornadoes Fast Facts', *CNN Editorial Research*, [online] 7 February, Available from: https://edition.cnn.com/2013/05/20/us/tornadoes-fast-facts/index.html2013-05-21T17:14:45Znever0.5 [Accessed 3 May 2024].

35 https://education.nationalgeographic.org/resource/tornadoes-and-climate-change/.

36 Wahl-Alexander Z. and Sinelnikov, O.A. (2016) 'Examining instructor's and student's perceptions in an after school program focused on emotional recovery following a natural disaster', *Athens Journal of Sport*, 3(1): 7–24.

37 Wetzel, C., Kneebone, R.L., Woloshynowych, M., Nestel, D., Moorthy, K. Kidd, J. et al (2006) 'The effects of stress on surgical performance', *American Journal of Surgery*, 191: 5–10.

38 Beaton, R., Murphy, S., Williamson, C., Pike, K. and Corneil, W. (1999) 'Coping responses and posttraumatic stress symptomatology in urban fire service personnel', *Journal of Traumatic Stress*, 12: 293–307.

39. Weinberg, R.S. (1988) *The Mental Advantage: Developing your Psychological Skills in Tennis*, Champaign, IL: Human Kinetics.
40. Zinsser, N., Bunker, L. and Williams, J. (2006) 'Cognitive techniques for building confidence and enhancing performance', in J.M. Williams (ed) *Applied Sport Psychology: Personal Growth to Peak Performance* (5th ed), New York: McGraw Hill, pp 349–381.
41. Hardy, J., Roberts, R. and Hardy, L. (2009) 'Awareness and Motivation to Change Negative Self-Talk', *The Sport Psychologist*, 23: 435–450.
42. Zinsser, N., Bunker, L. and Williams, J. (2006) 'Cognitive techniques for building confidence and enhancing performance', in J.M. Williams (ed) *Applied Sport Psychology: Personal Growth to Peak Performance* (5th ed), New York: McGraw Hill, pp 349–381.
43. Hardy, J., Roberts, R. and Hardy, L. (2009) 'Awareness and Motivation to Change Negative Self-Talk', *The Sport Psychologist*, 23: 435–450.
44. Van Raalte, J.L., Brewer, B.W., Lewis, B.P., Linder, D.E., Wildman, G. and Kozimor, J. (1995) 'Cork! The effects of positive and negative self-talk on dart throwing performance', *Journal of Sport Behavior*, 18: 50–57.

Chapter 5

1. Affleck, G. and Tennen, H. (1996) 'Construing benefits from adversity: adaptational significance and dispositional underpinnings', *Journal of Personality*, 64: 899–922.
2. Lazarus, R.S. and Folkman S. (1984) *Stress, Appraisal, and Coping*, New York: Springer.
3. Gross, J.J. (1998) 'Antecedent- and response-focused emotion regulation: Divergent consequences for experience, expression, and physiology', *Journal of Personality and Social Psychology*, 74(1): 224–237.
4. Gross, J.J. (1999) 'Emotion regulation: past, present, future', *Cognition and Emotion*, 13: 551–573.
5. Uusberg, A., Taxer, J.L., Yih, J., Uusberg, H. and Gross, J.J. (2019) 'Reappraising Reappraisal', *Emotion Review*, 11(4), 267–282.
6. Cassidy, T., McLaughlin, M. and Giles, M. (2014) 'Benefit finding in response to general life stress: measurement and correlates', *Health Psychology and Behavioral Medicine*, 2(1): 268–282.
7. Tennen, H. and Affleck, G. (2002) 'Benefit-finding and benefit-reminding', *Handbook of Positive Psychology*, 1: 584–597.
8. Tedeschi, R.G. and Calhoun, L.G. (1995) *Trauma and Transformation: Growing in the Aftermath of Suffering*, Thousand Oaks, CA: Sage.

9. McMillen, J.C., Smith, E.M. and Fisher, R.H. (1997) 'Perceived benefit and mental health after three types of disaster', *Journal of Consulting and Clinical Psychology*, 65(5): 733.
10. Mishra, V. and Shah, H.L. (2018) 'Hydroclimatological perspective of the Kerala flood of 2018', *Journal of the Geological Society of India*, 92: 645–650.
11. Panigrahi, G.S. and Suar, D. (2021) 'Resilience among survivors in the aftermath of the 2018 Kerala flood: An avenue toward recovery', *International Journal of Disaster Risk Reduction*, 64, 102477.
12. McRae, K., Ciesielski, B. and Gross, J.J. (2012) 'Unpacking cognitive reappraisal: goals, tactics, and outcomes', *Emotion*, 12(2): 250–255.
13. Garnefski, N., Kraaij, V. and Spinhoven, P. (2001) 'Negative life events, cognitive emotion regulation and emotional problems', *Personality and Individual Differences*, 30(8): 1311–1327.
14. https://disasterphilanthropy.org/disasters/2019-australian-wildfires/.
15. https://www.theguardian.com/world/2023/nov/09/canada-wildfire-record-climate-crisis.
16. NPR (2023) '2023 was a tragic and bizarre year of wildfires. Will it mark a turning point?' *NPR*, [online] 21 December, Available from: https://www.npr.org/2023/12/21/1220594184/2023-was-a-tragic-and-bizarre-year-of-wildfires-will-it-mark-a-turning-point [Accessed 9 February 2024].
17. Hayes, C., Granville, S. and Vardy, E. (2025) 'How LA fires devastation shaped this year's Grammys', *BBC News*, [online] 2 February, Available from: https://www.bbc.co.uk/news/articles/c4g76x194jpo [Accessed 2 March 2025].
18. Hayes, C. (2025) 'Firefighters battle huge blaze near Los Angeles as winds pick up' *BBC News*, [online] 22 January, Available from: https://www.bbc.co.uk/news/articles/cj029138n4zo [Accessed 2 March 2025].
19. https://www.latimes.com/business/story/2025-01-24/estimated-cost-of-fire-damage-balloons-to-more-than-250-billion.
20. Felix, E., Afifi, T., Kia-Keating, M., Brown, L., Afifi, W. and Reyes, G. (2015) 'Family functioning and posttraumatic growth among parents and youth following wildfire disasters', *American Journal of Orthopsychiatry*, 85(2), 191–200.
21. Garnefski, N., Kraaij, V. and Spinhoven, P. (2001) 'Negative life events, cognitive emotion regulation and emotional problems', *Personality and Individual Differences*, 30(8): 1311–1327.
22. Raio, C.M., Orederu, T.A., Palazzolo, L., Shurick, A.A. and Phelps, E.A. (2013) 'Cognitive emotion regulation fails the stress test', *Proceedings of the National Academy of Sciences*, 110(37): 15139–15144.

[23] Sheppes, G. (2020) 'Transcending the "good & bad" and "here & now" in emotion regulation: Costs and benefits of strategies across regulatory stages', *Advances in Experimental Social Psychology*, 61: 185–236.
[24] Affleck, G. and Tennen, H. (1996) 'Construing benefits from adversity: adaptational significance and dispositional underpinnings', *Journal of Personality*, 64: 899–922.
[25] Affleck, G. and Tennen, H. (1996) 'Construing benefits from adversity: adaptational significance and dispositional underpinnings', *Journal of Personality*, 64: 899–922.
[26] Danoff-Burg, S. and Revenson, T.A. (2005) 'Benefit-finding among patients with rheumatoid arthritis: Positive effects on interpersonal relationships', *Journal of Behavioral Medicine*, 28: 91–103.

Chapter 6

[1] Kay, S.A. (2016) 'Emotion regulation and resilience: Overlooked connections', *Industrial and Organizational Psychology*, 9(2): 411–415.
[2] Tugade, M.M. and Fredrickson, B.L. (2007) 'Regulation of positive emotions: Emotion regulation strategies that promote resilience', *Journal of Happiness Studies*, 8(3): 311–333.
[3] Gross, J.J. (1998) 'Antecedent- and response-focused emotion regulation: Divergent consequences for experience, expression, and physiology', *Journal of Personality and Social Psychology*, 74(1): 224–237.
[4] Sheppes, G. and Gross, J.J. (2012). 'Emotion regulation effectiveness: What works when', *Handbook of Psychology*, 5: 391–406.
[5] Rovenpor, D.R., Skogsberg, N.J. and Isaacowitz, D.M. (2013) 'The choices we make: An examination of situation selection in younger and older adults', *Psychology and Aging*, 28(2): 365.
[6] Rovenpor, D.R., Skogsberg, N.J. and Isaacowitz, D.M. (2013) 'The choices we make: An examination of situation selection in younger and older adults', *Psychology and Aging*, 28(2): 365.
[7] Gross, J.J. (2008) 'Emotion regulation', *Handbook of Emotions*, 3(3): 497–513.
[8] Gross, J.J. (1999) 'Emotion regulation: Past, present, future', *Cognition and Emotion*, 13: 551–573.
[9] Troy, A.S. and Mauss, I.B. (2011) 'Resilience in the face of stress: Emotion regulation as a protective factor', *Resilience and Mental Health: Challenges Across the Lifespan*, 1(2): 30–44.
[10] Gross, J.J. (1999) 'Emotion regulation: Past, present, future', *Cognition and Emotion*, 13: 551–573.
[11] Webb, T.L., Lindquist, K.A., Jones, K., Avishai, A. and Sheeran, P. (2018) 'Situation selection is a particularly effective emotion

regulation strategy for people who need help regulating their emotions', *Cognition and Emotion*, 32(2): 231–248.
12. Sheppes, G. and Gross, J.J. (2012). 'Emotion regulation effectiveness: What works when', *Handbook of Psychology*, 5: 391–406.
13. Gross, J.J. (1998) 'Antecedent- and response-focused emotion regulation: Divergent consequences for experience, expression, and physiology', *Journal of Personality and Social Psychology*, 74: 224–237.
14. Gross, J.J. (1998) 'Antecedent- and response-focused emotion regulation: Divergent consequences for experience, expression, and physiology', *Journal of Personality and Social Psychology*, 74: 224–237.
15. Aldao, A., Nolen-Hoeksema, S. and Schweizer, S. (2010) 'Emotion-regulation strategies across psychopathology: A meta-analytic review', *Clinical Psychology Review*, 30(2): 217–237.

Chapter 7

1. Lazarus, R.S. and Folkman, S. (1984) *Stress, Appraisal and Coping*. New York: Springer.
2. Wells, J.D., Hobfoll, S.E. and Lavin, J. (1999) 'When it rains, it pours: The greater impact of resource loss compared to gain on psychological distress', *Personality and Social Psychology Bulletin*, 25(9): 1172–1182.
3. Hobfoll, S.E. (1989) 'Conservation of resources: a new attempt at conceptualizing stress', *American Psychologist*, 44(3): 513–524.
4. Lazarus, R.S. and Folkman S. (1984) *Stress, Appraisal, and Coping*, New York: Springer.
5. Hobfoll, S.E. (1989) 'Conservation of resources: a new attempt at conceptualizing stress', *American Psychologist*, 44(3): 513–524.
6. Antonovsky, A. (1979) *Health, Stress, and Coping*. San Francisco: Jossey Bass.
7. Hobfoll, S.E. (2002) 'Social and psychological resources and adaptation', *Review of General Psychology*, 6: 307–324.
8. Institute for Economics and Peace (2024) 'Global Terrorism Index 2024', Institute for Economics and Peace, [online] February, Available from: https://www.economicsandpeace.org/wp-content/uploads/2024/02/GTI-2024-web-290224.pdf [Accessed 27 February 2025].
9. Naval History and Heritage Command (2023) 'The 9/11 terrorist attacks: 11 September 2001', *Naval History and Heritage Command*, [online] 7 September, Available from: https://www.history.navy.mil/browse-by-topic/wars-conflicts-and-operations/sept-11-attack.html [Accessed 8 July 2024].
10. United States Government Accountability Office (2004) 'Health Effects in the Aftermath of the World Trade Center Attack', *United*

States Government Accountability Office, [online] 8 September, Available from: https://www.gao.gov/assets/gao-04-1068t.pdf [Accessed 11 March 2025].

11 Bonanno, G.A., Galea, S., Bucciarelli, A. and Vlahov, D. (2007) 'What predicts psychological resilience after disaster? The role of demographics, resources, and life stress', *Journal of Consulting and Clinical Psychology,* 75(5): 671.

12 Hobfoll, S.E. (1989) 'Conservation of resources: a new attempt at conceptualizing stress', *American Psychologist,* 44(3): 513–524.

13 Hobfoll, S.E. and Shirom, A. (2000) 'Conservation of resources theory: Applications to stress and management in the workplace', in R.T. Golembiewski (ed), *Handbook of Organization Behavior* (2nd Revised Ed.) New York: Dekker, pp 57–81.

14 Grandey, A.A. and Cropanzano, R. (1999) 'The conservation of resources model applied to work–family conflict and strain', *Journal of Vocational Behavior,* 54(2): 350–370.

15 Westman, M. and Eden, D. (1997) 'Effects of a respite from work on burnout: vacation relief and fade-out', *Journal of Applied Psychology,* 82(4): 516.

16 Hobfoll, S.E. (2001) 'The influence of culture, community, and the nested-self in the stress process: Advancing conservation of resources theory', *Applied Psychology,* 50(3): 337–421.

17 Hobfoll, S.E. (2001) 'The influence of culture, community, and the nested-self in the stress process: Advancing conservation of resources theory', *Applied Psychology,* 50(3): 337–421.

18 Wells, J.D., Hobfoll, S.E. and Lavin, J. (1999) 'When it rains, it pours: The greater impact of resource loss compared to gain on psychological distress', *Personality and Social Psychology Bulletin,* 25: 1172–1182.

19 Wells, J.D., Hobfoll, S.E. and Lavin, J. (1999) 'When it rains, it pours: The greater impact of resource loss compared to gain on psychological distress', *Personality and Social Psychology Bulletin,* 25(9): 1172–1182.

20 Ironson, G., Wynings, C., Schneiderman, N., Baum, A., Rodriguez, M., Greenwood, D. et al (1997) 'Post–traumatic stress symptoms, intrusive thoughts, loss, and immune function after Hurricane Andrew', *Psychosomatic Medicine,* 59: 128–141.

21 Baltes, M.M. and Lang, F.R. (1997) 'Everyday functioning and successful aging: The impact of resources', *Psychology and Aging,* 12(3): 433–443.

22 Norris, F.H. and Kaniasty, K. (1996) 'Received and perceived social support in times of stress: Aa test of the social support deterioration deterrence model', *Journal of Personality and Social Psychology,* 71(3): 498.

23. Hobfoll, S.E. (1998) *Stress, Culture, and Community: The Psychology and Philosophy of Stress*, New York: Plenum.
24. Hirsch, B.J. and Rapkin, B.D. (1986) 'Multiple roles, social networks, and women's well-being', *Journal of Personality and Social Psychology*, 51(6): 1237–1247.
25. Wells, J.D., Hobfoll, S.E. and Lavin, J. (1999) 'When it rains, it pours: The greater impact of resource loss compared to gain on psychological distress', *Personality and Social Psychology Bulletin*, 25(9): 1172–1182.
26. Updegraff, J.A. and Taylor, S.E. (2000) 'From vulnerability to growth: Positive and negative effects of stressful life events', in J.H. Harvey and E.D. Miller (eds), *Handbook of Loss and Trauma*, New York: Bruner/Mazel, pp 3–28.
27. Freedy, J.R. and Hobfoll, S.E. (1994) 'Stress inoculation for reduction of burnout: A conservation of resources approach', *Anxiety, Stress and Coping*, 6(4): 311–325.

Chapter 8

1. Cohen, S. (2004) 'Social relationships and health', *American Psychologist*, 59: 676–684.
2. Sippel, L.M., Pietrzak, R.H., Charney, D.S., Mayes, L.C. and Southwick, S.M. (2015) How does social support enhance resilience in the trauma-exposed individual? *Ecology and Society*, 20(4).
3. Southwick, S.M. and Charney, D.S. (2012) *Resilience: The Science of Mastering Life's Greatest challenges: Ten Key Ways to Weather and Bounce Back from Stress and Trauma*, Cambridge University Press.
4. Sippel, L.M., Pietrzak, R.H., Charney, D.S., Mayes, L.C. and Southwick, S.M. (2015) How does social support enhance resilience in the trauma-exposed individual? *Ecology and Society*, 20(4).
5. Revilla, J.C., Martín, P. and de Castro, C. (2018) 'The reconstruction of resilience as a social and collective phenomenon: poverty and coping capacity during the economic crisis', *European Societies*, 20(1): 89–110.
6. Coghlan, E., McCorkell, L. and Hinkley, S. (2018) 'What really caused the great recession?' *Institute for Research on Labour and Employment*, [online] Available from: https://irle.berkeley.edu/publications/irle-policy-brief/what-really-caused-the-great-recession/ [Accessed 12 February 2024].
7. Loo, A. (unknown) 'The Great Recession', *Corporate Finance Institute*, [online] Available from: https://corporatefinanceinstitute.com/resources/economics/2008-2009-global-financial-crisis/ [Accessed 5 December 2024].

8. Royo, S. (2020) 'From boom to bust: the economic crisis in Spain 2008–2023', in S Royo (ed) *Why Banks Fail? The Political Roots of Banking Crises in Spain*, New York: Springer, pp 119–140.
9. Revilla, J.C., Martín, P. and de Castro, C. (2017) 'The reconstruction of resilience as a social and collective phenomenon: poverty and coping capacity during the economic crisis', *European Societies*, 20(1), 89–110.
10. Bonanno, G.A. and Diminich, E.D. (2013) 'Annual Research Review: Positive adjustment to adversity – trajectories of minimal – impact resilience and emergent resilience', *Journal of Child Psychology and Psychiatry*, 54: 378–401.
11. Aldrich, D.P. (2012) *Building Resilience: Social Capital in Post-Disaster Recovery*, University of Chicago Press.
12. Visentin, M., Reis, R.S., Cappiello, G. and Casoli, D. (2021) 'Sensing the virus. How social capital enhances hoteliers' ability to cope with COVID-19', *International Journal of Hospitality Management*, 94L 102820.
13. Holahan, C.J. and Moos, R.H. (1990) 'Life stressors, resistance factors, and improved psychological functioning: An extension of the stress resistance paradigm', *Journal of Personality and Social Psychology*, 58(5): 909–917.
14. Brewin, C.R., Andrews, B. and Valentine, J.D. (2000) 'Meta-analysis of risk factors for posttraumatic stress disorder in trauma-exposed adults', *Journal of Consulting and Clinical Psychology*, 68: 748–766.

Chapter 9

1. Janoff-Bulman, R. and Timko, C. (1987) 'Coping with traumatic events: The role of denial in light of people's assumptive worlds', in C.R. Snyder and C.E. Ford (eds) *Coping with Negative Life Events: Clinical and Social Psychological Perspectives*, New York: Plenum, pp 135–159.
2. Lazarus, R.S. (1983) 'The costs and benefits of denial', in S. Bresnitz (ed) *Denial of Stress*, New York: International Universities Press.
3. Miller, D. (1992) 'The Icarus paradox: How exceptional companies bring about their own down-fall', *Business Horizons*, 35(1): 24–35.
4. Sheaffer, Z., Richardson, B. and Rosenblatt, Z. (1998) 'Early-warning-signals management: A lesson from the Barings crisis', *Journal of Contingencies and Crisis Management*, 6(1): 1–70.
5. Argenti, J. (1976) *Corporate Collapse*, New York: Halstead.
6. Kets de Vries, M.F.R. and Miller, D. (1984) 'Neurotic Style and Organizational Psychology', *Strategic Management Journal*, 5(1): January/February, pp 35–55.

7 Drummond, H. (2002) 'Living in a fool's paradise: the collapse of Barings' Bank', *Management Decision*, 40(3): 232–238.
8 Spillan, J. and Hough, M. (2003) 'Crisis Planning in Small Businesses: Importance, Impetus and Indifference', *European Management Journal*, 21(3): 398–407.
9 Weick, K.E. and Sutcliffe, K.M. (2007) *Managing the Unexpected: Assuring High Performance in an Age of Complexity*, San Francisco, CA: Jossey-Bass.
10 Wlodarczyk, A., Basabe, N., Páez, D., Amutio, A., García, F. E., Reyes, C. et al (2016) 'Positive effects of communal coping in the aftermath of a collective trauma: The case of the 2010 Chilean earthquake', *European Journal of Education and Psychology*, 9, 9–19.
11 Parker, J. and Davies, B. (2020) 'No blame no gain? From a no blame culture to a responsibility culture in medicine', *Journal of Applied Philosophy*, 37(4): 646–660.

Chapter 10

1 Kemp, E., Kennett-Hensel, P.A. and Williams, K.H. (2014) The calm before the storm: Examining emotion regulation consumption in the face of an impending disaster, *Psychology and Marketing*, 31(11): 933–945.
2 Xu, Y., Wu, J., Li, Q., Zeng, W., Wu, C., Yang, Y. et al (2022) 'The impact of intrusive rumination on college students' creativity during the COVID-19 pandemic: the mediating effect of posttraumatic growth and the moderating role of psychological resilience', *Frontiers in Psychology*, 13: 789844.
3 Nolen-Hoeksema, S. (1991) 'Responses to depression and their effects on the duration of depressive episodes', *Journal of Abnormal Psychology*, 100: 569–582.
4 Martin, L.L. and Tesser. A. (1996) 'Some ruminative thoughts', in R.S. Wyer (ed) *Advances in Social Cognition*, Hillsdale, NJ: Erlbaum, Vol. 9, pp 1–47.
5 Wade, N.G., Vogel, D.L., Liao, K.Y.H. and Goldman, D.B. (2008) 'Measuring state-specific rumination: Development of the rumination about an interpersonal offense scale', *Journal of Counseling Psychology*, 55(3): 419–426.
6 Nolen-Hoeksema, S. and Morrow, J. (1991) 'A prospective study of depression and posttraumatic stress symptoms after a natural disaster: The 1989 loma prieta earthquake', *Journal of Personality and Social Psychology*, 61(1): 115–121.
7 Nolen-Hoeksema, S., Wisco, B.E. and Lyubomirsky, S. (2008) 'Rethinking rumination', *Perspectives on Psychological Science*, 3(5): 400–424.

8. Gross, J.J. (1999). Emotion regulation: Past, present, future. *Cognition & Emotion*, 13(5): 551–573.
9. Nolen-Hoeksema, S., Wisco, B.E. and Lyubomirsky, S. (2008) 'Rethinking rumination', *Perspectives on Psychological Science*, 3(5): 400–424.
10. Watkins, E. R. and Roberts, H. (2020) 'Reflecting on rumination: Consequences, causes, mechanisms and treatment of rumination', *Behaviour Research and Therapy*, 127: 103573.
11. Seligowski, A.V., Lee, D.J., Bardeen, J.R. and Orcutt, H.K. (2015) 'Emotion regulation and posttraumatic stress symptoms: A meta-analysis', *Cognitive Behaviour Therapy*, 44(2): 87–102.
12. Murray, J., Ehlers, A. and Mayou, R.A. (2002) 'Dissociation and posttraumatic stress disorder: Two prospective studies of road traffic accident survivors', *The British Journal of Psychiatry*, 180(4): 363–368.
13. Birkeland, M.S., Blix, I. and Thoresen, S. (2021) 'Trauma in the third decade: Ruminative coping, social relationships and posttraumatic stress symptoms', *Journal of Affective Disorders*, 278: 601–606.
14. Holroyd, M. (2021) 'Danish MPs agree to a new investigation into deadly 1990 ferry fire', *Euronews*, [online] Available from: https://www.euronews.com/2021/05/12/danish-mps-agree-to-new-investigation-into-deadly-1990-ferry-fire [Accessed 15 January 2024].
15. Birkeland, M.S., Blix, I. and Thoresen, S. (2021) 'Trauma in the third decade: Ruminative coping, social relationships and posttraumatic stress symptoms', *Journal of Affective Disorders*, 278: 601–606.
16. Kemp, E., Kennett-Hensel, P.A. and Williams, K.H. (2014) The calm before the storm: Examining emotion regulation consumption in the face of an impending disaster, *Psychology and Marketing*, 31(11): 933–945.
17. Nolen-Hoeksema, S. and Morrow, J. (1991) 'A prospective study of depression and posttraumatic stress symptoms after a natural disaster: The 1989 loma prieta earthquake', *Journal of Personality and Social Psychology*, 61(1): 115–121.
18. Nolen-Hoeksema, S. and Larson J. (1999) *Coping with Loss*, Mahwah, NJ: Erlbaum.
19. Nolen-Hoeksema, S. (2001) 'Ruminative coping and adjustment to bereavement', in M.S. Stroebe, R.O. Hansson, W. Stroebe and H. Schut (eds) *Handbook of Bereavement Research: Consequences, Coping, and Care*, American Psychological Association, pp 545–562.
20. Di Schiena, R., Luminet, O., Chang, B. and Philippot, P. (2013). 'Why are depressive individuals indecisive? Different modes of rumination account for indecision in non-clinical depression', *Cognitive Therapy and Research*, 37: 713–724.

[21] Kang, H.S. and Kim, B.N. (2021) 'The role of event-related rumination and perceived social support on psychological distress during the COVID-19 pandemic: results from greater Daegu region in South Korea', *Psychiatry Investigation*, 18(5): 392–399.

[22] Puterman, E., DeLongis, A. and Pomaki, G. (2010) 'Protecting us from ourselves: Social support as a buffer of trait and state rumination', *Journal of Social and Clinical Psychology*, 29(7): 797–820.

[23] Teasdale, J.D., Segal, Z.V. and Williams, J.M.G. (1995) 'How does cognitive therapy prevent depressive relapse and why should attentional control (mindfulness) training help?' *Behaviour Research and Therapy*, 33: 25–39.

[24] Nolen-Hoeksema, S., Wisco, B.E. and Lyubomirsky, S. (2008) 'Rethinking rumination', *Perspectives on Psychological Science*, 3(5): 400–424.

[25] Nolen-Hoeksema, S., Wisco, B.E. and Lyubomirsky, S. (2008) 'Rethinking rumination', *Perspectives on Psychological Science*, 3(5): 400–424.

[26] Hilt, L.M. and Pollak, S.D. (2012) 'Getting out of rumination: Comparison of three brief interventions in a sample of youth', *Journal of Abnormal Child Psychology*, 40(7): 1157–1165.

[27] New York Times (2023) 'How to stop ruminating', [online] Available from: https://www.nytimes.com/2023/02/01/well/mind/stop-rumination-worry.html [Accessed 21 August 2024].

Chapter 11

[1] Waugh, C.E., Shing, E.Z. and Furr, R.M. (2020) 'Not all disengagement coping strategies are created equal: positive distraction, but not avoidance, can be an adaptive coping strategy for chronic life stressors', *Anxiety, Stress, & Coping*, 33(5): 511–529.

[2] Skinner, E.A., Edge, K., Altman, J. and Sherwood, H. (2003) 'Searching for the structure of coping: A review and critique of category systems for classifying ways of coping', *Psychological Bulletin*, 129(2): 216–269.

[3] Carver, C.S., Scheier, M.F. and Weintraub, J.K. (1989) 'Assessing coping strategies: A theoretically based approach', *Journal of Personality and Social Psychology*, 56(2): 267–283.

[4] Littleton, H., Horsley, S., William, S. and Nelson, D.V. (2007) 'Trauma coping strategies and psychological distress: A meta-analysis', *Journal of Traumatic Stress: Official Publication of the International Society for Traumatic Stress Studies*, 20(6): 977–988.

[5] Hamilton, N. and Ingram, C. (2001) 'Self-focused attention and coping: Attending to the right things', in C.R. Snyder (ed) *Coping*

with Stress: Effective People and Processes, Oxford: Oxford University Press, pp 178–195.
6. Dijkstra, M.T.M., De Dreu, C.K.W., Evers, A. and van Dierendonck, D. (2009) 'Passive responses to interpersonal conflict at work amplify employee strain', European Journal of Work and Organizational Psychology, 18(4): 405–423.
7. Graber, R., Turner, R. and Madill, A. (2016) 'Best friends and better coping: Facilitating psychological resilience through boys' and girls' closest friendships', British Journal of Psychology, 107(2): 338–358.
8. Foster, A. D. (2014) Traumatic Life Events and Symptoms of Anxiety: Moderating Effects of Adaptive Versus Maladaptive Coping Strategies, Doctoral dissertation, East Tennessee State University.
9. Ferreira, M.J., Sofia, R., Carreno, D.F., Eisenbeck, N., Jongenelen, I. and Cruz, J. F.A. (2021) 'Dealing with the pandemic of COVID-19 in Portugal: On the important role of positivity, experiential avoidance, and coping strategies', Frontiers in Psychology, 12: 647984.
10. Dijkstra, M.T.M., De Dreu, C.K.W., Evers, A. and van Dierendonck, D. (2009) 'Passive responses to interpersonal conflict at work amplify employee strain', European Journal of Work and Organizational Psychology, 18(4): 405–423.
11. Dijkstra, M.T. and Homan, A.C. (2016) Engaging in rather than disengaging from stress: Effective coping and perceived control. Frontiers in Psychology, 7: 1415.
12. Burker, E.J., Evon, D., Loiselle, M.M., Finkel, J. and Mill, M. (2005) 'Planning helps, behavioral disengagement does not: Coping and depression in the spouses of heart transplant candidates', Clinical Transplantation, 19(5): 653–658.

Chapter 12

1. Gross, J.J. (2002) 'Emotion regulation: Affective, cognitive, and social consequences', Psychophysiology, 39: 281–291.
2. Carver, C.S., Scheier, M.F. and Weintraub, J.K. (1989) 'Assessing coping strategies: A theoretically based approach', Journal of Personality and Social Psychology, 56(2): 267–283.
3. Hayes, S.C., Luoma, J.B., Bond, F.W., Masuda, A. and Lillis, J. (2006) 'Acceptance and commitment therapy: Models, processes and outcomes', Behaviour Research and Therapy, 44(1): 1–25.
4. Ciarrochi, J., Robb, H. and Godsell, C. (2005) 'Letting a little non-verbal air into the room: Insights from acceptance and commitment therapy, Part I: Philosophical and theoretical underpinnings', Journal of Rational-Emotive and Cognitive-Behavior Therapy, 23: 79–106.

5   Williams, V., Ciarrochi, J. and Deane, F.P. (2010) 'On being mindful, emotionally aware, and more resilient: Longitudinal pilot study of police recruits', *Australian Psychologist*, 45(4): 274–282.
6   Meichenbaum, D. (2017) 'Resilience and posttraumatic growth: A constructive narrative perspective', in *The Evolution of Cognitive Behavior Therapy*, London: Routledge, pp 157–171.
7   Hobfoll, S.E. (2002) 'Social and psychological resources and adaptation', *Review of General Psychology*, 6: 307–324.

Appendix B: Additional Commentary for Studying Entrepreneurs in Crisis and Resilience

1   Doern, R. (2017) 'Strategies for resilience in entrepreneurship: Building resources for small business survival after a crisis', in T. Vorley and N. Williams (eds) *Creating Resilient Economies: Entrepreneurship, Growth and Development in Uncertain Times*, London: Edward Elgar.
2   Meliou, E. (2020) 'Family as a eudaimonic bubble: Women entrepreneurs mobilizing resources of care during persistent financial crisis and austerity', *Gender Work and Organization*, 27: 218–235.
3   De Cock, R., Denoo, L. and Clarysse, B. (2020) 'Surviving the emotional rollercoaster called entrepreneurship: The role of emotion regulation', *Journal of Business Venturing*, 35(2): 105936.
4   Fang He, V., Sirén, C., Singh, S., Solomon, G. and von Krogh, G. (2018) 'Keep calm and carry on: Emotion regulation in entrepreneurs' learning from failure', *Entrepreneurship Theory and Practice*, 42(4): 605–630.
5   Li, N., Sun, Y., Jiang, D.K. and Yang, X. (2021) 'Exploring the moderating effect of interpersonal emotion regulation between the integration of opportunity and resource and entrepreneurial performance', *Frontiers in Psychology*, 12: 1–14.
6   Sirén, C., He, V.F., Wesemann, H., Jonassen, Z., Grichnik, D. and von Krogh, G (2020) 'Leader emergence in nascent venture teams: The critical roles of individual emotion regulation and team emotions', *Journal of Management Studies*, 57: 931–961.
7   Bonanno, G.A., Galea, S., Bucciarelli, A. and Vlahov, D. (2007) 'What predicts psychological resilience after disaster? The role of demographics, resources, and life stress', *Journal of Consulting and Clinical Psychology*, 75(5): 671–682.
8   Wlodarczyk, A., Basabe, N., Páez, D., Amutio, A., García, F.E., Reyes, C. and Villagrán, L. (2016) 'Positive effects of communal coping in the aftermath of a collective trauma: The case of the 2010 Chilean earthquake', *European Journal of Education and Psychology*, 9(1), 9–19.

[9] Felix, E., Afifi, T., Kia-Keating, M., Brown, L., Afifi, W. and Reyes, G. (2015) 'Family functioning and posttraumatic growth among parents and youth following wildfire disasters', *American Journal of Orthopsychiatry*, 85(2): 191–200.

[10] Wahl-Alexander, Z. and Sinelnikov, O.A. (2016) 'Examining instructor's and student's perceptions in an after school program focused on emotional recovery following a natural disaster', *Athens Journal of Sport*, 3(1): 7–24.

[11] Wilson, M., Rankin, K., Ludi, D. and Sweeny, K. (2022) 'Emotional, cognitive, and physical well-being during the wait for breast biopsy results', *Psychology and Health*, 1–20.

[12] Aldao, A., Nolen-Hoeksema, S. and Schweizer, S. (2010) 'Emotion-regulation strategies across psychopathology: A meta-analytic review', *Clinical Psychology Review*, 30(2): 217–237.

Index

References to figures appear in *italic* type; those in **bold** type refer to tables.
References to endnotes show both the page number and the note number (214n3).

9/11 attacks 119

A

acceptance-based coping strategies 97, 193
acceptance-based distraction 34, 36–38, **41**, **42**, 44
active planning 184, 186
adaptation 18–19, 67
adjustments 191–193
affect, definition 13
anxiety 49, 54, 55
Argenti, J. 156
athletes, and self-talk 66
attention-led adjustments 191, 192
avoidance/avoidant strategy 102, 112, 165
avoidance-based distraction 38–40, **41**, 43, 44
avoidant coping strategies 177, 193, 194
Ayduk, O. 34

B

Baring Brothers and Co. Ltd 156
Beaton, R. 69
behavioural disengagement 174, 183–184, **183**, **184**, 185–186, 204
  actionable takeaways 185
  description of 176–179
  monitoring 179
  protecting ourselves from in a crisis 182–184
  role of 179–182
benefit finding 81–82, 97, 98

benefit reminding 82, 97, 98
Birkeland, M.S. 168
Blix, I. 168
Bonanno, George 12, 13, 18, 119, 214n3

C

California, and wildfires 83
Calvete, E. 68
Cardenoso, O. 68
cautious optimism 58, 63
checking vitals 163–164
Cheng, Cecilia 18
Chile, and earthquake 33
coaches 77, 205
cognitive behavioural therapy (CBT) 172
communal coping 163
conservation of resources (COR) theory 120
Constitución, devastated by tsunami 33
constructive thinking 66–67, 78, 196
contingency planning 64
coping behaviours/strategies 21, 55, 67
  acceptance-based 193
  avoidant 194
  behavioural disengagement 185
  benefit reminding 82
  communal 163
  and positive reappraisal 83
COVID-19 pandemic 6–8, 29–31, 64–65, 118
  and active planning 184

and behavioural disengagement 179, 182–184
and building resources 124, 125–126, 127–128
and denial 159–160
and distraction 34, 36, 39, 195
and effect of humour 32
and growth-centred framing 91–94
and low expectations 52–54
and optimizing resources 121–123
and other event-centred framing 88
and other victim-centred framing 85–86
and positive expectations 56–59
and positive self-talk 71–72, 194, 202
and situation modification 109
and situation selection 104–107
and social support 135–136, 138, 141–142, 143–144
and support-centred framing 90
crisis
definition 4, 190
see also COVID-19 pandemic; London riots
crossword puzzles, as form of distraction 40

D

de-catastrophizing 22
Deepwater Horizon oil spill 18
denial **162**, 163–165, 204
actionable takeaways 164–165
description of 153–157
monitoring 156–157
protecting ourselves from in a crisis 161–164
role of 157–161
denial busting 161, **162**, 164
depression 16, 34
Desert Island Discs 84
destructive thinking 66, 74
disaster survivors 82
distraction 25, **41–43**, 43–44, **198**, **199**
actionable takeaways 43–44
and adjusting to the environment 192
avoidance strategy 102
avoidant coping strategy 193
and behavioural disengagement 177–178
can help to shift our attention in the short term 192

description of 31–35
effectiveness 32–34
emotion regulation 210
engaging in more effectively in a crisis 40–43
monitoring 34–35
and negative emotions 195, 196
role of 35–40
and rumination 172–173, 175
sub-strategies
acceptance-based with a lower case 'd' 35–38, 40, **41**, **42**, 43–44
avoidance-based with a capital 'D' 35, 38–40, **41**, 44
and uncertainty 47
distress 128, 193
and behavioural disengagement 185
and expectation management 48, 210
and reappraisal 82
and situation modification 107, 109
and situation selection 113

E

earthquakes 33
emotional intelligence 23–24
emotional support 144–145, 146, **149**, 150, 196
emotion regulation 22, 24, 209–210
and distraction 31, 34, 44
and reappraisal 81
and rumination 175
and situation modification 107, 113
and situation selection 113
emotions *see* negative emotions; positive emotions
entrepreneur, definition 3–4
environment, adjusting 192–193
Epstein, S. 66–67, 224n18
expectation management **61**, 62, 192, 197, **198**, **199**
actionable takeaways 63
engaging in expectation more effectively in a crisis 60–63
description of 43, 46–50
and distress 210
effectiveness 49–50
monitoring 50
role of 50–60

sub-strategies
  maintain caution expectations, cautious optimism 56–60
  maintaining low expectations 52–56
  and uncertainty 194

F

Federation of Small Businesses 47
Felix, E. 83, 210
flexible adaptation 13, 18–19, 67
flooding 47, 82
Foster, A.D. 178
Fredrickson, Barbara 14
functional support 137, 146
furlough scheme 30, 54, 85, 104, 118, 205

G

'gain spirals' 120
Gazermy, N. 16
Giancola, P.R. 66–67
Global Financial Crisis (GFC) of 2008 138–139
Global Terrorism Index 119
Gordy, C.C. 66–67
gratitude journal 98
Gross, James 81, 101
growth-centred framing 91–94, **96**

H

Hamilton, R.A. 66
hardiness 19
Hardy, James 66, 75, 76
Hartmann, S. 24
healthy functioning 13–16
High Street Fund 116, 126, 129, 139, 195
  difficult to continue without money from 120
  made up for financial losses not reimbursed by insurers 130
  and negative emotions 196
Hobfoll, Stevan 120
hospitality industry 29–30, 125–126, 141–142, 182, 205, 206
  built an online community for support 147
  and London riots 45
  made adjustments to make business stronger 91
  qualifying for grants 127–128
  re-arranging the workspace to take advantage of existing resources and generate new resources 122
  uncertainty during lockdown 52–53
humour, as form of distraction 32

I

informational support 141–142, 146, **149**, 150
Inside Out (film) 14–15
interpersonal therapy 172

J

job loss 48–49, 67, 81, 178

K

Karoly, P. 68
Kemp, E. 168
Kets de Vries, M.F.R. 156
Korber, S. 23, 24
Kross, E. 34

L

Lavin, J. 120, 230n18
leaning into social support
  actionable takeaways 150
  effectiveness 139–140
  engaging in more effectively in a crisis 145–148
  monitoring 140–141
Leeson, Nick 156
Libya, and flooding 47
lockdowns 6–8, 29–31
  and distraction 34, 36
  and growth-centred framing 91–94
  and low expectations 52–54
  and positive expectations 56–58
  and self-talk 64–65, 194
  and situation modification 109
  and situation selection 104–107
  and social support 135–136, 141–142
locus of control orientation 19
London riots 1–2, 5, 8–9, 21–22, 45–46, 128–129, **173–174**
  and acceptance-based distraction 36–37
  and active planning 184
  and attention-led adjustments 191
  and avoidance-based distraction 38–39

and behavioural
 disengagement 180–182
and building resources 126, 127
and denial 153–155, 157–159,
 160–161
and expectation management 192
and growth-centred framing 92
and maintaining low
 expectations 54–56
and negative emotions 196
and negative self-talk 73–74
and offsetting resource
 losses 115–116
and optimizing resources 123
and other event-centred
 framing 87–88
and other victim-centred framing 85
and positive reappraisal 79–80
and positive self-talk 72–73
and resource substitution 195
and rumination 166, 170–171
and situation modification 99–100
and social support 137–138,
 144–145
and support-centred framing 89, 91
'loss spirals' 120
Ludi, D. 48, 49, 50

M

maladaptive coping 21, 67, 178
Martin, L.L. 167
material support 137, 142–144, 146,
 149, 150, 196
McNaughton, R.B. 23, 24
Meliou, Elina 209
mental health, and behavioural
 disengagement 179, 182
mentors 77, 205
Miller, D. 156
mindfulness 172, 175
Morrow, J. 34, 167, 168

N

negative emotions 193, 196
 and acceptance 97
 and COVID-19 pandemic 57
 and humour 32
 interrupting or subverting 194
 and low expectations 51
 and other event-centred
  framing 87
 and positive reappraisal 80, **95**

signal something wrong and
 deserving of our attention 14
and situation modification 100, 107,
 108, 109, 113, 114, 197
and situation selection 102, 103,
 104–105, 109, 113, 210
and support-centred framing 89
see also distraction
negative self-talk 67, 68, 69, 73–74,
 75, 76, 78
negative stress 117, 133, 195
network building 147, 150
no-blame culture 163
Nolen-Hoeksema, S. 34, 167,
 168, 172

O

offsetting resource losses 130–131,
 131, 132–134, **132**, 193, 194, **198**,
 201
 actionable takeaways 133
 effectiveness 119–120
 description of 119–121
 engaging in more effectively in a
  crisis 130–132
 monitoring 120–121
 and resource substitution 195
 role of 121–124
 and stress 195, 196
online community 146–147
optimism 50, 59, 61–62, 63
organizational resilience 23, 24, 189
other event-centred framing
 86–88, **96**
other victim-centred framing
 85–86, **96**

P

Park, R.J. 34
personality traits 19–20, 24
pessimism 61–62
physical environment 109, 113
physical health 14–15, 47, 82
planning, active 184, 186
policy makers, how they can help
 entrepreneurs 205–206
positive adaptation 17, 18, 67
positive emotions 14, 80, 100,
 109, 196
 and distraction 33, 37, 38
 and expectations 54, 55
 and humour 32

and other event-centred framing 87
and positive reappraisal **95**
and situation modification 107, 110, 113, 197
and situation selection 104, 105–107, 110, 113
and support-centred framing 89
positive expectations 50, **51**, 56–60, 62
  associated with a sense of hope and a kind of cautious optimism 52, 63
  can co-exist with low expectations 58, 59, 60–61, 191
  minimize distress in the short term 48, 56
positive reappraisal **95–96**, 97–98, 173, 183, 194–195, **198**, **200**
  actionable takeaways 98
  effectiveness 82–84
  engaging in more effectively in a crisis 94–97
  description of 77, 80–84
  monitoring 84
  role of 84–94
  and stress resistance 197
  sub-strategies
    growth-centred framing 91–94
    other event-centred framing 86–88
    other victim-centred framing 85–86
    support-centred framing 89–91
positive self-talk 67, 68–69, 76, 77, 78, 194, **198**, **199**, 202
  actionable takeaways 77
  effectiveness 68–69
  monitoring 69–70
  engaging in more effectively in a crisis 74–77
  role of 70–73
posttraumatic growth (PTG) 15, 20, 89, 123
  and distraction 33
  and positive reappraisal 82, 83
posttraumatic stress disorder (PTSD) 15–16, 82
posttraumatic stress symptomology (PTSS) 14–15, 17, 167–168
problem solving 135, 169
  and constructive thinking 67
  and distraction 32, 37
  and rumination 171, 173
protective factors 16–17, 18, 23, 67, 197

protective thinking 164
psychological health 14–15, 82, 210
psychological resilience 24
psychopathology 112, 210

Q
Al Qaeda 119

R
'Raise the Bar' 128
Rankin, K. 48, 49, 50
reappraisal 34, 173
  see also positive reappraisal
redundancy 22, 48–49, 67, 81, 178
resilience
  entrepreneurs and 23–25
  definition 12–13
  and healthy functioning 13–16
  as an outcome 20–21
  as a personality trait 19–20
  and positive adaptation and flexible adaptation 18–19
  as a process 21–25
  and protective factors 16–17
resiliency model 20
resilient functioning 22
resource-led adjustments 191, 192
resources 116–118
  building 124–128, 133, 193
  optimizing 121–124, 133
  substitution 128–130, 133, 195
  see also offsetting resource losses
reverse listing 76
Revilla, J.C. 139
Riot Damages Act of 1886 205
riots, London *see* London riots
Ruehlman, L.S. 68
rumination 172–175
  actionable takeaways 175
  description of 166–169
  monitoring 169
  protecting ourselves from in a crisis 172–174
  role of 169–171
Rutter, M. 16

S
Scandinavian Star ferry fire 168
self-efficacy 19, 65, 78
self-esteem 17, 19, 20, 117
self-regulation 65, 78

self-talk 75–78, **75**, 183, 194, 197
  description of 64–70
  role of 70–74
  and stress resistance 195–196
  see also positive self-talk
sensemaking 82, 197, **200**
September 11 attacks 119
Sheppes, G. 101
Sinelnikov, O.A. 68
situational depression 16
situation-led adjustments 191, 192
situation modification 100–101, **111**, 112–114, **112**, 195, **198**, **201**
  description of 107–108
  effectiveness 107–108
  monitoring 108
  and negative emotions 110
  and positive emotions 197
  and psychopathology 210
  role of 108–109
situation selection 109–110, **111**, 112–114, **112**, 193, 195, **198**, **200**
  effectiveness 102–103
  description of 101–103
  monitoring 103
  and negative emotions 196, 210
  role of 103–107
  sub-strategies
    approaching situations to increase positive emotions 105–107
    avoiding situations to diminish negative emotions 104–105
  situation selection and modification
    actionable takeaways 113
    engaging in more effectively in a crisis 109–112
small to medium-sized enterprises (SMEs) 8
social cognitive theory 65
social support 146–148, **148**, **149**, 150, 194, **198**, **201**, 210
  description of 135–141
  role of 141–145
  and rumination 168, 172, 175
  and stress 195, 196
Smith, R. 16
Spain, economic crisis 139
Spirrison, C.L. 66–67
stakeholders, how they can help entrepreneurs 204–205
Stephens, Simon 24
Storm Daniel 47
stress 63, 109, 110, 113, 119
  and conservation of resources (COR) theory 120
  and constructive thinking 66
  and limited resources 117
  and positive self-talk 69, 77
  and social support 140, 150
stress resistance 77, 117, 118, 195–196, 197
Strick, M. 32
structural support 137, 146
success-breeds-failure syndrome 156
support-centred framing 89–91, **96**
Sweeny, Kate 48, 49, 50, 58, 60–61

T

terrorist attacks 119
Tesser. A. 167
Thoresen, S. 168
thought-led adjustments 191, 192
thought stopping 76
tornadoes 68

U

uncertainty 47, 51, 52–53, 63, 141, 194
United States
  disaster survivors 82
  and tornadoes 68
  wildfires 83

V

Van Raalte, J.L. 66, 68
vitals, checking 161, **162**, 163–164, 165

W

Wade, N.G. 167
Wahl-Alexander, Z. 68
Webb, Robert 84
wellbeing
  and acceptance 193
  affect of loss of a home or business 47
  and benefit finding and benefit reminding 97
  and checking vitals 163
  and distraction 210
  and healthy functioning 13
  and offsetting resource losses 121
  and resources 117, 127
  and rumination 169, 171, 175
  and self-talk 68, 75
  and situation modification 112

Wells, J.D. 120, 230n18
Werner, E. 16
Wetzel, C. 69
wildfires 82–83
Wilson, M. 48, 49, 50

Wlodarczyk, A. 33, 210
World Trade Center attacks 119

Z

Zinsser, N. 75

www.ingramcontent.com/pod-product-compliance
Lightning Source LLC
Chambersburg PA
CBHW051535020426
42333CB00016B/1944